HOTELS OF CHARACTER
AND CHARM IN PARIS

While every care has been taken to ensure the accuracy of the information in this guide, time brings change, and consequently the publisher cannot accept responsibility for errors that may occur. Prudent travelers will therefore want to call ahead to verify prices and other perishable information.

Hotels of Character and Charm in Paris

Translators: Anne Norris, Oliver Langhorne
Rewriting: Marie Gastaut
Cover design: Fabrizio La Rocca
Front cover photograph: Hôtel des Grandes Écoles (Paris 5ᵉ),
photo by François Tissier
Back cover: Hôtel San Régis (Paris 8ᵉ)

Special Sales

Fodor's Travel Publications are available at special discounts for bulk purchases for sales promotions or premiums. Special editions, including personalized covers, excerpts of existing guides, and corporate imprints, can be created in large quantities for special needs. For more information, contact your local bookseller or Special Markets, Fodor's Travel Publications, 201 E. 50th Street, New York, NY 10022.

Printed in Italy by Printer
10 9 8 7 6 5 4 3 2 1

Fodor's RIVAGES

HOTELS
of Character
and Charm
IN PARIS

Conceived by
Jean and Tatiana de Beaumont, Michelle Gastaut

Project editors
Jean and Tatiana de Beaumont

Fodor's Travel Publications, Inc.
New York • Toronto • London • Sydney • Auckland
www.fodors.com/

Photographic Credits

Nr. 1, 2, 12, 13, 33, 34, 42, 95, 123 and 209: photos by Ingrid Hoffmann.
Nr. 16, 38, 58, 66, 70, 72, 76, 81, 83, 89, 106, 120, 136, 138, 210,
212, 218 and 227: photos by Eliophot - Aix-en-Provence.
Nr. 49: © Vincent Knapp - Nr. 63: © Éric Avenel - Nr. 84 and 246:
© Dannie A. Launay - Nr. 156: © Guy Hervais - Nr. 178: © Laurent Weyl.

Acknowledgememts

Marie Gastaut and Véronique Jollé.

PRATICAL INFORMATION

Hotels are listed by district ('arrondissement') and in alphabetical order by hotel name, with a summary listing at the front of the Guide.

Flags on the map of Paris indicate the hotel location and page number where you will find its photo and description.

Different listings at the back of the Guide are there to help you in your research, and we have grouped our hotels as follows:

- by name (alphabetical order);
- by district;
- good value ('petits prix') hotel (double rooms from 280-520F)
- with a restaurant in the hotel.

You should also note that the prices were given to us by the hotels for the 1998 season. However, it is always possible that some of them may have been changed in the meantime, and we would recommend that when making your reservation, you should ask for the latest detailed rates for your room.

We have also tried to give both the high season and low season rates for each hotel.

The low season for hotels is particularly well aligned for the tourist calendar. In general it varies around July and August, and from November to February (except when the professional trade shows are on in Paris). So before reserving, do not hesitate to ask about the exact dates, while you should also note that many hotels offer very attractive promotional rates at weekends.

In both such cases, the differences in rates can be significant.

ATTENTION !

From 13 June to 15 July 1998, Paris will host the Football World Cup.

The rates given in this Guide will NOT apply during this period and it would be advisable to make direct contact with your selected hotel to check out their rates for this exceptional four-week period.

INTRODUCTION

Once again this year we went out to look for those small hotels that continue the tradition of 'Paris of the Poets' ('Paris des poètes'), and so much delight their loyal clientele.

This third edition describes 254 hotels, all carefully visited and selected in line with criteria that are difficult to define, but which you are ever more numerous in looking for : 'charm'.

This ideal 'hotel of charm' has retained a few eloquent features witnessing the past, such as a lovely stone staircase, wood-beamed ceilings, or tall windows giving onto a garden. It will also offer a reasonable number of rooms, all different and prettily decorated with elegant fabrics, framed prints and some antique furniture. Renovated on a regular basis, notably with ragard to the beds and bedding, it avoids any hint of "the dated" and above all offers the best of modernity in the bathrooms. In these hotels you feel a little bit like being at home thanks to the quality of the welcome, that corner saloon inviting you to take a drink or just quietly read, a dining room perfect for taking your breakfast when the weather does not allow you to have it outside …

The hotels selected for this Guide all have something in common with the "ideal picture": some of them correspond to it perfectly, others match the charm of the welcome, irreproachable standards and charming decorative details compensating a sometimes rather too standardized style; others have a marvellous way of exploiting the contemporary trends; yet others pleased us by their peace and quiet and surrounding greenery - while all proved to us that 'charm' also calls for diversity.

Simple or luxury, all the hotels chosen thus have real qualities. By carefully reading our introductory texts on each hotel, we are confident you will find that special one to meet your tastes; and providing you do not expect a 'two-star' hotel to offer those same services of a 'palace', you always run the chance of being surprised, as we were, by some of these rare gems ('perles rares') …

PLEASE LET US KNOW ...

Do not hesitate to write to us with your opinions about these hotels that we have recommended.

In addition, if you are attracted by any hotel not listed in this our 1998 guide, and you think it worthy of selection, please tell us about it so that the author may visit it and possibly add it in to the next edition. You should know that we do not accept any financial contribution from the hotel owner as we insist on our complete independence to select and list our hotels - or to remove them from our list.

With our thanks in advance, please send your comments and/or suggestions to:

Tatiana de Beaumont
Guide des Hôtels de Charme de Paris
Éditions Payot & Rivages
106, Boulevard Saint-Germain
75006 Paris - France

C O N T E N T S

C I N Q U I E M E

S I X I E M E

S E P T I E M E

H U I T I E M E

N E U V I E M E

D I X I E M E

O N Z I E M E

D O U Z I E M E

T R E I Z I E M E

Q U A T O R Z I E M E

Q U I N Z I E M E

S E I Z I E M E

D I X – S E P T I E M E

D I X - H U I T I E M E

N E U I L L Y - L A D É F E N S E

MAPS

KEY TO THE MAPS

Scale: 1:18,500
Maps 1 & 2: scale: 1:12,500

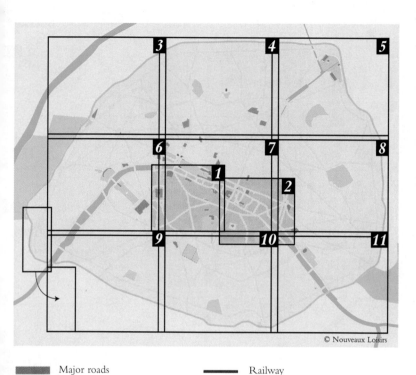

© Nouveaux Loisirs

Major roads		Railway	
Pedestrianized street		Police station	
One-way street		Post office	
P Parking		Hospital	
Gas station		RER station	
Rail station		Metro station	
Garden		Catholic, Orthodox, Protestant	
Cemetery		Synagogue	
Space not build		Mosque	
Monuments and visiting places			

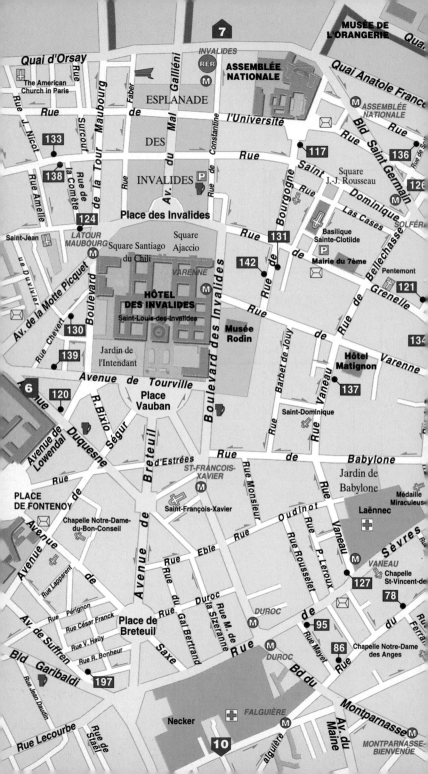

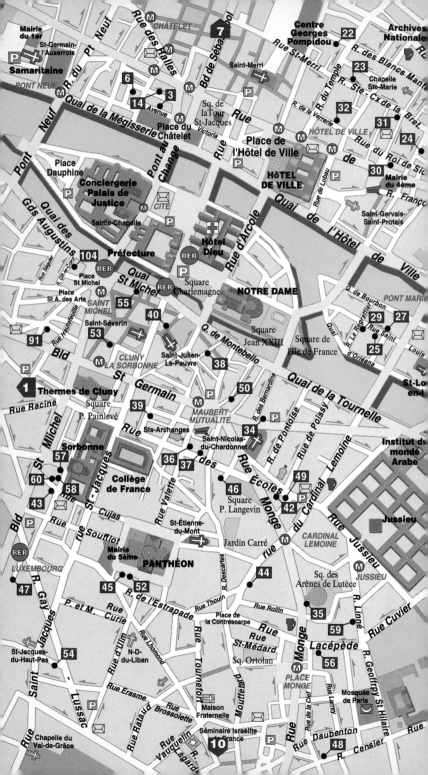

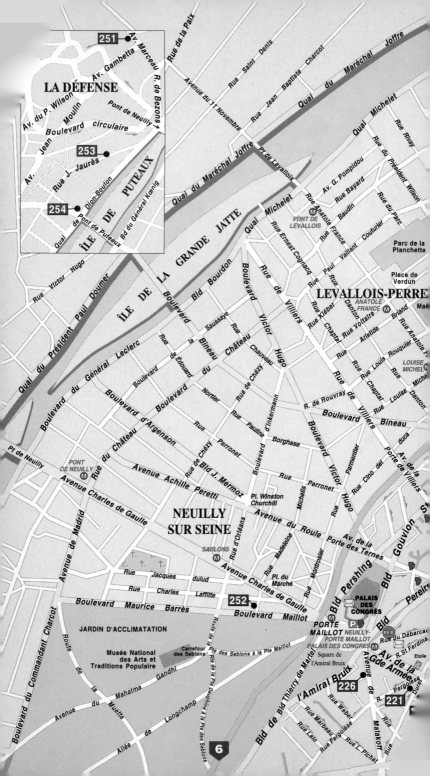

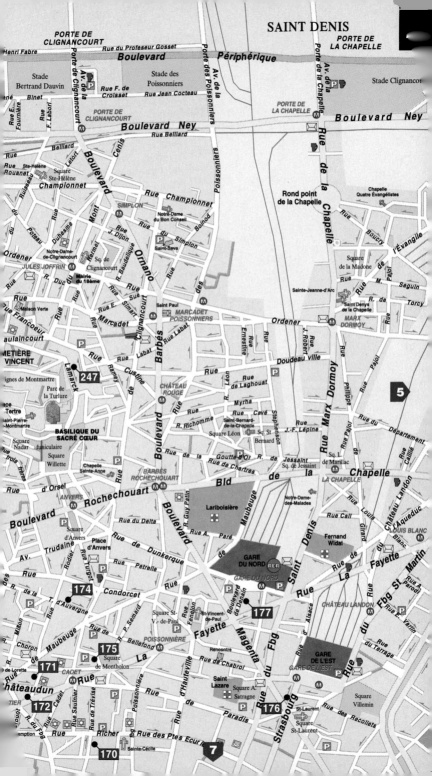

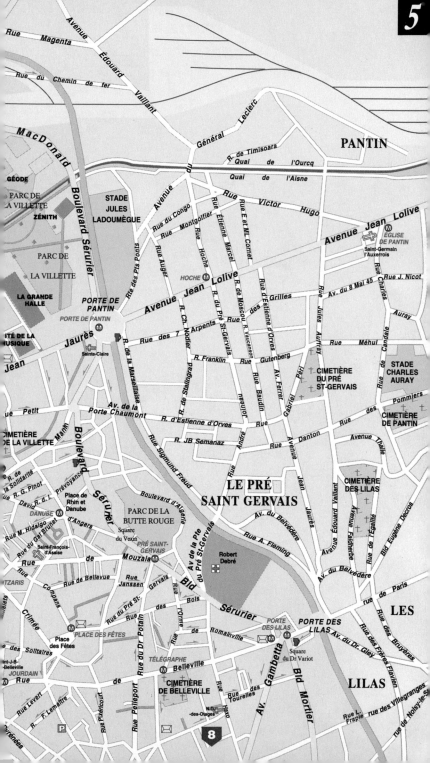

Rue Magenta
Avenue
Édouard
Vaillant
Rue
Rue du Chemin de fer
Général Leclerc
du

PANTIN

MacDonald
R. de Timisoara
Quai de l'Ourcq
Quai de l'Aisne

GÉODE
PARC DE LA VILLETTE
ZÉNITH

STADE JULES LADOUMÈGUE

Boulevard Sérurier

Avenue
Rue du Congo
Rue Montgolfier
Rue Auger
Rue Étienne Marcel
Rue E et M L Cornet

Victor Hugo

Avenue Jean Lolive
ÉGLISE DE PANTIN
Saint-Germain l'Auxerrois
Rue J. Nicot
Rue Charles
Rue J. Nicot

PARC DE LA VILLETTE

LA GRANDE HALLE

PORTE DE PANTIN
PORTE DE PANTIN
Jaurès
Sainte-Claire

CITÉ DE LA MUSIQUE
Jean

HOCHE
Avenue Jean Lolive
Rue Hoche
R. Ch. Nodier
R. de Moscou
R. du Pré St-Gervais
Rue des Grilles
Rue d'Estienne d'Orves
Rue Jules Auffray
Av. du 8 Mai 45
Rue de Candie
Rue Méhul

STADE CHARLES AURAY

Auray
Pommiers
CIMETIÈRE DE PANTIN

Rue des 7 Arpents
R. de la Marseillaise
R. de Stalingrad
R. Franklin
Rue Gutenberg
Av. Ferrer
Av. Baudin
Gabriel Péri

CIMETIÈRE DU PRÉ ST-GERVAIS
Rue des
Avenue Thaïe

R. Petit
CIMETIÈRE DE LA VILLETTE
Mann
Boulevard
Av. de la Porte Chaumont
R. d'Estienne d'Orves
R. JB Semanaz
Rue André
Rue
Avenue Danton
Avenue
Rue

CIMETIÈRE DES LILAS

R. de la Solidarité
R. G. Pinot
David R.d.I.
Prévoyance
Place de Rhin et Danube
DANUBE
d'Angers
Sérurier
Rue Sigmund Freud
Boulevard d'Algérie
PARC DE LA BUTTE ROUGE
Square du Vexin

LE PRÉ SAINT GERVAIS

Av. du Belvédère
Rue A. Fleming
Jean Jaurès
Avenue Édouard Vaillant
Avenue Faidherbe
Rue de l'Égalité
Bld Eugène Decros
Rue Eugène Decros

Rue M. Hidalgo
Rue du Gal Brunet
Saint-François-d'Assise
Rue
de
Mouzaïa
PRÉ SAINT-GERVAIS
Av. de la Pré du Pré St-Gervais
Robert Debré

Av. du Belvédère
rue de Paris
LES
Rue des Bruyères

TZARIS
Rue de Bellevue
Rue Janssen
Gervais
Rue du Pré St
des
Bld
Bois
Rue l'Orme
Sérurier
Romainville
PORTE DES LILAS
PORTE DES LILAS Av. du Dr. Gley
Rue des Frères Flavien

Crimée
Compans
PLACE DES FÊTES
Place des Fêtes
Rue du Dr Potain
de
Av. Gambetta
Square du Dr Variot
Bld Mortier

LILAS

des Solitaires
Saint-J-B-Belleville
JOURDAIN
Rue
Rue Levert
R. - F. Lemaître
Rue Pixérécourt
Rue Pelleport
TÉLÉGRAPHE
Belleville
CIMETIÈRE DE BELLEVILLE
N.Dm-des-Otages
Rue Haxo
Rue des Tourelles
Rue L. Fraple rue des Villegranges
rue de Noisy-le-S

Pyrénées
P

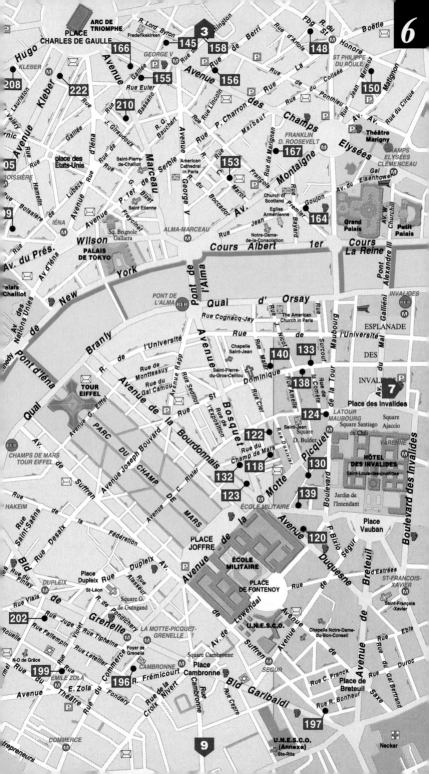

Sainte-Cécile
Rue Ste Cécile
169
RUE MONTMARTRE
Bld Montmartre
Bld Poissonnière
BONNE NOUVELLE
Rue du Fbg Poissonnière
Rue d' Hauteville
Rue d'Enghien
Rue de l'Echiquier
4
CHÂTEAU D'EAU
Rue du fbg St Denis
Bld de Strasbourg
Rue de Metz
Rue des Vinaigriers
Rue de Nancy
Mairie du 10ème
Rue du Château d'Eau
Bld de Magenta
R. Sampaix
Rue de Lancry
JACQUES BONSERGENT
St-Martin-des-Champs
Rue A. Thomas
Rue Beaurepaire
Rue Dieu
Rue Yves Toudic
Rue d'Uzes
Rue du Sentier
Rue des Jeuneurs
Bourse des Valeurs
BOURSE
Notre-Dame-de-Bonne-Nouvelle
Rue de Cléry
Rue d'Aboukir
La Pentecôte
SENTIER
STRASBOURG ST DENIS
Rue du Fbg
Rue Bouchardon
Rue Taylor
Bld St-Martin
RÉPUBLIQUE
PLACE DE LA RÉPUBLIQUE
Rue Meslay
Rue N.D. de Nazareth
Rue du Vertbois
TEMPLE
Rue Réaumur
Rue du Mail
Basilique N.-D. des Victoires
Place des Victoires
Rue Montmartre
Rue L. Bellan
R. Mandar
Rue St Sauveur
R. Greneta
17
Rue Montorgueil
Square E. Chautemps
RÉAUMUR SÉBASTOPOL
Conservatoire des Arts et Métiers
Square du Gal Morin
ARTS ET MÉTIERS
Rue Turbigo
Sainte-Elisabeth
R. Béranger
Bld du Temple
Rue Dupetit-Thouars
Square du Temple
Carreau du Temple
Mairie du 3ème
Rue du Louvre
Hôtel des Postes
Rue Etienne Marcel
ÉTIENNE MARCEL
Saint-Nicolas-des-Champs
Rue St Martin
Rue Coquillière
Saint-Eustache
Rue de Turbigo
Rue de Beaubourg
Rue de Montmorency
Rue du Temple
Rue des Archives
Rue de Charlot
Rue de Saintonge
Rue de Bretagne
Rue de Poitou
LES HALLES
Saint-Leu-Saint-Gilles
CHÂTELET LES HALLES
Bld de Sébastopol
Rue St Denis
Bourse du Commerce
Forum des Halles
RER
Rue Saint Honoré
12
LOUVRE
Sq. des Innocents
CHÂTELET
Rue Saint Denis
1
Boulevard
RAMBUTEAU
Jardin St Aignan
Rue Rambuteau
Centre Georges Pompidou
Cathédrale Ste-Croix
Rue de Turenne
Archives Nationales
Rue des 4 fils
Rue Vieille du Temple
Jardin de l'Hôtel Salé
Musée Picasso
Saint-Denys-du-St-Sacrement
Mairie du 1er
St-Germain-l'Auxerrois
PONT NEUF
Rue des Halles
Rue St-Merri
Saint-Merri
R. des Blancs Manteaux
Chapelle Ste-Marie
N-D-des-Blancs-Manteaux
Rue Barbette
8
Square L. Achille
Sq. G. Cain
Musée Carnavalet
R. du Pt Neuf
Quai de la Mégisserie
Sq. de la Tour St-Jacques
Place du Châtelet
Rue de Rivoli
HÔTEL DE VILLE
Billettes
R. Ste-Cx de la Bret.
Rue Elzevir
Rue des Francs Bourgeois
Rue de Sévigné
Pont Neuf
Place Dauphine
Conciergerie Palais de Justice
Pont au Change
Place de l'Hôtel de Ville
HôTEL DE VILLE
Rue du Roi de Sicile
Rue des Rosiers
Mairie du 4ème
R. F. Miron
SAINT-PAUL
Saint-Paul-Saint-Louis
Quai des Gds Augustins
CITÉ
Sainte-Chapelle
Hôtel Dieu
Rue d'Arcole
Quai de l'Hôtel de Ville
Saint-Gervais-Saint-Protais
Square A. Schweitzer
Préfecture
SAINT MICHEL
Quai St Michel
Square Charlemagne
NOTRE DAME
PONT MARIE
Rue St Paul
Rue Beautreillis
Rue du Pt Musc
St-André-des-Arts
Sq. de l'Ave Maria
Quai des Célestins
Saint-Séverin
Square R. Viviani
Saint-Julien-Le-Pauvre
Square Jean XXIII
Square de l'Ile de France
Rue Le Regrattier
Rue Saint-Louis-en-l'Ile
Square H. Galli
SULLY-MORLAND
CLUNY LA SORBONNE
Bld St-Germain
Quai de la Tournelle
St-Louis-en-l'Ile
Pont Sully
Rue de Sully
Thermes de Cluny
Rue Racine
Square P. Painlevé
MAUBERT MUTUALITÉ
Square Barye
Quai Henri IV
Rue Morland
Boulevard St-Michel
Rue M. le Prince
Sorbonne
Sts-Archanges
Saint-Nicolas-du-Chardonnet
R. de Pontoise
R. de Poissy
Rue du Cardinal Lemoine
Institut du monde Arabe
Quai St-Bernard
Collège de France
Rue St-Jacques
St-Ephrem
Rue des Ecoles
N-D-Joie-des-Affligés
Square P. Langevin
R. Monge
Rue Valette
Rue Cujas
Jussieu
Rue Soufflot
Mairie du 5ème
PANTHÉON
St-Etienne-du-Mont
Jardin Carré
CARDINAL LEMOINE
Rue Jussieu
Rue Cuvier
LUXEMBOURG
Sq. des Arènes de Lutèce
JARDIN DES PLANTES
R. de l'Estrapade
Rue P. et M. Curie
10
Place Valhubert

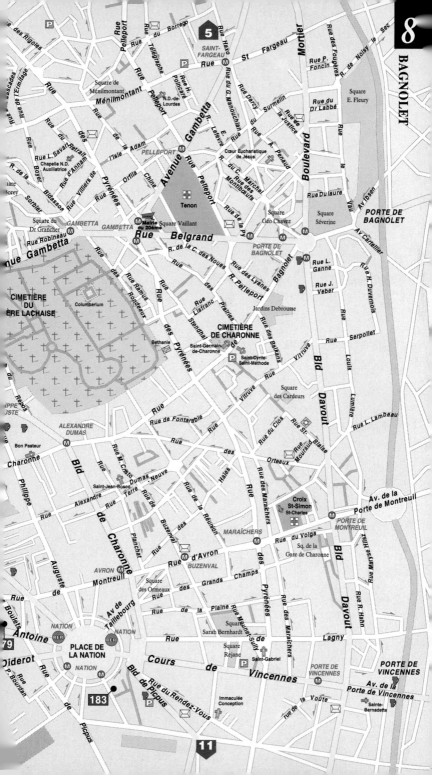

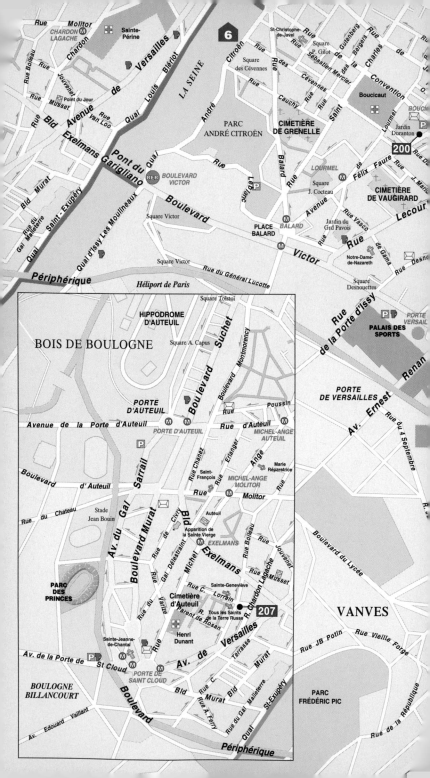

COMMERCE

des Entrepreneurs

Rue Lakanal

Rue de la Croix Nivert

Rue

Rue A.

Rue Mademoiselle

Résurrection

ronne

Lecourbe

U.N.E.S.C.O. (Annexe)

F. Bolvin

Ste-Rita Notre-Dame-du-Lys

Rue de Staël

Rue Ernest Renan

M PASTEUR

c

St-Jean-Baptiste-de-Grenelle

Rue

Rue L. Lhermitte

Rue T. Renaudot

Rue Roussin

St-Séraphin-de-Sarov

Blomet

Rue Copreaux

Rue des

Square Blomet

Rue E. Duclaux

VOLONTAIRES

Pasteur St Jacques

Rue du Docteur Roux

201

Bld

FÉLIX FAURE

Rue de Javel

Rue C. Lecocq

de l'Abbé

Square St-Lambert

Rue J. Formigé

Pécot

Mairie du 15ème

P

Les Trois Saints Hiérarques

Rue

Vaugirard

Volontaires

M Regnier

Rue

St-Jean-Baptiste-de-Salle

d'Arsonval

Pasteur

203

St-Jean-de-Dieu

N-D-de-Charité

Blomet

St-Lambert-de-Vaugirard

P

Vaugirard

Rue Ste F. Tessier

P. Quintinie

Dutot

Rue du Cotentin

de

VAUGIRARD

M

Rue R. Bourseul

des

la

Bargue

Gide

Rue E. Millon

Rue A. Charlier

F. Fabre

St-Charles

Rue d'Alleray

St-Sauveur

Favorites

Square Alleray-Quintinie

Barrel

Procession

Rue A.

St-Lambert

Rue Blomet

la

Corbon

Rue d'Alleray

R. St-Amand

Rue

CONVENTION

Convention

Dombasle

N-D-d'Espérance

Thiboumery

Branchion

Labrouste

Rue G. Pluad

Rue A. Bertillon

Olier

Rue E. Gibez

Rue Leriche

Rue

Rue Jobbé Duval

Danzig

Rue

Vouillé

Rue d'Alésia

Rue Lacretelle

Rue Vaugelas

de Sèvres

Rue de Cronstadt

N-D-de-la-Salette

des

Castagnary

PLAISANCE

M

Square Alésia Ridder

Rue F. Gillot

Olivier

R. de la Saïda

des

Morillons

Rue Santos Dumont

Rue du Lieuvin

Rue de Ridder

Rue

Square Losserand-Suisses

10

Présentation de la Sainte Vierge

Rue Rosenwald

M. Rouvroy

Raymond

Saint-Joseph

Jonquoy

Pierre Larousse

PARC DES EXPOSITIONS

Boulevard

Parc Georges Brassens

Branchion

Rue J. Baudry

Notre-Dame-du-Rosaire

Broussais

Square Cardinal Verdier

St-Antoine-de-Padoue

Stade des Périchaux

Square Castagnary

Rue

Bld Brune

Square de la Pte de la Plaine

Square du Dr Calmette

Lefèbvre

Rue

PORTE DE VANVES

Avenue M. d'Ocagne

Stade de la Porte de la Plaine

Avenue de

Rue J. Bartet

Av. de la Porte de Vanves

PORTE DE VANVES

Square M. Nogues

Avenue M. Sangnier

Av. Victor Hugo

Rue Sadi Carnot

Jean

Bleuzen

Gaulle

Square de la Porte de Vanves

Boulevard

Avenue G. Lafenestre

Adolphe

Pinard

Stade Jules Noël

CIMETIÈRE DE VANVES

Rue

M

de

Charles

Bd

MALAKOFF PLATEAU DE VANVES

Pierre

Larousse

Avenue

Rue de la Tour

Rue Victor Hugo

Rue

Gambetta

PORTE DE CHÂTILLON

R. E. Laval

MALAKOFF

Bd

Gabriel

Péri

Rue Savier

Rue Vincent Morris

Avenue Augustin Dumont

Avenue

Pierre

Brossolette

Rue

Maurice

Arnoux

6

P

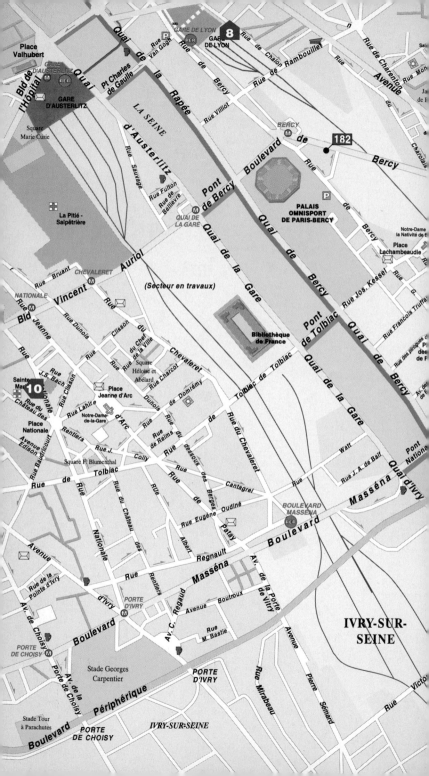

8

ITGALLET
Diaconesses

CIMETIÈRE DE PICPUS
Rothschild

Av. de Saint Mandé   Av Courteline

Rue Mousset Robert   Arnold
Rue Lasson
Rue   Trousseau

Rue Santerre
Rue Dagorno

Bld de Picpus

Rue   du   Dr.   Goujon

BEL AIR

Rue de la Gare de Reuilly

Rue   de

Rue Sibuet

Rue V. Chevreuil
Rue du
Rue
Rue Messidor
Braille
Rue Sahel
Rue de Montempoivre

Square E. Cohl
Square G. Méliès

Boulevard Soult

A.V. J. Phil.
Boulevard Carnot
Rue Édouard Lartet

Périphérique

SAINT-MANDÉ

Rue Taine
JGOMMIER

Place Félix Éboué
Reuilly
de

DAUMESNIL
Avenue

St-Esprit

Square du Donom

Michel Bizot
la Vega
Rue de Tour.

Square Charles Peguy
Rottembourg

CIMETIÈRE DE ST MANDÉ

Rue de la Brêche aux Loups
Rue de la Lancette
Rue de
Claude
R. de
Gravelle
Wattignies
Rue des
Meuniers
du
Rue

E. Robert
Fécamp
Général
Picpus
Décaen
Avenue

MICHEL BIZOT
Daumesnil

PORTE DORÉE
PORTE DORÉE

Square P. Pasquier
Square des Comb. d'Indochine

PORTE DORÉE

Coriolis
Charenton

CIMETIÈRE DE BERCY

PORTE DE CHARENTON

Stade Léo Lagrange

Square Van Vollenhoven
Square P. Blanchet
Square L. Gentil

Boulevard

LAC DAUMESNIL

Boulevard Poniatowski

Av. de la Porte de Charenton

PORTE DE CHARENTON

Cimetière Valmy

BOIS DE VINCENNES

R. M. Delcher

Rue de Valmy
Rue de Paris
LIBERTÉ

Av. Winston Churchill
Rue de Verdun

Quai de Bercy

Rue du Nouveau Bercy

Rue de l'Entrepôt

Liberté

R. du Port aux Lions
Rue de l'Arcade
Rue de la

Rue
de
Rue de l'Archevêché

Rue de Paris

Av. Anatole France
Rue Jean Jaurès

R. St-Pierre

CHARENTON ÉCOLES

Quai de Bercy

CHARENTON-LE-PONT

Avenue
Rue de Conflans

Rue des Bordeaux
Rue de la Cerisaie
Saint-Pierre
R. P. Éluard
Villa
Rue Victor Hugo

Rue Jean - Jacques - Rousseau

Boulevard Paul Vaillant Couturier

Quai Jean Compagnon

Quai des Carrières

AUTOROUTE A4

Rue de Reuilly
Vivaldi
umesnil
Rue
Rue
P

Hôtel Agora

7, rue de la Cossonnerie
75001 Paris
Tel. (0)1 42 33 46 02 - Fax (0)1 42 33 80 99
M. De Marco

Category ✶✶ **Rooms** 29 with soundproofing, bath or shower, WC, TV, safe. **Price** Single 435-585F, double 540-640F, extra bed 100F - Special rates in July-August: −10%. **Meals** Breakfast 40F, served 7:00-9:30. **Credit cards** Amex, Visa, Eurocard, MasterCard. **Pets** Dogs not allowed. **Facilities** Elevator. **Parking** Forum des Halles. **How to get there** (Map 7): Bus: 21, 29, 38, 39, 47, 58, 67, 69, 70, 72, 74, 75, 76, 81 - Metro and RER: Châtelet-Les Halles. **Open** All year.

The Agora is on a bustling street in Les Halles very near the Les Innocents Square and Fountain, where trendy clothes shops rub elbows with lively restaurants. The Centre Beaubourg is also in this area, one of the most touristed quarters of Paris. A stairway leads to the reception area on the second floor. The somewhat mixed decor, created by an accumulation of furniture and flea market finds, creates an atmosphere of joyous disorder. Adjacent to the reception area is a small country-style lounge where breakfast is served. A very small elevator takes you to the bedrooms; they are well kept and decorated with old-fashioned charm, including flowery wallpapers, mirrors with gilt or painted borders, and basic but functional washrooms. The rooms on the highest floor have lovely mansard roofs, those on the *cinquième étage* have a balcony, and the large corner rooms are illuminated by two large windows; all overlook the street. In winter, double–glazed windows effectively soundproofs the rooms, but in good weather, it's best to stay on the top floors. This is a small, simple, typically Parisian hotel–the kind you might see in an American movie from the 1940s.

PREMIER

Hôtel Brighton

218, rue de Rivoli
75001 Paris
Tel. (0)1 47 03 61 61 – Fax (0)1 42 60 41 78
M. Shimizu

Category ★★★ **Rooms** 70 (including suites) with soundproofing, bath or shower, WC, telephone, TV, minibar. **Price** Single 545-915F, double 580-950F, triple 1025-1125F, suite 1400F. **Meals** Breakfast included. **Credit cards** All major. **Pets** Dogs not allowed. **Facilities** Room-service. **Parking** At place Vendôme and place du Marché-Saint-Honoré. **How to get there** (Map 7): Bus: 68, 69, 72. - Metro: Tuileries, Concorde. **Open** All year.

Ahotel which despite a full renovation has managed to retain everything that gave it charm, that is the Brighton: Marble, velvets, carpets, crystal, and the muffled atmosphere and silence of its lounges where the discreet personnel look after your every need. All the rooms are very different in size, comfort, and decor. But one of the main attractions of this hotel is the quite exceptional view from the rooms on the upper floors, with their small balconies overlooking the Tuileries Gardens of course, and also with a view stretching from Notre-Dame cathedral to the modern La Défense quarter.

Hôtel Britannique

20, avenue Victoria – 75001 Paris
Tel. (0)1 42 33 74 59 – Fax (0)1 42 33 82 65
web: http://www.hotel-britannique.fr
M. Danjou

Category ★★★ **Rooms** 40 with soundproofing, telephone, bath or shower, WC, hairdryer, TV satellite, minibar, safe. **Price** Single 527-659F, double 631-898F. **Meals** Breakfast (buffet) 55F, served 7:00-10:30. **Credit cards** All major. **Pets** Dogs not allowed. **Facilities** Elevator, bar, laundry service. **Parking** At Hôtel de Ville and quai de Gesvres. **How to get there** (Map 2): Bus: 21, 38, 47, 58, 67, 69, 70, 72, 75, 76, 81, 85 - Metro: Châtelet - RER Châtelet-Les Halles. **Open** All year.

A plaque at the entrance to the Hotel Britannique informs you that it was built in 1840 and has been run to this day by a family of English origin: It has always been a favorite hotel with Anglo-Saxon tourists. The lounge downstairs is faithful to this British influence, with leather chesterfields and Turner reproductions. The cozy, elegant ambience is heightened by figured carpets in the corridors, and bouquets of fresh flowers throughout the hotel. The bedrooms are of varying sizes, from singles and small doubles to more spacious rooms on the courtyard. But all are pleasant, comfortable, bright, and well decorated. The Hôtel Britannique is next door to the *Cèdre Rouge,* one of the most famous garden stores in Paris, and near many other flower and horticultural shops off the Place du Châtelet and the Quai de la Messagerie. Scattered among the flower shops on the quay are other shops selling billy goats, roosters, rabbits, turtles, rods and reels—you name it. Tourists and Parisians alike love it.

Hôtel du Continent

30, rue du Mont–Thabor
75001 Paris
Tel. (0)1 42 60 75 32 – Fax (0)1 42 61 52 22
M. Jean-Pierre Gamelon

Category ★★★ **Rooms** 28 with air-conditioning, soundproofing, bath or shower, telephone, hairdryer, WC, cable TV and minibar. **Price** Single 596-756F, double 722-872F, extra bed 166F. **Meals** Breakfast (buffet) 65F, served 7:00-10:30. **Credit cards** All major. **Pets** Dogs allowed. **Facilities** Elevator, laundry service, room-service, safe at reception. **Parking** At rue du Mont-Thabor. **How to get there** (Map 7): Bus: 24, 42, 72, 73, 84, 94 - Metro: Concorde. **Open** All year.

It is certainly true that with the Tuileries, Opera and Place Vendôme as neighbors, this small hotel can boast of its location. Simple and well-run, the Hôtel du Continent also offers good comfort and attention to detail. On the ground floor, the space is all well used with an attractive breakfast room and TV-lounge grouped around the reception area. The ambiance is warm, thanks to the worked-wood pieces and salmon pink walls. The same color is found in the rooms, brightened by flowery curtains and bedspreads. The rooms are rather small but have comfortable bathrooms. The largest have full-size bathtubs, as do all those rooms with a number ending in a '6'; these also face onto the street.

Hôtel Costes

239, rue Saint-Honoré
75001 Paris
Tel. (0)1 42 44 50 00 - Fax (0)1 42 44 50 01
M. Costes

Category ★★★★ **Rooms** 85 with air-conditioning, soundproofing, bath, WC, hairdryer, telephone and fax, TV, CD player, safe and minibar - 3 for disabled persons. **Price** Single 1750F, double 2000-2250F, suite 2750-3750F. **Meals** Breakfast 130F, served from 7:00. **Credit cards** All major. **Pets** Dogs allowed. **Facilities** Elevator, laundry service, swimming pool, sauna, hammam, health center. **Restaurant** À la carte; tea room. **Parking** At place Vendôme. **How to get there** (Map 7): Bus: 24, 42, 72, 73, 94 - Metro: Concorde. **Open** All year.

On the Rue Saint-Honoré close to the Place Vendôme, only the name Costes indicates this discreet facade is a hotel. A gallery of red-trimmed windows leads you to the reception area where lounges open onto a large courtyard in the Italian style of terraces decorated with antique statues. This well of light contrasts with the cosy and theatrical ambiance of the small lounges around the patio. The decor comes from the La Traviata opera, with deep armchairs and 'confidante' chairs in dark pearwood arranged around the lampstands, and an imposing ceramic fireplace to create cosy corners for any conversation. The same 'fin de siècle' decor is in the rooms with cases in red brocade, a subtle mix of colors for the topstitched bedspreads, beautiful monogrammed bathroom linen, and an amusing reusage of former 'bourgeois' furniture. The suites are more luxurious and even more baroque.

Grand Hôtel de Champagne

13, rue des Orfèvres
75001 Paris
Tel. (0)1 42 36 60 00 – Fax (0)1 45 08 43 33
Mme Herbron - M. and Mme Lauferon

Category ★★★ **Rooms** 40 and 3 suites (with minibar), with telephone, bath, WC, TV satellite. **Price** Single 590-715F, double 640-800F, triple 810-970F, suite 990-1230F. **Meals** Breakfast (buffet) 55F, served 7:00-11:00. **Credit cards** All major. **Pets** Dogs allowed (+50F). **Facilities** Elevator, laundry service, bar. **Parking** Quai de Gesvres, Hôtel de Ville. **How to get there** (Map 2): Bus: 21, 28, 38, 47, 58, 67, 69, 70, 72, 74, 75, 76, 81, 85 - Metro: Châtelet - RER: Châtelet-Les Halles. **Open** All major.

Dating from 1647, the Grand Hôtel de Champagne has an inviting entrance and reception area, leading to a convivial bar and lounge. The adjacent breakfast room is in a Louis XIII style, which harmonizes well with the hotel's architecture. The bedrooms are decorated in different styles; the most remarkable are the suites, which vary from Japanese to 1970s, while paintings and frescos depicting 1930s Paris add color to other bedrooms. Our favorite floors are the *troisième étage,* where the bedrooms are larger, and the *cinquième étage,* whose rooms have mansard roofs and large balconies where you can enjoy breakfast with a view over the Paris rooftops. Note that to get to the small Rue des Orfèvres (meaning goldsmiths, who were located here from the 15th to the 19th centuries) you take the Rue Jean-Liantier, which continues on the other side of the Rue des Lavandières Sainte-Opportune. History buffs will be interested to know that the hotel was once home to tailors belonging to the prestigious skilled-workers guild called the *Compagnons du Tour de France,* which still exists.

Hôtel Louvre Saint-Honoré

141, rue Saint-Honoré
75001 Paris
Tel. (0)1 42 96 23 23 - Fax (0)1 42 96 21 61
M. Toulemonde

Category ✷✷✷ **Rooms** 40 with air-conditioning, soundproofing, telephone, bath, WC, hairdryer, safe, cable TV, minibar. **Price** Single 670-770F, double 780-880F. **Meals** Breakfast (buffet) 75F. **Credit cards** Amex, Visa, Eurocard, MasterCard. **Pets** Dogs allowed. **Facilities** Elevator. **Parking** Louvre, Louvre des antiquaires, rue Croix-des-Petits-Champs, Forum des Halles. **How to get there** (Map 1): Bus: 21, 67, 69, 74, 75, 76, 81, 85 - Metro: Louvre-Rivoli - RER: Châtelet-Les Halles. **Open** All year.

Next to the Louvre and Les Halles, this hotel comprises two buildings connected by a skylight under which an honor bar has been set up where clients can serve their own drinks. The breakfast room is also found here, and small exhibitions of pictures are organized. The decor and accommodations are modern without being austere. The bedrooms are bright, quiet (20 overlook the courtyard) and the bathrooms are well equipped. In the rooms you find a tray set for tea or coffee so that you can relax in full privacy on return home in the late afternoon. The staff is very friendly. The hotel is in an extremely picturesque neighborhood where, on Sunday morning, an open-air market takes place on the Rue Montorgueil. Nearby, around the Place des Victoires, you will find the fashionable boutiques of the city's leading *créateurs*.

Hôtel Mansart

5, rue des Capucines – 75001 Paris
Tel. (0)1 42 61 50 28 – Fax (0)1 49 27 97 44
e-mail: espfran@micronet.fr
M. Dupain

Category ★★★ Rooms 57 (some with air-conditioning) with telephone, bath, WC, TV satellite, safe, minibar. **Price** Single 550-980F, double 700-980F, suite 1250-1600F. **Meals** Breakfast 55F; snacks available. **Credit cards** Amex, Visa, Eurocard, MasterCard, JCB. **Pets** Dogs not allowed. **Facilities** Elevator. **Parking** At place Vendôme. **How to get there** (Map 7): Bus: 21, 27, 52, 68, 81, 95 - Metro: Opéra, Madeleine, Concorde, Tuileries - RER: Auber. **Open** All year.

On the corner of the Place Vendôme and the Rue des Capucines, the Hôtel Mansart has an idyllic location. The refurbishment was conceived in homage to Louis XIV's architect, Jules Mansart; thus, you will find tasteful baroque decor in the lobby, with mauve damask-covered 18th-century furniture and large paintings inspired by the famous formal gardens of Le Nôtre, Mansart's contemporary. The spacious bedrooms are comfortable, as are their bathrooms which have kept their original sizes. The flowery wallpapers and rustic furniture pieces give the rooms a certain provincial charm. For more style, and if you want to enjoy the view over Place Vendôme, ask for the Mansart suite with its 'Grand Siècle' styling.

Hôtel Opéra-Richepanse

14, rue Richepanse
75001 Paris
Tel. (0)1 42 60 36 00 - Fax (0)1 42 60 13 03
Mme Laporte - M. Jacques

Category **** **Rooms** 35 and 3 suites, with air-conditioning, soundproofing, bath, WC, hairdryer, telephone, TV satellite, minibar and safe. **Price** Single 1250F, double 1250-1450F, triple 1650F, suite 2050F. **Meals** Breakfast (buffet) 85F, served 7:00-10:30; snacks available on request. **Credit cards** All major. **Pets** Dogs allowed (+60F). **Facilities** Elevator, laudry service, room-service, sauna. **Parking** At place de la Madeleine. **How to get there** (Map 7): Bus: 24, 42, 52, 84, 94 - Metro: Madeleine. **Open** All year.

This new luxury hotel is two paces away from the Madeleine and Concorde, and displays the full aesthetics and opulence of Art Deco. All the acajou furniture was specially designed for the hotel from drawings that copied the typical forms of the 1920's, while their brown-red tones perfectly harmonize with the two other dominant colors, royal-blue and a golden-orange. Very comfortable and perfectly sound-proofed, the rooms vary in size and it seems that the bigger ones, with two beds, are a better deal. You will also appreciate the comfort and beauty of the bathrooms with their white faience enhanced by a frieze of gilt, silver or colored cabochons, large three-panelled mirrors, and perfect lighting. A small vaulted room for the copious breakfasts, a sauna and on the ground floor and a very warm little lounge are also available to you in this welcoming hotel.

Hôtel de la Place du Louvre

21, rue des Prêtres-Saint-Germain-l'Auxerrois - 75001 Paris
Tel. (0)1 42 33 78 68 - Fax (0)1 42 33 09 95
e-mail: espfran@micronet.fr
M. Chevalier

Category ★★★ **Rooms** 20 with telephone, bath, WC, TV satellite, safe, hairdryer. **Price** Single 510-700F, double 700-790F, duplex 830F. **Meals** Breakfast 40-50F. **Credit cards** All major. **Pets** Dogs allowed. **Facilities** Elevator, bar. **Parking** At place du Louvre, Saint-Germain-l'Auxerrois. **How to get there** (Map 1): Bus: 21, 24, 27, 67, 69, 74, 76, 81, 85 - Metro: Louvre-Rivoli, Pont-Neuf - RER: Châtelet-Les Halles. **Open** All year.

A room with a view awaits you at this hotel. And what a view! Rooms overlook the famous Louvre itself (which you can see by leaning from the windows) and the gargoyles and spires of the church of Saint-Germain-l'Auxerrois. A few vestiges of this ancient building have been preserved and successfully incorporated with modern decorative elements. The lounge and bar are located beneath a glass roof, while breakfast is served in a beautiful vaulted cellar called the *Salle des Mousquetaires,* which once was connected with the Louvre. Bright, comfortable and functional, the rooms vary in elegant cameos of beiges and white. Each has the name of a modern painter and lithographs on the walls. As always, the quieter rooms are on the courtyard but they lack the view. The welcome is attentive.

Le Relais du Louvre

19, rue des Prêtres-Saint-Germain-l'Auxerrois
75001 Paris
Tel. (0)1 40 41 96 42 – Fax (0)1 40 41 96 44
Mlle Aulnette

Category ★★★ Rooms 18 and 2 suites with soundproofing, telephone, bath or shower, WC, cable TV, safe, hairdryer, minibar. **Price** Single 600-750F, double 820-950F, suite 1280-1450F - Weekends (including Sunday night) and longs stays: –10%; August: –20%. **Meals** Breakfast 50F, served from 6:30. **Credit cards** All major. **Pets** Small dogs allowed. **Facilities** Elevator, room-service. **Parking** 2 private locations (70F per day) and at place du Louvre-Saint-Germain-l'Auxerrois. **How to get there** (Map 1): Bus: 21, 24, 27, 58, 67, 69, 70, 74, 76, 81, 85 - Metro: Louvre-Rivoli, Pont-Neuf - RER: Châtelet-Les Halles. **Open** All year.

One can guess the charm of the hotel from the reception area's pretty lighting and warm colors which complement the chairs and antique furniture to a lovely effect. The rooms are not particularly large apart from those designated suites, where particular attention has been given to both decor and comfort. Most rooms can be converted into small apartments for families. The hotel is in one of the most prestigious areas of Paris, near the Grand Louvre and in the shadow of the church of Saint-Germain-l'Auxerrois, the former parish of the Kings of France. Lastly, breakfasts are prepared with great care while the welcome is very friendly

Tonic Hôtel Louvre

12-14, rue du Roule
75001 Paris
Tel. (0)1 42 33 00 71 - Fax (0)1 40 26 06 86
M. Frédéric Boissier

Category ★★★ Rooms 34 with soundproofing (14 in the Roule section) telephone, bath with whirlpool and steam bath, WC, hairdryer, TV satellite, minibar - 1 for disabled persons. **Price** Single 590-690F, double 690-850F, triple 890F. **Meals** Breakfast (buffet) included, served 7:00-11:00. **Credit cards** All major. **Pets** Small dogs allowed. **Facilities** Elevator, laundry service, patio, room-service. **Parking** Les Halles, access: rue du Pont-Neuf. **How to get there** (Map 7): Bus: 21, 38, 47, 58, 67, 69, 70, 72, 75, 76, 81, 85 - Metro and RER: Châtelet-Les Halles. **Open** All year.

The Hotel Tonic was formed out of two earlier hotels, and in the section known as the 'Tonic' the rooms are decorated identically, with beautiful beamed ceilings, and walls of exposed stones. The dark, Spanish-style furniture goes well with the predominantly red color scheme. The rooms are spacious, with modern bathrooms. As for the 'Roule' section, it has just been renovated with both decor and comfort much improved. The reception area and breakfast room are in the 'Tonic' section. Down on the Rue du Roule, you will have a beautiful view of the Les Halles Gardens and Saint Eustache Church. Looking the other way, you'll see the busy Rue de Rivoli with its large department stores.

Hôtel des Tuileries

10, rue Saint-Hyacinthe - 75001 Paris
Tel. (0)1 42 61 04 17 - Fax (0)1 49 27 91 56
web: http://www.webscapades.com/france/paris/tuilerie.htm
Family Poulle-Vidal

Category ★★★ **Rooms** 26 with air-conditioning, telephone, bath, WC, hairdryer, TV satellite. **Price** Single 590-890F, double 690-1200F - Special rates on request. **Meals** Breakfast 60F, served 6:30-12:00. **Credit cards** All major. **Pets** Dogs allowed. **Facilities** Elevator, laundry service, room-service. **Parking** At place du Marché-Saint-Honoré and place Vendôme. **How to get there** (Map 7): Bus: 21, 27, 68, 69, 72 - Metro: Tuileries, Pyramides. **Open** All year.

The Hôtel des Tuileries is tucked away in a small street off the Rue du Faubourg Saint-Honoré, between the Place du Marché Saint-Honoré and Saint-Roch Church (by car, you arrive via the Rue Saint-Honoré and the Rue du 29 Juin). The street is somewhat dark, but very quiet; the bustling Palais-Royal and Les Halles are but a few steps away. The reception area is very inviting, leading to the basement sitting rooms, a small reading room, and the breakfast room, where guests can enjoy a buffet with favorite foods from their own country (cereals, toast, cheeses, etc.). The bedrooms are individually decorated, some with Polish-style beds and tapestries in an 18th-century Chinese style, others with painted furniture and pastel colors. Rooms are quiet because of double-glazing and air-conditioning and they can be combined to form an apartment for four people. The bathroom facilities include whirlpool tubs and separate toilets. It is said that Marie-Antoinette stayed in this pleasant place. Note the proximity of the Saint-Roch Church, one of the most beautiful baroque churches in Paris, with its Virgin's Chapel designed by Louis XIV's architect, Jules Hardoin-Mansart.

Hôtel Violet

7, rue Jean-Lantier
75001 Paris
Tel. (0)1 42 33 45 38 - Fax (0)1 40 28 03 56
M. Hakim Sifaoui

Category ★★★ **Rooms** 30 with sounproofing, telephone, bath or shower, WC, hairdryer, cable and satellite TV, minibar, safe - 1 for disabled persons. **Price** Single 550-660F, double 730F, triple 900F - Special rates in low season. **Meals** Breakfast (buffet) 50F, served 7:30-10:00. **Credit cards** All major. **Pets** Dogs not allowed. **Facilities** Elevator, laundry service. **Parking** At Hôtel de Ville and quai de Gesvres. **How to get there** (Map 2): Bus: 21, 38, 47, 58, 67, 69, 70, 72, 75, 76, 81, 85, 96 - Metro: Châtelet - RER: Châtelet-Les Halles. **Open** All year.

Via an alternating combination of windows and glass doors, the Hôtel Violet is wide open onto the quiet Rue Jean Lantier running between the Châtelet Theater and the Rue de Rivoli. Reception, lounge and bar are on the large and airy ground floor, along with a winter garden. The rooms are all decorated on the same model : painted classical-style furniture and quilted cottons for the bedsteads, along with matching curtains. Some will comfortably take three people without needing the traditional emergency bed. These are genuine 'triples' with the 'double' part giving onto the street, and the 'single' area onto the courtyard, to allow sharing without too much proximity. The breakfast buffet is laid out in a 16th-century, cut-stone vaulted room, but you can also be served your traditional 'continental' breakfast in your room if you wish. The welcome is young and charming.

Demeure Hôtel Castille

37, rue Cambon
75001 Paris
Tel. (0)1 44 58 44 58 – Fax (0)1 44 58 44 00
M. Langlois

Category ★★★★ **Rooms** 111 with air-conditioning, bath, telephone, hairdryer, WC, TV satellite, minibar, safe. **Prices** Rooms 2100-2750 F, duplex and suite 3050F and 3600F. **Meals** Breakfast 140F, served 7:00-10:30. **Credit cards** All major. **Pets** Dogs allowed. **Facilities** Elevator, laundry service, room-service. **Garage** 8 parking places (150F). **Restaurant** "Il Cortile": closed Sunday - Service 12:00-14:00, 19:00-22:00; menu 195F, also à la carte (about 250F). Specialties: Italian cooking. **Parking** At place de la Madeleine. **How to get there** (Map 7): Bus: 24, 42, 52, 84, 94 - Metro: Concorde, Madeleine. **Open** All year.

The Hotel Castille adjoins the famous couture house of Coco Chanel on the Rue Cambon. The Opera wing was once the annex of the equally famous Ritz Hotel. The hotel was extensively redesigned in an Italian style, with engraved mirrors, clouded patinas, painted furniture and lamps, and a large Roman mosaic. The bedrooms are decorated with red and green brocades and damasks recreating Renaissance motifs; the bathroom marbles pick up the same rich colors. The neighboring 18th-century building, called the Rivoli Wing (our favorite), offers some twenty rooms and suites. Decorated by Jacques Grange, they are done in a totally different style: minimalist chic. In the small sitting room, you will find faux marble patina, deep sofas, cane armchairs, and various antiques such as painted metal lamps and Aubusson carpets. The bedrooms are decorated in green and burgundy stripes, checks, or plaids, with dark, 19th-century–style furniture, and photos of Paris by Robert Doisneau. A very good Italian restaurant in the hotel serves summer meals in a charming courtyard painted in *trompe-l'œil*, beautified with a fountain and cypress trees. You can even see the models from Chanel there, perpetuating the legend of "Coco" and the Ritz.

Hôtel Favart

5, rue Marivaux
75002 Paris
Tel. (0)1 42 97 59 83 – Fax (0)1 40 15 95 58
M. Éric Champetier

Category ★★★ Rooms 37 with soundproofing, telephone, bath or shower, WC, hairdryer, TV satellite, radio, minibar, safe. **Price** Single 515F, double 640F, 3 pers. 750F. **Meals** Breakfast included, served 6:45-11:00. **Credit cards** All major. **Pets** Dogs allowed. **Facilities** Elevator, laundry service. **Parking** Boulevard des Italiens. **How to get there** (Map 7): Bus: 39, 48 - Metro: Quatre-Septembre, Richelieu-Drouot - RER: Auber. **Open** All year.

The Hôtel Favart reminds us that before becoming the Opéra-Comique the pretty theater facing us was the Salle Favart, which twice had to make a fresh start in its life, and the present hotel dates from the last reconstruction. The entrance is spacious and very attractive, with its naive panoramas on the staircase, its marble columns and reception area leading into the breakfast room. The best rooms are on the front, with a clear view over the very quiet little street. On the first floor the low ceilings with beams and the arched windows create a cosy effect; one room is named the Goya Room to remind you that the painter stayed in it. From the second floor the rooms are really large with light watered fabrics and painted ceilings to give a lot of light. As for the comfortable bathrooms, they have a certain liking for 'trompe-l'oeil' effects and depending on your taste, you can opt for cork panelling or a more aquatic ambiance. Between the Palais-Royal and the Grands Boulevards, you will appreciate this central site that reconciles culture and shopping.

Grand Hôtel de Besançon

56, rue Montorgueil
75002 Paris
Tel. (0)1 42 36 41 08 – Fax (0)1 45 08 08 79
M. Boudaa

Category ★★★ Rooms 9 and 11 junior suites, with soundproofing, telephone, bath or shower, WC, hairdryer, TV satellite, radio. **Price** Single 620F, double 650F, junior suite 680-720F (3 pers.), triple 870-900F. **Meals** Breakfast 40F, served 7:00-11:30. **Credit cards** All major. **Pets** Dogs not allowed. **Facilities** Elevator, laundry service. **Parking** Saint-Eustache (rue de Turbigo) and rue Saint-Denis. **How to get there** (Map 7): Bus: 29 - Metro: Étienne-Marcel, Sentier - RER: Châtelet-Les Halles. **Open** All year.

The Rue Montorgueil is one of those historical streets of the capital that you should visit in this district once known as the 'Belly of Paris'; it has kept all the life and noises of Parisian markets. So if you decide to stay at the Grand Hôtel de Besançon you will have to cope with the robust street noises, unless you take a room on the courtyard. You reach the reception area on the first floor via a rather steep (especially if you have heavy baggage) staircase. Fully renovated, identical rooms have are simple and in good taste: Louis Philippe-style furniture and floral cotton fabrics give them an incontestable provincial charm, while those on the back are light and charming. It is better to take your breakfast in your room as the reception-lounge is not very attractive for starting the day. Even bette, especially on a Sunday, go and have coffee and 'tartines' on the Rue Montorgueil where you will meet the last street urchins of Paris, among others.

Hôtel de Noailles

9, rue de la Michodière
75002 Paris
Tel. (0)1 47 42 92 90 - Fax (0)1 49 24 92 71
Mme Falck

Category ★★★ **Rooms** 58 with soundproofing (45 with air-conditioning), telephone, bath, WC, hairdryer, cable TV. **Price** Single 706F, double 880F. **Meals** Breakfast (buffet) 40F, served 7:00-11:00; snacks available, room-service until 22:00. **Credit cards** All major. **Pets** Dogs allowed. **Facilities** Elevator, laundry service, patio and terraces. **Parking** At place du Marché-Saint-Honoré and rue de la Chaussée-d'Antin. **How to get there** (Map 7): All bus for Opéra - Metro: Opéra, Quatre-Septembre. **Open** All year.

In the very animated neighborhood around the Opéra, popular with tourists for its proximity to the Grand Louvre and the large department stores, the Hôtel de Noailles is a haven of tranquillity and comfort. Decorated in contemporary and Japanese styles, the hotel is centered around a small garden and a terrace on the *deuxième étage*. The reception area is very large, with a lounge/library for non-smokers; the bar/breakfast room opens onto the garden, where breakfast and drinks are served in good weather. You will find a modern style in the bedrooms, with a different color scheme on each floor: grey-black (a surprisingly bold decorative touch), midnight blue, and yellow. The rooms are very comfortable; some are air-conditioned, others open onto the terrace, and those on the top floor have a balcony where you can enjoy your breakfast. On each floor, there is a small lounge for entertaining guests, and a soft drink machine. The staff is very friendly, and the same can be said of the house dog, Emile.

Le Stendhal Hôtel

22, rue Danielle-Casanova
75002 Paris
Tel. (0)1 44 58 52 52 - Fax (0)1 44 58 52 00
Mme Nelly Frey

Category ★★★★ **Rooms** 17 and 3 suites with air-conditioning, soundproofing, telephone, bath or shower, WC, hairdryer, minibar, safe, cable TV. **Price** Single and double 1380-1560F (July 15 – August 31: 900F, breakfast included), suite 1700 and 1900F (3 pers.). **Meals** Breakfast 95F, served from 6:30 (weekend: from 7:00). **Credit cards** All major. **Pets** Dogs allowed. **Facilities** Elevator, laundry service, bar, room-service. **Parking** At place Vendôme. **How to get there** (Map 7): All bus to Opéra - Metro: Opéra, Tuileries - RER: Auber. **Open** All year.

Rue Saint-Honoré, Place Vendôme and Rue de la Paix - the whole district stands for the French luxury and chic of the leading 'couturiers' and prestige jewellers. The Stendhal Hôtel is in a discreet building on the quiet Rue Danielle-Casanova, right next to this world center for window-shopping. In this small hotel a lot of care has been given to decor quality and the well-being of the rooms, which differ in size. Those with a number ending in a '3' are in yellow and blue with large window-lit bathrooms. Just as pretty are others in reds and greens, along with the suites; one of them plays on 'The red and the black' theme in tribute to Stendhal. Double-glazing and air-conditioning guarantee quiet. Along with a fine basement for breakfast service, this is a refined address.

Hotel Les Chevaliers

30, rue de Turenne
75003 Paris
Tel. (0)1 42 72 73 47 – Fax (0)1 42 72 54 10
Mme Truffaut

Category ★★★ **Rooms** 24 with soundproofing, telephone, bath, WC, hairdryer, TV satellite, safe. **Price** Single and double 600-830F, triple 824-1004F. **Meals** Breakfast 50F (offered in August), buffet 80F, served 7:00-10:30. **Credit cards** Amex, Visa, Eurocard, MasterCard. **Pets** Dogs allowed. **Facilities** Elevator, laundry service, room-service. **Parking** At 16 rue Saint-Antoine. **How to get there** (Map 2): Bus: 20, 29, 65, 96 - Metro: Chemin-Vert, Saint-Paul, Bastille. **Open** All year.

Very near the famous Place des Vosges, the Carnavalet Museum, and the Picasso Museum in the historic Marais quarter, the Chevaliers occupies a 17th-century building of which there are still original vestiges, like the half-timbering in the stairwell, and the well in the basement. The recent renovation has brightened up the lounge walling and chairs in their yellow and blue prints, which go well with the new style furniture in cherry wood. All the rooms are different and a discreet stylisation of the furniture pieces has been adopted, which gives full decorative effect to the prettily coordinated drapes and bedspreads. Many thoughtful details further add to guests' pleasure: fresh flowers in the rooms, baskets of fruit, chocolates on the pillows, toiletries in the baths–things you'd normally expect in a more luxurious hotel.

Pavillon de la Reine

28, place des Vosges
75003 Paris
Tel. (0)1 40 29 19 19 – Fax (0)1 40 29 19 20
Mme Véronique Ellinger

Category ★★★★ **Rooms** 34, 13 appartments and 8 duplex, with air-conditioning, sounproofing, telephone, bath, WC, cable TV, hairdryer, minibar - 4 for disabled persons. **Price** Single 1650F, double, "luxe room" and duplex 1850-2300F, suite 2900F (double) and 3400F (triple). **Meals** Continental breakfast 110F, buffet 135F, served 7:00-10:30 (in room at any time). **Credit cards** All major. **Pets** Dogs allowed. **Facilities** Elevator, laundry service, bar, patio, room-service (24h/24). **Parking** Private garage (25 places). **How to get there** (Map 2): Bus: 20, 29, 65, 69, 76, 96 - Metro: Bastille, Saint-Paul. **Open** All year.

This is an admirable hotel in a historic setting. The hotel consists of two buildings, one dating from the 17th century and the other harmoniously rebuilt around a small courtyard. The entry lobby is superb, all green with its Virginia creeper and geraniums. The Haute Epoque interiors reflect the architectural style, with worked oak covering the lounge walls, beautiful antique pieces, and deep armchairs in smart polished leather. The rooms, and above all the suites, have very fine fittings and offer a very warming comfort, with colors and materials of great refinement. Whichever side they are on, looking over the garden or the flowery courtyard, all are very quiet. The service is discreet and stylish, and the welcome personal. This is a very fine address with one of the most exceptional sites of all Paris.

Hôtel Beaubourg

11, rue Simon-Lefranc - 75004 Paris
Tel. (0)1 42 74 34 24 - Fax (0)1 42 78 68 11
web: http://www.paris-hotel.com/beaubourg
M. and Mme Morand

Category ★★★ **Rooms** 28 with telephone, bath or shower, WC, hairdryer, TV satellite, minibar. **Price** Single 490-580F, double 490-700F. **Meals** Breakfast 40F, served 7:00-11:00. **Credit cards** All major. **Pets** Dogs allowed. **Facilities** Elevator. **Parking** Beaubourg. **How to get there** (Map 2): Metro: Rambuteau - RER: Châtelet-Les Halles. **Open** All year.

Rue Simon-Lefranc is right behind the Georges-Pompidou Center and its facade of colored piping, shafts and air-conditioning vents. In contrast, the Hôtel Beaubourg is in an old house that has conserved its ceiling beams, fine samples of exposed stonework and a vaulted basement. The decor is classical, with leather sofas and armchairs in the entrance-reception-lounge area. Most of the rooms are large and equipped with functional furniture, bedheads in copper, cane, or bamboo, enhanced by the flowery fabrics of the curtains and bedspreads. The whole effect is cosseted and well maintained. One room on the ground floor has a small semi-private terrace, particularly attractive in summertime. If you are lucky to find it free then take it, but do not embarrass the owner by insisting on it as the others are all just as comfortable and pleasant. The welcome appears a little reserved but this is only a first impression soon forgotten as M. and Mme. Morand are attentive to ensure that all goes well.

Hôtel de la Bretonnerie

22, rue Sainte-Croix-de-la-Bretonnerie
75004 Paris
Tel. (0)1 48 87 77 63 - Fax (0)1 42 77 26 78
Mlle Sagot

Category ★★★ **Rooms** 27 and 3 suites with soundproofing, bath, WC, hairdryer, telephone, cable TV, safe, minibar. **Price** Single and double 640-790F, suite 980F. **Meals** Breakfast 50F, served 7:15-10:30. **Credit cards** Visa, Eurocard, MasterCard. **Pets** Small dogs allowed. **Facilities** Elevator. **Parking** Hôtel-de-Ville, Baudoyer (rue de Rivoli/place Baudoyer) and garage nearby. **How to get there** (Map 2): Bus: 29, 38, 47, 58, 67, 69, 70, 72, 74, 75, 76 - Metro: Hôtel-de-Ville. **Open** All year except Aug.

In a private residence dating from the 17th century, just a few steps from the Pompidou Center and Picasso Museum, the Hôtel de la Bretonnerie has pleasant surprises in store for visitors. In fact, each year the owners transform and redecorate a few rooms and thus they all acquire their own special atsosphere and decor. Most of them are vast and those with mezzanine ceilings will sleep three people. Bright colors for some, softer lines for others, just now favorites are numbers 20 and 21, along with the small number 14 bathed in sunshine. The bathrooms are very well equipped and some have large windows opening onto the courtyard. A cosy atmosphere of comfort reigns throughout the hotel and the welcome is very friendly.

Hôtel Caron de Beaumarchais

12, rue Vieille-du-Temple
75004 Paris
Tel. (0)1 42 72 34 12 - Fax (0)1 42 72 34 63
M. Bigeard

Category ★★★ **Rooms** 19 with air-conditioning, soundproofing, bath or shower, WC, telephone, TV satellite, hairdryer, minibar. **Price** Single and double 690-770F. **Meals** Breakfast 54F, brunch 78F, served 7:30-12:00. **Credit cards** All major. **Pets** Dogs not allowed. **Facilities** Elevator. **Parking** Baudoyer (rue de Rivoli/place Baudoyer) and at rue Lobau. **How to get there** (Map 2): Bus: 54, 68, 74, 80, 81, 95 - Metro: Hôtel-de-Ville, Saint-Paul-le-Marais. **Open** All year.

This comfortable 18th-century house has been restored in homage to the famous author of *The Marriage of Figaro,* who lived on this street in the Marais district. The decoration was carried out by Alain Bigeard, who researched and took inspiration from documents of the time. Thus, in the lobby, the walls are covered with embroidered fabric reproduced from original designs, and there are Burgundian stone floors and period furniture. The same elegance is found in the comfortable bedrooms and the bathrooms, whose tiles are modeled on those made in Rouen and Nevers. The welcome is attentive while the location is ideal on the corner of Rue de Rivoli, right between the Marais quarter and the Ile Saint-Louis.

Hôtel des Deux Îles

59, rue Saint-Louis-en-l'Île
75004 Paris
Tel. (0)1 43 26 13 35 – Fax (0)1 43 29 60 25
M. Buffat

Category ✦✦✦ **Rooms** 17 with air-conditioning, bath or shower, WC, telephone, cable TV, hairdryer. **Price** Single 730F, double 840F. **Meals** Breakfast 47F, snacks available. **Credit cards** Visa, Eurocard, MasterCard, Amex. **Pets** Dogs not allowed. **Facilities** Elevator. **Parking** At 2 rue Geoffroy-l'Asnier and square in front of Notre-Dame. **How to get there** (Map 2): Bus: 24, 63, 67, 86, 87 - Metro: Pont-Marie. **Open** All year.

Monsieur and Madame Buffat have converted two buildings into hotels of charm: the Hôtel des Deux Iles and the Lutèce, set between a former Archbishop's Palace, the Church of Saint-Louis-en-l'Ile, and Bertillon, famous for its ice cream. We have chosen the Deux Iles for its atmosphere – English with a tinge of exoticism: Flowery fabrics and painted cane and bamboo furniture are the main features of the decor. The bedrooms are not very large, but they are delightful. Provençal fabrics replace the chintzes used in the lounge, and the bathrooms are lined with gleaming blue tiles. Everything here is comfortable, including the beautiful vaulted breakfast room. This hotel has maintained a clientele loyal to a house that is so much in harmony with the whole of Ile Saint-Louis.

Grand Hôtel Jeanne d'Arc

3, rue de Jarente
75004 Paris
Tel. (0)1 48 87 62 11 – Fax (0)1 48 87 37 31
M. and Mme Mesenge

Category ★★ **Rooms** 36 with telephone, bath or shower, WC, hairdryer, cable TV. **Price** Single 300-395F, double 305-490F, triple 530F, 4 pers. 590F. **Meals** Breakfast 35F, served 7:00-11:00. **Credit cards** Visa, Eurocard, MasterCard. **Pets** Dogs allowed. **Facilities** Elevator. **Parking** At rue Saint-Antoine. **How to get there** (Map 2): Bus: 29, 69, 76, 96 - Metro: Saint-Paul. **Open** All year.

The Marais is famous for its historic Place des Vosges, prestigious town houses, and the Picasso and Carnavalet Museums. It's less known for the small "village" just off the noble square: the Place du Marché Sainte-Catherine and the Rue de Jarente, where you'll find the small Hôtel Jeanne d'Arc. Named after the Jeanne d'Arc Convent, which was demolished in the 18th century to make way for a market, the hotel reflects the simple charm of the neighborhood, which abounds with picturesque cafés and outdoor restaurants on tree-lined sidewalks. The hotel's reception area/lounge and the breakfast room with white crocheted tablecloths give it the feel of a family home. There are four small bedrooms, but they are reasonably priced, especially if there are two of you. Other rooms are larger, some are very large, like Room 63, which is on the top floor and can accommodate four people; it has an immense bathroom and mansard roof. Most rooms are decorated in blue, which you'll find repeated in the *trompe-l'œil* bathroom tiles. And from most of the rooms you will have a view over the flower-filled inner courtyards and the rooftops of this enchanting neighborhood.

Hôtel du Jeu de Paume

54, rue Saint-Louis-en-l'Île
75004 Paris
Tel. (0)1 43 26 14 18 - Fax (0)1 40 46 02 76
Mme Prache

Category ★★★★ **Rooms** 32 with bath, WC, telephone, cable TV, hairdryer, minibar.
Price Double 895-1395F. **Meals** Breakfast 80F; snacks available. **Credit cards** All major.
Pets Dogs allowed. **Facilities** Elevator, secretariat, sauna, gym, patio, bar. **Parking** At 2 rue
Geoffroy-l'Asnier and square in front of Notre-Dame. **How to get there** (Map 2): Bus: 24, 63,
67, 86, 87 - Metro: Pont-Marie. **Open** All year.

This hotel is on the site of an authentic old palm-tennis court. The spacious interior has been entirely and artfully restructured by creating a series of galleries and mezzanines to form a dynamic and decorative architectural arrangement. On the ground-floor is an intimate lounge-bar and a warm, inviting breakfast room; on the mezzanine you will find a reading room, and off the galleries are the elegant and comfortable rooms. They are not very large but have beautiful bathrooms. The delicious breakfasts include excellent homemade preserves.

Hôtel Libertel Grand Turenne

6, rue de Turenne
75004 Paris
Tel. (0)1 42 78 43 25 - Fax (0)1 42 74 10 74
Mme Biagini

Category ★★★ **Rooms** 41 and 5 suites with soundproofing, telephone, bath or shower, WC, hairdryer, minibar, cable TV - 2 for disabled persons. **Price** Single 650-780F, double 700-840F, triple 990F, suite 990F (2 pers.). **Meals** Breakfast 75F, served 7:00-10:30. **Credit cards** All major. **Pets** Dogs allowed. **Facilities** Elevator, laundry service, safes at reception. **Parking** At rue Saint-Antoine. **How to get there** (Map 2): Bus: 29, 67, 69, 76, 96 - Metro: Saint-Paul, Bastille. **Open** All year.

There is nothing to criticize about this comfortable hotel in Le Marais, just a few steps from the Place des Vosges, with a welcoming reception area enlivened by energetic and qualified personnel. It leads into a colorful lounge opening wide onto the street. The rooms are rather standardized and not large, but again there is nothing to criticize as they are well maintained, pleasantly furnished with good comfort, as are the bathrooms. Please note that some are reserved for non-smokers and that two of them have a view over the gardens of the Hôtel de Sully.

Hôtel de Lutèce

65, rue Saint-Louis-en-L'Île
75004 Paris
Tel. (0)1 43 26 23 52 - Fax (0)1 43 29 60 25
M. Buffat

Category ★★★ **Rooms** 23 with air-conditioning, telephone, bath or shower, WC, cable TV. **Price** Single 720F, double 840F, triple 980F. **Meals** Breakfast 45F, served 7:30-12:00. **Credit cards** All major. **Pets** Dogs not allowed. **Facilities** Elevator. **Parking** At 2, rue Geoffroy-l'Asnier and square in front of Notre-Dame. **How to get there** (Map 2): Bus: 24, 63, 67, 86, 87 - Metro: Pont-Marie, Cité, Hôtel-de-Ville. **Open** All year.

The intimate lighting, the beautiful bouquet of fresh flowers, the ancient floor in polished tiles, the fire burning in the hearth - all tempt you to pass in through the reception door. Everything has been thought out with taste and care. The rooms are not very large and furnished 'à minima' but always with a certain note to personalize each: a Braun Van Velde lithograph, a fine mirror, and so on. A choice of pretty fabrics livens up the rooms which have kept their fine ceiling beams. The top floor has mansard ceilings. On this long street in old Paris the beautiful private houses of the 17th and 18th centuries do not inhibit the real life of the district with its genuine old shops, booksellers and tearooms. Bertillon with their famous icecreams are at No. 31, and chocolate-lovers will also find La Charlotte de l'Isle close by. For dinner close to the hotel we would name L'Orangerie at No. 28, and Au Gourmet de l'Isle to get to know the oldest restaurant of the capital. This hotel and district summarize all the charms of Paris.

Hôtel de Nice

42 *bis*, rue de Rivoli
75004 Paris
Tel. (0)1 42 78 55 29 - Fax (0)1 42 78 36 07
M. and Mme Vaudoux

Category ✶✶ **Rooms** 23 with soundproofing, telephone, bath, WC, TV. **Price** Single 380F, double 480F, triple 600F. **Meals** Breakfast 35F, served 7:00-10:00. **Credit cards** Visa, Eurocard, MasterCard. **Pets** Dogs not allowed. **Facilities** Elevator. **Parking** Hôtel-de-Ville. **How to get there** (Map 2): Bus: 47, 67, 69, 70, 72, 74, 76, 96 - Metro: Hôtel-de-Ville. **Open** All year.

Despite the turquoise-painted door, at first you do not spot the entrance of the Hôtel de Nice with its reception on the first floor. On the other hand you straight away realize that you are in a hotel with atmosphere as the binding paper on the walls, with its graphics repeated on the kilims covering the floors, is a handsome backing for the numerous cover pages of 'Le Petit Journal' that decorate the walls. The lounge also serves as breakfast room, and has the same ambiance of a private house with its very personal choice of antique furniture and a fine collection of 19t-century paintings, including one very large portrait. The rooms also reflect the owners' whims with Napoleon III chairs, a Louis-Philippe desk, cupboards, old doors, and always lots of prints, pastels and so on. The top-floor rooms have mansard ceilings and a small balcony, and are among the largest, able to sleep several guests. The rooms on the courtyard are the quietest, and you find here an unexpected atmosphere right in the center of Paris between Le Marais and the Hôtel de Ville.

Hôtel Rivoli Notre-Dame

19, rue du Bourg-Tibourg
75004 Paris
Tel. (0)1 42 78 47 39 - Fax (0)1 40 29 07 00
Mme Capdeville

Category ★★★ Rooms 31 with bath, WC, hairdryer, telephone, TV satellite, minibar, safe. **Price** Single 525F, double 660F, triple 715F. **Meals** Breakfast 42F, served 7:00-10:30. **Credit cards** All major. **Pets** Dogs not allowed. **Facilities** Elevator. **Parking** Hôtel-de-Ville. **How to get there** (Map 2): Bus: 67, 69, 70, 72, 74, 76, 96 - Metro: Hôtel-de-Ville. **Open** All year.

The Hôtel Rivoli Notre-Dame is quite simply charming and in good taste, in this attractive district on the edge of Le Marais, Les Halles, the Beaubourg and the Hôtel de Ville. The rooms are on six floors with white molded ceilings, fine stripes on the walls and bedspreads in quilted Vichy. Select your color depending on whether you prefer blues, browns or greens; all are successful. The bathrooms are comfortably equipped and some also enjoy direct daylight. The rooms on the corner with numbers ending with a '6' are the largest, while on the top floor the small balcony along the facade allows you a better view of the roofs of Paris. Fine vaulted basements serve as the breakfast room. The welcome is full of good humor in a hotel offering you a very good quality-price deal.

Hotel Saint-Merry

78, rue de la Verrerie
75004 Paris
Tel. (0)1 42 78 14 15 - Fax (0)1 40 29 06 82
M. Crabbe

Category ★★★ Rooms 11 and 1 suite with soundproofing, telephone, bath or shower, 9 with WC. **Price** Single or double 450-1100F, suite (2 pers., free for children under 12 years) 1800F, suite (3-4 pers.) 2400F. **Meals** Breakfast 50F. **Credit cards** Visa, Eurocard, MasterCard. **Pets** Dogs allowed. **Parking** Saint-Merry/Rivoli, access: rue Saint-Bon. **How to get there** (Map 2): Bus: 58, 70, 72, 74, 76 - Metro: Châtelet, Hôtel-de-Ville - RER: Châtelet-Les Halles. **Open** All year.

This hotel is named after the Saint-Merry Church, which was built in the Renaissance in the flamboyant Gothic style. The hotel occupies the building adjoining the church, once the residence of the nuns of Saint-Merry. The owner, Monsieur Crabbe, has restored the hotel to its original splendor. Room 9 is traversed from one side to the other by a magnificent flying buttress, which you should see even if you're not staying in this room. He spent years gathering period pieces from the Drouot Auction Rooms, like furniture and old panels, which were reconstructed as headboards and closet doors. Ironwork, another major Gothic art form, is also well represented in the chandeliers and large candelabras that have been transformed into beautiful lamps. The bathrooms are decorated with small panes of stained glass. The result is one of great taste and proportion. The suite known as the 'Apotheosis of Saint Merry' has its own private entrance on the top floor, leading into a genuine apartment.

Hôtel Saint-Paul-Le Marais

8, rue de Sévigné
75004 Paris
Tel. (0)1 48 04 97 27 – Fax (0)1 48 87 37 04
Mme Leguide

Category ★★★ **Rooms** 27 with soundproofing, bath or shower, WC, telephone, cable TV, hairdryer, safe. **Price** Single 510-590F, double 630-690F, "Luxe" with whirlpool 850-990F, triple 790-890F, suite with whirlpool 1360-1580F. **Meals** Breakfast (buffet) 55F, served 7:00-10:15. **Credit cards** All major. **Pets** Dogs not allowed. **Facilities** Elevator, laundry service, patio, bar, Whirlpool. **Parking** At place Baudoyer and 16, rue Saint-Antoine. **How to get there** (Map 2): Bus: 29, 69, 76, 96 - Metro: Saint-Paul. **Open** All year.

For those who love the Marais district with its private mansions, craftwork boutiques next door to the fashion kinds, and proximity to the world-famous Place des Vosges, then this hotel is ideal. Only a few pillars and some worked wood remain from the earlier building and a contemporary style has been chosen with the reception area opening widely onto the street, both bright and airy with its black leather armchairs contrasting the pastel wall shades. Some of the rooms still display their ancient ceiling beams but all have been renovated in combined blues and pinks, with pictures to match. The decoration is simple and rather standard but there are welcome extras such as an electric kettle with tea and coffee-bags. Another novelty, the young women of the family have opened a beauty salon in the basement, and plan soon a sauna for any envious husbands.

Hôtel Abbatial Saint-Germain

46, boulevard Saint-Germain
75005 Paris
Tel. (0)1 46 34 02 12 - Fax (0)1 43 25 47 73
M. Sahuc

Category ★★★ **Rooms** 43 with air-conditioning, bath or shower, WC, telephone, minibar, safe, TV. **Price** Single 590-650F, double 680-820F, triple 950F. **Meals** Breakfast (buffet) 50F, served 7:00-10:30. **Credit cards** Visa, Eurocard, MasterCard, Amex, JCB. **Pets** Dogs not allowed. **Facilities** Elevator. **Parking** Maubert. **How to get there** (Map 2): Bus: 24, 63, 86, 87 - Metro: Maubert-Mutualité - RER: Saint-Michel. **Open** All year.

Two-hundred yards from Notre-Dame (six bedrooms overlook the cathedral) the Abbatial Saint Germain, formerly the Grand Hôtel de Lima, has just had a facelift. The lobby, with its beautifully upholstered Louis XVI-style furniture, gives a hint of the refinement and attention to detail to be found in the bedrooms: pink wall fabrics coordinated with thick piqué bedspreads, Louis XVI-style white lacquered furniture, effective double-glazing (to quieten the busy Boulevard Saint Germain), and well-kept bathrooms and showers, with all the amenities you would expect in an establishment of this kind. Breakfasts are served in a barrel-vaulted room in the basement where the rustic stones have been softened with beautiful Louis-Philippe medallion-back chairs and a large mural landscape. The effect is lovely, and it is a welcome change from the rustic coldness of many hotels with an overdone decor of exposed stones. There is a small lounge and bar next to the reception area.

Hôtel des Arènes

51, rue monge
75005 Paris
Tel. (0)1 43 25 09 26 – Fax (0)1 43 25 79 56
M. Balouka

Category ✱✱✱ **Rooms** 52 with bath or shower, WC, telephone, minibar, TV - 2 for disabled persons. **Price** Single 650F, double 805F, triple 1065F. **Meals** Breakfast included, served 7:00-10:30. **Credit cards** All major. **Facilities** Elevator. **Parking** Private (84F per day), 300m. **How to get there** (Map 2): Bus: 47, 67, 89 - Metro: Cardinal-Lemoine, Monge. **Open** All year.

As its name suggests, the Arènes overlooks the ruins of the immense Gallo-Roman amphitheater where, in the first century A.D., 15,000 spectators came to the circus and the theater. They were progressively pillaged and then buried until their remains were discovered by chance around 1865 when the Rue Monge was opened. For the best view, ask for one of the 15 rooms overlooking the back: Beneath your windows, you can see the ancient stage, and the remains of several walls surrounded by lawns, flower beds, and large trees where neighborhood children come to play. Modern comforts have not been neglected in the pleasant, quiet rooms; those on the street (with double-glazing) do not have the same charming view. Breakfast is served in a basement room designed somewhat like a conservatory, whose mirrored walls create an impression of spaciousness.

Hôtel des Carmes

5, rue des Carmes
75005 Paris
Tel. (0)1 43 29 78 40 - Fax (0)1 43 29 57 17
M. Paul Dauban

Category ★★ **Rooms** 30 with soundproofing, bath or shower, WC, telephone, TV - 1 for disabled persons. **Price** Single 455-555F, double 510-610F, triple 780F. Special rates in low season on request. **Meals** Breakfast 35F, served 7:00-11:30. **Credit cards** All major. **Pets** Dogs not allowed. **Facilities** Elevator. **Parking** At rue Lagrange. **How to get there** (Map 2): Bus: 24, 47, 63, 84, 86, 87, 89 - Metro: Maubert-Mutualité. **Open** All year.

After eight months of work, the Hôtel des Carmes has refound its youth. The entry hall is spacious with a corner lounge which is agreeable but without surprises, along with a breakfast room. The rooms themselves are much warmer while their vivid and attractive colors form the basis of a functional decor : small furniture in yellow and Sienna red, both modern and practical, go well with the curtains and bedcovers mainly in blues. The rooms on the street are generally larger and also have an attractive view on the ancient Convent of the Carmelites. Don't be afraid of any noise as the street is narrow with little traffic. On the courtyard side the rooms are smaller and less expensive apart from some which are designed for three people. Those on the sixth floor are nice and large. The small bathrooms have also been renovated and most of them have showers. All is impeccably maintained while welcome and service are always available. On coming out of the hotel one has a very pleasant direct view of the Panthéon.

Hôtel Claude Bernard

43, rue des Écoles - 75005 Paris
Tel. (0)1 43 26 32 52 - Fax (0)1 43 26 80 56
web: http://www.webscapades.com/france/paris/bernard.htm
M. Trévoux

Category *** **Rooms** 34 with bath or shower, WC, telephone, minibar, cable TV. **Price** Single 530-620F, double 760-980F, suite (3 pers.) 1100F, 4 pers. 1220F. Extra bed 120F. **Meals** Breakfast (buffet) 50F, served 7:30-10:30. **Restaurant** and Tea room "Mascara": 7.30-22:00 (15:00 Saturday, 18:00 Monday); menus 75-120F. **Credit cards** All major. **Pets** Small dogs allowed. **Facilities** Elevator, room-service 7:30-20:00 (15:00 Sunday), sauna. **Parking** Saint-Germain (300m.). **How to get there** (Map 2): Bus: 27, 38, 63, 81, 84, 85 - Metro: Maubert-Mutualité. **Open** All year.

At No. 43 of the Rue des Ecoles a frontage completely painted in 'bull's blood' red provides a perfect sample of the universe you will discover once you cross the threshold of the Hôtel Claude Bernard. You'll finds a cosy ambiance in the lounge with its salmon-pink walls enhanced by a frieze in this same intense red, and superb furniture including a Renaissance cabinet and a major 17th-century picture. Next door a very elegant tearoom is used also as breakfast room or for serving light meals; meals can also be taken on the terrace. Fully renovated in 1996, the pretty rooms are mostly of a large size with English polished pine furniture, and light and bright wallpapers matching the curtains and bedspreads. The suites are vast with corner lounges and they always provide extra bedding for family use. This is a charming and well-located address, with very reasonable prices.

Hôtel Colbert

7, rue de l'Hôtel-Colbert
75005 Paris
Tel. (0)1 43 25 85 65 – Fax (0)1 43 25 80 19
Mme Sylvie Alvarez

Category ★★★ **Rooms** 36 with bath, WC, telephone, minibar, safe, TV. **Price** Single 890F, double 1030F, suite (1-4 pers.) 1650F, appart. (1-4 pers.) 1950F. **Meals** Breakfast 70F, served 7:00-11:00. **Credit cards** Visa, Eurocard, MasterCard, Amex. **Pets** Dogs not allowed. **Facilities** Elevator, laundry service, bar. **Parking** At 1, rue Lagrange. **How to get there** (Map 2): Bus: 21, 24, 27, 38, 47, 85, 96 - Metro: Saint-Michel, Maubert-Mutualité - RER: Cluny-Saint-Michel. **Open** All year.

The Colbert has the quiet air of a private hotel with its entry court and elegant reception rooms. You find this same elegance in the rooms with their blue 'Toile de Jouy' paper and 'Persian' decor; they are fitted with a small alcove in white moulded wood with blue set-offs. The rooms have Mansard ceilings on the top floor. Rooms with a number ending with a '5' or '7' are decorated with a beautiful mottled carpeting, furniture pieces in polished oak, a stylish armchair and bathrooms in marble. They are pleasant and more modern but possibly rather lacking in character. Those with numbers ending with a '1' or '2' have a view of Notre-Dame and some of the Seine 'quais'. In this previously popular district the rooms were often small,and this is also the case with those of the Colbert. For this reason and because many of them could do with bathroom renovations, we did find them rather expensive, but it is still true that the service is very attentive, while Notre-Dame and the Ile de la Cité are only a few meters away.

Hôtel du Collège de France

7, rue Thénard
75005 Paris
Tel. (0)1 43 26 78 36 - Fax (0)1 46 34 58 29
Mme Georges

Category ★★ Rooms 29 with soundproofing, bath or shower, WC, hairdryer, telephone, safe, TV satellite - 1 for disabled persons. **Price** Single 480F, double 500F, triple 630F, 4 pers. 1030F, 5 pers. 1130F. **Meals** Breakfast 33F, served 7:00-10:30. **Credit cards** All major. **Pets** Dogs not allowed. **Facilities** Elevator, laundry service. **Parking** At 1, rue Lagrange. **How to get there** (Map 2): Bus: 21, 24, 27, 38, 47, 63, 85, 86, 87 - Metro: Maubert-Mutualité, Cluny-La Sorbonne - RER: Saint-Michel, Notre-Dame. **Open** All year.

Founded in 1530 by Francis I, the Collège de France allows free access to its classes by the best-known intellectuals and scientists of France. The hotel is very close by, hidden in a small street linking the Boulevard Saint-Germain and the Rue des Ecoles. A statue of Joan of Arc welcomes you in the entry hall that stretches into a very pleasing small lounge, with comfortable Louis XVI-style armchairs in front of a perfect fireplace for winter evenings. Right behind is a cosy dining room for a pleasant start to the day. The small rooms are all in the same style: plain cream wallpaper with elegant gilded brass wall-lamps. Only the pretty fabrics of the curtains and bedcovers are varied. All is certainly very simple but one feels at home and the prices really reflect this as a result.

Hôtel Esmeralda

4, rue Saint-Julien-le-Pauvre
75005 Paris
Tel. (0)1 43 54 19 20 - Fax (0)1 40 51 00 68
Mme Bruel

Category ★★ **Rooms** 19 with telephone, bath, shower or washstand, WC. **Price** Single and double 160-490F. **Meals** Breakfast 40F, served 7:00-10:30. **Credit cards** Not accepted. **Pets** Dogs allowed. **Parking** At 1, rue Lagrange, Notre-Dame. **How to get there** (Map 2): Bus: 21, 24, 27, 38, 85, 96 - Metro: Saint-Michel - RER: Cluny-Saint-Michel. **Open** All year.

On crossing the cloister of Saint-Julien-le-Pauvre, you'll be enchanted by the softened light and the intimacy of this little house. A rather faded charm reigns over all the hotel, a little tired and a little jaded : floral wallpapers, waxed parquets, and basic furniture bought from the second-hand dealers decorate each of the small rooms. Do not fail to make a priority reservation for a room facing Notre-Dame cathedral, for these are a bit more comfortable and some can sleep up to four people. For a more modest rate you can sleep on the courtyard side or take a room without bathroom. A very well situated address that has remained "dans son jus", to use an expression well known to lovers of old furniture, and with one of the most charming views of the capital.

Hôtel de l'Espérance

15, rue Pascal
75005 Paris
Tel. (0)1 47 07 10 99 - Fax (0)1 43 37 56 19
M. and Mme Aymard

Category ★★ **Rooms** 38 with soundproofing (some with air-conditioning), bath or shower, WC, telephone, hairdryer, cable TV - 1 for disabled persons. **Price** Single 360F, double 390-430F. Extra bed 70F. **Meals** Breakfast 35F, served 7:30-11:00. **Credit cards** All major. **Pets** Dogs not allowed. **Facilities** Safes at reception, elevator, bar, 2 patios. **Parking** 50m., rue des Patriarches. **How to get there** (Map 10): Bus: 27, 47, 83, 91 - Metro: Censier-Daubenton, Gobelins. **Open** All year.

In a quiet spot near the Rue Mouffetard and its famous open-air market, this is one of the most charming hotels in Paris. Hospitable Monsieur and Madame Aymard have decorated the bright, immaculately-kept bedrooms with taste and care: patinated furniture, beautiful figured carpets, solid-color wallpaper coordinated with fabrics in pastel shades of blue, yellow, and salmon-pink, and lovely marble baths. The twenty-two four-poster beds have elegantly draped cotton canopies, and the larger rooms have a convertible sofa convenient for families. The rooms at the rear of the hotel get the morning sun. You can enjoy your breakfast in the pretty dining room on the garden, on one of the patios, or on a flower-filled balcony. There is a large lounge and bar where drinks are served at all hours. The Espérance (meaning "expectation") offers excellent value for the price.

Familia Hôtel

11, rue des Écoles
75005 Paris
Tel. (0)1 43 54 55 27 - Fax (0)1 43 29 61 77
M. Éric Gaucheron

Category ★★ **Rooms** 30 with bath or shower, WC, telephone, minibar, cable TV - 1 for disabled persons. **Price** Single 380-520F, double 420-520F. **Meals** Breakfast 35F, served 7:00-10:00. **Credit cards** All major. **Pets** Small dogs allowed. **Facilities** Elevator. **Parking** At rue Lagrange, Maubert. **How to get there** (Map 2): Bus: 24, 47, 63, 67, 86, 89 - Metro: Maubert-Mutualité, Jussieu - RER: Cluny-La Sorbonne. **Open** All year.

The Familia is a genuine small district hotel surrounded by 'bouquinistes', bistros and stores for colors and paints. Under the lead of the young Eric Gaucheron and his family, the hotel is changing fast and in each room Eric has tried to add 'that little extra' in order to personalize them. In half of them he has got an artist to make some very pretty sepia wall frescos of Parisian scenes. Those with a tiny little balcony have been given a table and two chairs and you have the pleasure of breakfasting outside with your nose in the greenery, as there are flowering boxes at every window. Elegant fabrics have been chosen for some rooms, small pictures bought in the 'flea markets' hang in the redecorated corridors, and traditional carpeting is on the stairs. Lastly, the breakfast room with its Louis-Philippe chairs and cherry bookcase has all the airs of a lounge, to give a final family touch to the particularly attractive overall effect.

Grand Hôtel Saint-Michel

19, rue Cujas
75005 Paris
Tel. (0)1 46 33 33 02 - Fax (0)1 40 46 96 33
M. Belaid

Category ★★★ **Rooms** 39 and 7 suites with air-conditioning, soundproofing, telephone, bath or shower, WC, hairdryer, TV satellite, minibar, safe - 2 for disabled persons. **Price** Single 590F, double 690-790F, suite 1190F. **Meals** Breakfast 55F, served 7:00-10:30. **Credit cards** All major. **Pets** Small dogs allowed. **Facilities** Elevator, bar, laundry service, room-service. **Parking** At 20, rue Soufflot. **How to get there** (Map 2): Bus: 21, 27, 38, 63, 84, 85, 86, 89, 96 - Metro: Cluny-La Sorbonne - RER: Luxembourg, Cluny-Saint-Michel. **Open** All year.

At two paces from the Sorbonne and Boulevard Saint-Michel, the Grand Hôtel Saint-Michel has just been fully renovated. Two lounges face the entry door while one also shelters the bar. The floor is in beige marble and there are worked stuccos on the ceiling, for a very classical decor with Directory-style furniture along with reproductions of famous pictures. The whole effect is still rather stuffy and cold, but the rooms themselves are very attractive. With a blue, green or salmon dominant color, matching with painted furniture pieces and the curtains and bedspreads, they all have one or two elegant old prints of Parisian scenes. The bathrooms are white with just one touch of color from the large basins varying with the rooms. Breakfasts are served in the basement and despite the lack of any window, the room is comfortable and bright and a good place to start any day. The welcome is friendly and attentive.

Hôtel des Grandes Écoles

75, rue du Cardinal-Lemoine
75005 Paris
Tel. (0)1 43 26 79 23 – Fax (0)1 43 25 28 15
Mme Le Floch

Category ★★ **Rooms** 50 with bath or shower, WC, telephone - 3 for disabled persons. **Price** Double 510-620F. Extra bed 100F. **Meals** Breakfast 40F. **Credit cards** Visa, Eurocard, MasterCard. **Pets** Small dogs allowed. **Facilities** Elevator, garden. **Parking** Private locations, 12 places (100F per day). **How to get there** (Map 2): Bus: 47, 84, 89 - Metro: Cardinal-Lemoine, Monge - RER: Luxembourg. **Open** All year.

At the end of a private alleyway and sunk in its full garden (not just a few square yards of lawn but a genuine garden), this hotel is a small marvel. How indeed could one imagine that such a space could survive so close to the Panthéon and the Contrescarpe, true to itself and escaping the fevered attention of developers, and still hold its prices reasonable. This is however the case with these three houses forming the Hôtel des Grandes Ecoles. The place still keeps its unchangeable air of the 'provinces' which gives it their full charm. There is 19th-century furniture in fruitwood in the reception lounge, lace-skirted tables, straw-seated chairs and a piano in the breakfast room. The rooms mostly have flowered wallpaper but if you do not like such a dated ambiance, you can choose from those just installed in the annex buildings. You can have your breakfast outside in the greenery accompanied only by the twittering of the sparrows. Your welcome will be friendly, quite natural and in the family style.

Hôtel des Grands Hommes

17, place du Panthéon
75005 Paris
Tel. (0)1 46 34 19 60 – Fax (0)1 43 26 67 32
Mme Moncelli

Category ★★★ **Rooms** 32 with air-conditioning, bath, WC, telephone, cable TV, hairdryer, minibar. **Price** Single 700F, double 800F, room with terrasse 870F (1-3 pers), 4 pers. 1200F. **Meals** Breakfast (buffet) 50F. **Credit cards** All major. **Pets** Dogs allowed. **Facilities** Elevator, laundry service, room-service until 16:00. **Parking** At 20, rue Soufflot. **How to get there** (Map 2): Bus: 21, 27, 38, 82, 84, 85, 89 - Metro: Cardinal-Lemoine - RER: Luxembourg. **Open** All year.

If the Hôtel des Grands Hommes refers to those illustrious personages buried in the Panthéon, you should also not forget that in one of its rooms André Breton and Philippe Soupault invented so-called "automatic writing". The reception area has moulded pink-orange walls and 1930's armchairs covered in the same shades, expressing the 'bourgeois' decoration and comfort of the hotel. Its former owners, vigorous inventors of surrealism, might well have objected to this but it still remains very attractive to passing guests. All decorated in pastel shades, the rooms are comfortable, bright and prettily furnished, often with metal or gilt aluminium bedsteads. In addition to a sublime view over the famous square, the fifth and sixth floors offer a wide view over the roofs of Paris with the Sacré-Coeur in the distance. Excepting these two floors, the room numbers ending with a '4' are small, on the courtyard side, and less welcoming, while the fourth floor is rather less well furnished. There is a warming breakfast room in the former vaulted basement and the welcome is very friendly.

Hôtel-Résidence Henri IV

50, rue des Bernardins
75005 Paris
Tel. (0)1 44 41 31 81 – Fax (0)1 46 33 93 22
Mme Moncelli

Category ★★★ **Rooms** 8 (2 with air-conditioning) and 5 apartements with bath, WC, minibar, safe, telephone, cable TV, kitchen - 1 for disabled persons. **Price** Double 700-900F, appart. (1-4 pers.) 1000-1200F; in low season double 600-700F, appart. 800-1000F. **Meals** Breakfast 40F, served 7:30-10:30. **Credit cards** All major. **Pets** Dogs allowed. **Facilities** Elevator, laundry service. **Parking** Saint-Germain (200m.). **How to get there** (Map 2): Bus: 63, 67, 87, 24 - Metro: Maubert-Mutualité. **Open** All year.

On the corner of the Rue des Ecoles and the lush little Square Paul Langevin, there is a small, very quiet dead-end street where you will find the freestone building of the Hôtel Résidence Henri IV. All the bedrooms overlook the square and, to the right, the façade of the former Ecole Polytechnique. The interior has been totally renovated, with elegant, comfortable bedrooms, and apartments decorated with cheerful colors and thick carpets. Specially designed for the hotel, the oak furniture includes molded headboards in the shape of antique pediments, framed on each side by shelves, and a beautiful painted wardrobe in some rooms. The immaculate baths are modern and functional, and a number of them overlook a small, flower-filled courtyard. The two-room apartments can accommodate up to four people. Like the bedrooms, they have a well-equipped kitchenette with refrigerator, cooking plaques, microwave oven, and dishwasher. Needless to say, the Résidence Henri IV is convenient for those who are in Paris for a long stay, and who'd like to save on those pricey Paris restaurant tabs.

Hôtel des Jardins du Luxembourg

5, impasse Royer-Collar
75005 Paris
Tel. (0)1 40 46 08 88 - Fax (0)1 40 46 02 28
Mme Touber

Category ★★★ **Rooms** 27 with air-conditioning, soundproofing, bath or shower, WC, telephone, minibar, TV satellite, safe - 2 for disabled persons. **Price** Single and double 740-840F. **Meals** Breakfast (buffet) 50F, served 7:00-11:00. **Credit cards** All major. **Pets** Dogs not allowed. **Facilities** Elevator, laundry service, sauna, patio, bar. **Parking** At rue soufflot. **How to get there** (Map 1 and 2): Bus: 21, 27, 38, 82, 84, 85, 89 - RER: Luxembourg. **Open** All year.

Opened last year, this hotel is a model of taste and comfort. Morning joggers will enjoy its location on a small, quiet street just off the Luxembourg Gardens, which in summer open at 7:30 AM. In the lobby, kilims brighten the pale oak parquet floors; next to the mahogany reception desk are two Oriental-style armchairs, a Chinese cloisonné table, and an incandescent fireplace (for once, the flames look quite real). The bedrooms are small but comfortable and elegant, with textured wallpaper, friezes matching the drapes and bedspreads, bronze beds, contemporary wooden furniture, statuettes, and handsome sconces. Our favorites are those overlooking the street, which have a nice view; noise is no problem because the windows are double-glazed, and there is no traffic on the street. The bathrooms are decorated with gleaming tiles, as is the breakfast room, where you will find an extremely warm decor in tones of green and orange, and small bistro chairs.

Hôtel Libertel Maxim

28, rue Censier
75005 Paris
Tel. (0)1 43 31 16 15 - Fax (0)1 43 31 93 87
Mme Chantal Pécou

Category ★★ **Roopms** 36 with soundproofing, bath or shower, WC, telephone, minibar, cable TV - 1 for disabled persons. **Price** Single 510F, double 570F. **Meals** Breakfast (buffet) 45F, served 7:00-10:30. **Credit cards** All major. **Pets** Dogs not allowed. **Facilities** Elevator, laundry service, safes at reception, room-service. **Parking** At rue Censier. **How to get there** (Map 2 and 10): Bus: 47 - Metro: Censier-Daubenton - RER and rail station: gare d'Austerlitz. **Open** All year.

The Hôtel Libertel Maxim has an attractive location right next to the Jardin des Plantes and the National Museum of Natural History, while also being close to the Rue Mouffetard, the Gobelins and the Grande Mosquée, where you should not miss having tea. The entry hall sets the style of the decor: cosseted, comfortable and refined, mixing the classical with the modern. Classical with the old prints and 'Toiles de Jouy ' which are found both in the ravishing lounge in raspberry and in all the rooms, declined in pinks, blues or greys: Carefully modern in the furniture that makes best use of available space. The rooms are small (apart from two of them) but really sweet and very well sound-proofed. The bathrooms are just as well thought out with pretty designer basins. Despite clever arrangement, some rooms with showers do seem a bit too small. One third of the rooms give onto the courtyard. There is a pretty breakfast room lit by a glass roof, while the welcome is very friendly.

Hôtel Libertel Quartier Latin

9, rue des Écoles
75005 Paris
Tel. (0)1 44 27 06 45 - Fax (0)1 43 25 36 70
M. Philippe Roye

Category ★★★ **Rooms** 29 with air-conditioning, soundproofing, bath or shower, WC, hairdryer, telephone, minibar, safe, cable TV - 1 for disabled persons. **Price** Single 910F, double 975-1050F, triple 1200F. **Meals** Breakfast (buffet) 75F, served 7:00-10:30. **Credit cards** All major. **Pets** Dogs not allowed. **Facilities** Elevator, laundry service, room-service. **Parking** Boulevard Saint-Germain. **How to get there** (Map 2): Bus: 63, 86, 87 - Metro: Cardinal-Lemoine. **Open** All year.

Midway between the Panthéon and the Arab World Institute, this hotel is rather different from the traditional hotels of this quarter as it is completely contemporary, with a sober and soothing decor, but warmed by the velvet fabrics and sombre Lapacho ebony wood found throughout. The tall bookshelves in the entry-lounge, photos of writers and quotations printed on the carpeting – all celebrate the literary life of the quarter. The decorator Didier Gomez designed the furniture and lighting, as well as the desk-consoles in the rooms, the bedheads rich in carved wood and a whole series of accessory furniture all with pure lines. The curtains are linen while the bathrooms are superb in white, heightened by a wide frieze in molten glass. There are three ambiances : vanilla, off-white and sky-blue. All the rooms have a very high standard of comfort but we stress that the more expensive offer a better quality-price deal given their size. Breakfast is 'soigné' and served in the same ambiance as the rest of the hotel. Both welcome and service are fully competent.

Hôtel de Notre-Dame

19, rue Maître-Albert
75005 Paris
Tel. (0)1 43 26 79 00 - Fax (0)1 46 33 50 11
M. Fouhety

Category ★★★ **Rooms** 34 with soundproofing, bath or shower, WC, telephone, cable TV, hairdryer, safe, minibar. **Price** Double 690-790F. **Meals** Breakfast 40F. **Credit cards** All major. **Pets** Dogs not allowed. **Parking** At 1, rue Lagrange. **How to get there** (Map 2): Bus: 21, 24, 27, 38, 47, 85, 96 - Metro: Maubert-Mutualité, Saint-Michel - RER: Cluny-Saint-Michel. **Open** All year.

In this typical small street of the old quarter of Paris, one immediately notices the Hôtel de Notre-Dame which has retained its huge frontage, which in earlier days must have been the window of a shop. An assembly of modern panelling has now reshaped this area, with the original beams, some beautiful antique furniture pieces and a superb tapestry giving full character to the reception, bar and corner-lounges of the ground floor. The small rooms have retained their beamed ceilings from earlier times and some slabs of cut-stone walls. For the rest, some beautiful contemporary furniture in light oak mingles in full harmony with the pastel shades of the walls and the sanded glass of the panelling closing off the bathrooms. All is very comfortable and intimate. The place is in close proximity of Notre-Dame, the Seine and the small book stalls or 'bouquinistes'.

Hôtel Observatoire-Luxembourg

107, boulevard Saint-Michel
75005 Paris
Tel. (0)1 46 34 10 12 – Fax (0)1 46 33 73 86
M. Bonneau

Category ★★★ **Rooms** 37 (18 with air-conditioning) with bath or shower, WC, telephone, safe, cable TV. **Price** Single 650-710F, double 700-810F, triple 1030F; –15% from Monday to Friday (excluding salon periods). **Meals** Breakfast 49F. **Credit cards** All major. **Pets** Dogs allowed. **Facilities** Elevator, laundry service, foreign press. **Parking** At 20, rue Soufflot. **How to get there** (Map 10): Bus: 21, 27, 38, 82, 84 - RER: Luxembourg. **Open** All year.

Lovers of chlorophyll and the wide open spaces will surely appreciate this hotel situated facing the corner of the Luxembourg gardens, which are open to the public from 7.30 in summer time. Dependiing on floor and outlook, they can admire all the full greenery of the Luxembourg (room numbers ending with a '6' or '7'), the garden of the Institute for young deaf people (room numbers with a '3', '4' or '5'), or the generous leafiness of the trees of Boulevard Saint-Michel (all other rooms). Apart from their view, the rooms are pleasantly decorated in fall tones, with a few exceptions in yellow and grey, with cerused beech furniture and coordinated fabrics. All have carefully maintained bathrooms in grey marble. A marble floor is also in the reception area, and the lounge is very welcoming with its corner settee in rainbow colors. The breakfast room is in bistro style but a little cold, although delicately lit by a series of low-power lamps. The welcome is friendly and attentive.

Hôtel du Panthéon

19, place du Panthéon
75005 Paris
Tel. (0)1 43 54 32 95 – Fax (0)1 43 26 64 65
Mme Moncelli

Category ★★★ **Rooms** 34 with air-conditioning, soundproofing, telephone, bath or shower, WC, hairdryer, cable TV, minibar. **Price** Single 700F, double 800F. Extra bed 100F. **Meals** Breakfast (buffet) 50F, served 7:00-10:30. **Credit cards** All major. **Pets** Dogs allowed. **Facilities** Elevator, laundry service, room-service until 16:00. **Parking** At place du Panthéon, at 20, rue Soufflot **How to get there** (Map 2): Bus: 21, 27, 38, 82, 84, 85, 89 - Metro: Cardinal-Lemoine - RER: Luxembourg. **Open** All year except.

The Hôtel du Panthéon adjoins the Hôtel des Grands Hommes and both are managed by the same family. The entry and lounges of the ground floor are very welcoming with their vast and very cool areas, helped by the light wood furniture pieces and the floors in immaculate travertin, offsetting the bright colors of the carpets. Color is only provided by the carpeting and numerous green plants. Snug and cosy, the rooms are elegant and pleasant, while those with numbers ending with '1' are the largest. In contrast, those ending with a '4' or '5' lack space. Most of them look out over the majestic Panthéon. square and the former church, converted since the Revolution into a civilian monument to the memory of famous Frenchmen and women. Half of them will see major renovation both of decor and bathrooms in 1998. The welcome is friendly and alert to your every request; such as finding a baby-sitter should you want to go out without the children.

Hôtel Parc Saint-Séverin

22, rue de la Parcheminerie - 75005 Paris
Tel. (0)1 43 54 32 17 - Fax (0)1 43 54 70 71
e-mail: espfran@micronet.fr
M. Lebouc

Category ★★★ **Rooms** 27 (some with air-conditioning) with soundproofing, telephone, bath or shower, TV satellite, hairdryer, minibar. **Price** Single 510F, doubles 615-1530F. **Meals** Breakfast (buffet) 50F. **Credit cards** All major. **Pets** Dogs not allowed. **Facilities** Elevator. **Parking** Square in front of Notre-Dame and 1, rue Lagrange. **How to get there** (Map 2): Bus: 21, 24, 27, 47, 63, 67, 86, 87, 96 - Metro: Cluny-La Sorbonne - RER: Cluny-Saint-Michel. **Open** All year.

At the heart of the Latin Quarter, the Hôtel du Parc Saint-Séverin is on a pedestrian street free of the motor traffic of the Paris center. In this handsome building the large airy spaces have been preserved and the whole effect is very light. The sobriety of the colors and of the contemporary and 1930's furniture in the lounge again augment the sense of space. The same atmosphere is also found in the rooms : bright and often spacious, they are elegant and always agreeably decorated, while it is not uncommon to find antique furniture pieces and paintings fitting in easily with the more modern elements. If you want a view over the roofs, the Saint-Séverin cloisters and the gardens of the Cluny Museum, choose a room from the fifth floor upwards. Those on the corner of the two upper floors also have terraces, some of them particularly large. The peace and quiet, comfort and smiling service are qualities that make the Parc Saint-Séverin a hotel much sought after.

Le Relais Saint-Jacques

3, rue de l'Abbé-de-l'Épée
75005 Paris
Tel. (0)1 53 73 26 00 - Fax (0)1 43 26 17 81
M. Bonneau

Category ★★★★ **Rooms** 23 with air-conditioning, soundproofing, bath, WC, hairdryer, telephone, minibar, safe, TV satellite - 1 for disabled persons. **Price** Single and double 1080-1300F (in low season 900-1100F), triple 1200F (in low season 1080F). **Meals** Breakfast 66F, served 7:00-11:00. **Credit cards** All major. **Pets** Dogs not allowed. **Facilities** Elevator, bar, laundry service, room-service. **Parking** At rue Soufflot. **How to get there** (Map 2 and 10): Bus: 21, 27, 38, 82 - RER: Luxembourg. **Open** All year.

As confirmed by a commemorative plaque a few meters away affixed to the church of Saint-Jacques-du-Haut-Pas, the Relais Saint-Jacques is on the road taken throughout the centuries by the pilgrims to Saint-Jacques of Compostella in Spain. Modern-day travellers will also enjoy a very agreeable stay here. Fully renovated from top to bottom in 1996, the hotel now offers large rooms as cosy as you might like them. They have embroidered hangings and classical decor, Louis XVI - or Directory-style , or even more original furnishings like in the five astonishing 'Portuguese rooms'. All rooms are comfortable, perfectly equipped and sound-proofed even though there is very little traffic in this very green street, almost like a square. The rooms are reasonably priced when taking count of their facilities. The breakfast is refined, with a fine welcoming area and ravishing lounge with its antique furniture, and a corner-bar where one is only too happy to linger.

Les Rives de Notre-Dame

15, quai Saint-Michel
75005 Paris
Tel. (0)1 43 54 81 16 - Fax (0)1 43 26 27 09
M. Degravi and Mlle Grace

Category ✱✱✱✱ **Rooms** 9 and 1 suite with air-conditioning, soundproofing, telephone, bath or shower, TV satellite, minibar - 1 for disabled persons. **Price** Singles and doubles 950, 1100 and 1500F, suite 2350F (2-4 pers.). **Meals** Breakfast 85F, served from 7:00. **Credit cards** All major. **Pets** Small dogs allowed. **Facilities** Elevator, bar, safes at reception, small veranda. **Parking** Square in front of Notre-Dame and 1, rue Lagrange. **How to get there** (Map 2): Bus 21, 24, 27, 47, 63, 67, 86, 87, 96 - Metro and RER: Saint-Michel. **Open** All year.

Between the Place Saint-Michel and Notre-Dame, your windows will open out onto a real postcard scene: the quays of the Seine with their 'bouquinistes' and the banks lower down where the lovers watch the river boats passing by. Excellent sound-proofing allows you to profit from such a view without also suffering the noise. In each of the ten rooms a particular decorative effect has been sought via a mixing of motifs and colors. The rooms are spacious with corner lounges with a sofa converting into an extra bed, while the bathrooms are bright and elegant. On the first floor three just as charming small rooms are offered for single visitors, but they could also suit a couple. The top floor has just been fitted with an apartment, with a room and lounge, and enjoying a view in two directions. Les Rives de Notre-Dame is a hotel where you will appreciate a smiling welcome and particularly efficient service.

Hôtel-Résidence Saint-Christophe

17, rue Lacépède
75005 Paris
Tel. (0)1 43 31 81 54 – Fax (0)1 43 31 12 54
M. Ait

Category ★★★ **Rooms** 31 with bath or shower, WC, telephone, minibar, TV satellite - 1 for disabled persons. **Price** Double 500-650F - Weekend and July-Augst 400F. **Meals** Breakfast 50F, served 7:00-10:00. **Credit cards** All major. **Pets** Dogs allowed. **Facilities** Elevator, laundry service, room-service. **Parking** At 4, rue du Marché-des-Patriarches. **How to get there** (Map 2 and 10): Bus: 47, 67, 89 - Metro: Monge, Jussieu - RER and rail station: Gare d'Austerlitz. **Open** All year.

Many regulars return to this little hotel as they are sure to find Michèle seated at the cherry desk not far from an imposing 17th-century Normandy cupboard. From the lounge you can see the first trees of the Jardin des Plantes with its promise of morning joggings. The warm little rooms with their peach-colored walls have rustic-style furniture, curtains varying with the brown-red piqué bedspreads and pleasant bathrooms in beige marble. Families will want to reserve those that can be changed into suites, and for a long stay choose a room with a number ending with a '4' as the alcove framing the bed offers extra storage space. All are correctly sound-proofed but in summer, if you want to sleep with open windows, be sure to reserve a room giving onto Rue de la Clef as they are quieter. For dinner you will find the restaurants of the Contrescarpe district close by, and on the square at No. 1, a plaque indicates the cabaret where Ronsard, Du Bellay and the members of the first 'Pléiade' used to meet in the 17th century.

Sélect Hôtel

1, place de la Sorbonne - 75005 Paris
Tel. (0)1 46 34 14 80 - Fax (0)1 46 34 51 79
e-mail: select.hotel@wanadoo.fr
M. Chabrerie

Category ★★★ **Rooms** 68 (53 with air-conditioning) with soundproofing, bath or shower, WC, telephone, hairdryer, TV satellite. **Price** Single 530F, double 650-780F, suite 890F, duplex 1250F. **Meals** Breakfast (buffet) 30F, served 7:00-10:30. **Credit cards** All major. **Pets** Dogs allowed (+30F). **Facilities** Elevators, patio, bar, safes at reception, room-service. **Parking** At rue Soufflot (100m.). **How to get there** (Map 2): Bus: 21, 24, 27, 38, 63, 82, 84, 85 - Metro and RER: Cluny-La Sorbonne. **Open** All year.

With its façade adorned with flower boxes and a wrought-iron canopy, the Sélect looks like a classic hotel from the outside. Inside, however, the style is assuredly modern, with a pyramid-shape skylight illuminating the stairway, several corner lounges surrounding an interior garden, and a bar. Delicious breakfasts are served amid a decor of exposed stones. The overall effect is very tasteful. In most of the bedrooms, there is sleek, modern, beautifully made furniture. Some rooms have old exposed beams. From the *sixième étage* up, the view over the rooftops is magnificent; on lower floors, the rooms overlook the charming Place de la Sorbonne with its student bistros and linden trees. On the courtyard side rooms are darker but very quiet, decorated in blue or orange shades and combining antique and modern styles; they have a beautiful view of the courtyard's ochre walls covered in jasmin–a touch of Italy in the heart of Paris. The renovated bathrooms are superb. This is a fine address animated by an attentive and caring staff.

Hôtel de la Sorbonne

6, rue Victor Cousin
75005 Paris
Tel. (0)1 43 54 58 08 – Fax (0)1 40 51 05 18
Mme Poirier

Category ✶✶ **Rooms** 37 with soundproofing, bath or shower, WC, telephone, cable TV. **Price** Double 420-490F. In low season 360-450F. **Meals** Breakfast 35F, served 7:15-10:30 (offered for the reader of the guide for a weekend stay Sunday night included). **Credit cards** Visa, Eurocard, MasterCard, Amex. **Pets** Dogs allowed. **Facilities** Elevator. **Parking** At rue soufflot (100m.). **How to get there** (Map 2): Bus: 21, 27, 38, 85 - Metro: Cluny-La Sorbonne - RER: Luxembourg. **Open** All year.

Rue Victor-Cousin runs into Rue Soufflot with the Panthéon on its right. Since 1311, the quarter has been dominated by its student life and so the Hôtel de la Sorbonne situated just opposite the famous university, has certainly seen many generations of turbulent young people passing under its windows. You go in under the porch and then take the door to the left, where the reception area is without great interest, but it extends into a small corner-lounge with a glass roof, where a few green plants reflect the many flower beds found in the courtyard. Staircases and corridors have red carpeting and white embossed wallpapers, while the plinths and doors are painted in light blue. Simple, small and well cared-for, the rooms have comfortable beds and bathrooms, the latter sometimes rather narrow. Whether giving onto street or courtyard, all are sound-proofed with efficient double-glazing. Breakfast is served under the wise old eyes of an African statue in a room decorated in bistro-style. The welcome is friendly and natural, quite in the tone of this hotel with more than reasonable prices.

Timhôtel Jardin des Plantes

5, rue Linné
75005 Paris
Tel. (0)1 47 07 06 20 - Fax (0)1 47 07 62 74
Mme Martine Bourgeon

Category ** **Rooms** 33 with soundproofing, bath or shower, WC, telephone, hairdryer, TV.
Price Single 460F, double 560F. Extra bed 140F. **Meals** Breakfast 49F, served 7:00-11:00.
Snacks available. **Credit cards** All major. **Pets** Dogs allowed. **Facilities** Elevator, terrace,
10 individual safes at reception. **Parking** At rue Censier (100 m). **How to get there** (Map 2
and 10): Bus: 67, 89 - Metro: Jussieu. **Open** All year.

The hotel's entrance is just opposite the well-known Jardin des Plantes, and such proximity plays a considerable role in the establishment's choice of decor. Almost all the rooms give onto the street and the large trees of the park. They have all just been renovated in a variety of yellow shades mingled with bottle greens and dark reds, but they have kept their white-lacquered cane furniture. Without any great fantasy, the whole effect remains attractive and comfortable, with the rooms on the upper floors the most agreeable. The lounge is under the vaults of the basement level and retains the botanical theme with its collection of prints, while the bar opens wide onto the street and also adds its flowery aspect. Lastly, you should certainly not miss the small communal terrace on the top floor, where if you wish you can have your breakfast surrounded by roses and lavender (Room 50 opens straight onto it). This is a very welcoming address much appreciated by the professors and researchers of the National Museum of Natural History.

Hôtel des Trois Collèges

16, rue Cujas
75005 Paris
Tel. (0)1 43 54 67 30 - Fax (0)1 46 34 02 99

Category ★★ **Rooms** 44 with soundproofing, bath or shower, WC, telephone, hairdryer, TV. **Price** Single 380-540F, double 480-650F, suite 750F. **Meals** Breakfast 42F. Snacks available at lunchtime (aroud 80F) and Tea room. **Credit cards** All major. **Pets** Dogs not allowed. **Parking** At 20, rue Soufflot. **How to get there** (Map 2): Bus: 21, 27, 38, 63, 82, 84, 86, 87 - Metro: Cluny-La Sorbonne, Odéon - RER: Luxembourg, Cluny-Saint-Michel. **Open** All year.

For centuries this district has been the capital of knowledge and the most famous college of the Montagne Sainte-Geneviève is the Sorbonne, founded in the 13th century. The Sainte-Barbe College is the oldest private establishment in France while the College de France houses the most prestigious teaching chairs. In the shade of such historical buildings is found the small and discreet Hôtel des Trois Collèges. A widespread simplicity reigns throughout the establishment where white dominates, but the rooms lack for no comfort. The largest rooms have Mansard ceilings with a view over the Sorbonne and Panthéon. The ground floor was recently enlarged and renovated, with a charming tea room installed, which may turn into a 'thesis room' when students arrive to celebrate their exam results. Light and elegant, you can take your delicious breakfast with home-made jams in peace and quiet here, or a light meal later in the day. Next door a tiny lounge recalls the ancient origins of the place, and you can admire the well of the former Sainte-Geneviève Convent from the Middle Ages, as well as prints illustrating the district a few centuries ago.

À la Villa des Artistes

9, rue de la Grande-Chaumière
75006 Paris
Tel. (0)1 43 26 60 86 – Fax. (0)1 43 54 73 70
Mlle Marie Peugeot

Category ★★★ **Rooms** 59 (45 with air-conditioning) with bath or shower, WC, telephone, TV satellite, hairdryer, safe, minibar. **Price** "Standard room" 670-695F (490F in low season), "club room" 870-895F (540F in low season). **Meals** Breakfast (buffet) included, served 7:00-10:30. **Credit cards** All major. **Pets** Dogs not allowed. **Facilities** Elevator, laundry service, bar, patio. **Parking** At 116, boulevard du Montparnasse (50 m). **How to get there** (Map 10): Bus: 58, 82, 83, 91 - Metro: Vavin - RER: Port-Royal - Rail station (TGV): gare Montparnasse. **Open** All year.

From the times when Montparnasse was the center of all the trends in the arts, many famous souls have stayed here: Beckett, Fitzgerald, Fujita and Modigliani, who had his studio close by. Today you can see them again in the photos on the bar walls, alongside Kiki, Man Ray, Hemingway and many others. These days the Villa des Artistes still carries on the artistic traditions of the quarter with regular picture exhibitions when painters, friends and clients of the hotel can meet together over a glass at the *vernissage*. The lounge is perfect for this kind of event and you will appreciate the comfortable armchairs and sofas and the 1930's spirit of the design. The breakfast room next door looks out on a very attractive patio with tables and deckchairs. The rooms have seen recent renovation and all are fitted with elegant and modern furniture set off by quality fabrics. The lighting has been carefully thought out and the bathrooms are impeccable. This is a quiet place where you are received attentively and with concern.

Hôtel de l'Abbaye

10, rue Cassette
75006 Paris
Tel. (0)1 45 44 38 11 – Fax (0)1 45 48 07 86
M. Lafortune

Category ★★★ Rooms 42 and 4 suites (duplex with terrace) with air-conditioning, bath, WC, telephone, TV. **Price** Standard room 900-1000F, large room 1500-1600F, duplex and apartment 1860-1950F. **Meals** Breakfast included; snacks available. **Credit cards** Amex, Visa, Eurocard, MasterCard. **Pets** Dogs not allowed. **Facilities** Elevator, garden, bar. **Parking** At place Saint-Sulpice. **How to get there** (Map 1): Bus: 48, 63, 70, 84, 87, 95, 96 - Metro: Saint-Sulpice and Sèvres-Babylone. **Open** All year.

Having crossed the entry court of this elegant hotel in the Saint-Sulpice quarter, you will be won over by the ambiance found in the reception areas, where deep sofas and some fine antique furniture around an open fire make an ideal corner for winter days. Next to the lounge, which could be that of a very beautiful Parisian apartment, the high window doors of the bar open onto the patio. Several rooms open onto this luxuriant and flowery area, and some duplex units have semi-private terraces. The rooms decor reflects the style of the ground floor: warm, personalized and very often with antique furniture. To these aesthetical qualities are added an irreproachable comfort and apparently faultless maintenance. This is a welcoming and superb address with the good taste of having preserved full confidentiality.

Hôtel Alliance Saint-Germain-des-Prés

7/11, rue Saint-Benoît
75006 Paris
Tel. (0)1 42 61 53 53 - Fax (0)1 49 27 09 33
M. Albert Cacciamani

Category ★★★★ **Rooms** 117 with air-conditioning, bath, WC, telephone, minibar, safe, TV satellite - 2 for disabled persons. **Price** Double 990-1190F. From July 15 to August 31 790F. **Meals** Breakfast (buffet) 75F, served 7:00-10:30. **Credit cards** All major. **Pets** Dogs allowed. **Facilities** Elevator, laundry service, bar, jazz club. **Parking** Opposite 169, boulevard Saint-Germain. **How to get there** (Map 1): Bus: 39, 48, 63, 70, 86, 87, 95 - Metro: Saint-Germain-des-Prés. **Open** All year.

Just a few meters from Café du Flor and Les Deux Magots, the Hôtel Alliance is found on a former site of the entrance to the Abbey Saint-Germain. Shown on a large fresco, the old abbey door reminds modern-day travellers that pilgrims once came here looking for shelter. Apart from this historical reference the fittings of the hotel are fully modern. The vast marble hall conceals several little corner-lounges with leather sofas facing wing chairs in the Louis XVI-style, all in contemporary fabrics. The rooms are extremely comfortable, functional and perfectly sound-proofed. Those just renovated have bright and elegant colors, classical 'reworked' furniture and some fine worked wood pieces in light oakt. The other rooms are also pleasant, with their cerused furniture pieces and pretty printed fabrics. Lastly, in the basement the jazz club offers an eclectic program in a 1950's decor from Tuesday to Saturday.

Hôtel d'Angleterre

44, rue Jacob
75006 Paris
Tel. (0)1 42 60 34 72 – Fax (0)1 42 60 16 93
Mme Blouin

Category ★★★ **Rooms** 23, 1 suite and 3 apartments with soundproofing, bath, WC, telephone, hairdryer, cable TV, safe. **Price** Single and double 650-1200F, suite (with 2 bedrooms) 1500F, apartment 1500F. **Meals** Breakfast 52F, served 7:30-11:30. **Credit cards** All major. **Pets** Dogs not allowed. **Facilities** Elevator, garden. **Parking** Opposite 169, boulevard Saint-Germain. **How to get there** (Map 1): Bus: 39, 48, 63, 70, 86, 87, 95, 96 - Metro: Saint-Germain-des-Prés. **Open** All year.

This house has its history; it was here that the independence of the federal republic of the United States was recognized. Today it is a very beautiful hotel with a superb decor of high wainscotted ceilings, polished beams and antique furniture pieces. All the rooms are different and a good number of them are much larger than those one is used to finding in the Quarter. The most beautiful has a huge wall of bare stone that sets off the 17th-century furniture, with a canopied bed of turned wood and some Louis XIII 'mutton bone' chairs. You should note that the largest and the quietest give onto the garden but do not expect to find air-conditioning, which is a pity given the real luxury of some rooms. Lastly, the very attentive management will ease your stay in Paris by reserving shows, restaurants and so on. A very good address where you can also have the pleasure in the good weather of taking your breakfast outdoors in the flowery quiet of the patio garden.

L'Atelier Montparnasse

49, rue Vavin – 75006 Paris
Tel. (0)1 46 33 60 00 – Fax (0)1 40 51 04 21
web: http://www.webscapades.com/france/paris/atelier.htm
Mme Tible

Category ★★★ Rooms 17 with soundproofing, bath or shower, WC, telephone, TV, hairdryer, safe, minibar. **Price** Single 600F, double 700-750F, "Fujita room" (2-3 pers.) 950F. Extra bed 100F. **Meals** Breakfast 40F, served 7:00-11:00. **Credit cards** All major. **Pets** Small dogs allowed. **Facilities** Elevator, room-service. **Parking** At 116, boulevard du Montparnasse. **How to get there** (Map 10): Bus: 68, 82, 83, 91 - Metro: Notre-Dame-des-Champs, Montparnasse - RER: Port-Royal - Rail station (TGV): gare Montparnasse. **Open** All year.

Very close to La Coupole restaurant, L'Atelier Montparnasse has revived the life of the Quarter. The amusing mosaic carpet of the entrance sets the 1930's tone for the very warm decoration of the tiny corner lounge. You will appreciate the elegance of the furniture and the exhibition of paintings that livens up the walls at all times, recreating a link with the "Montparno" tradition. Despite their small size, (apart from the large 'Foujita'), the rooms are comfortable and soberly decorated in pink and cream shades. As for the bathrooms, they are astonishing, with their molten glass mosaics all reproducing the work of some famous painter representative of the great days of Montparnasse. The energy and 'know-how' of Mme. Tible are found throughout this attractive and welcoming hotel, and she knows well how to make one forget the very smallness of its facilities.

Hôtel Atlantis Saint-Germain-des-Près

4, rue du vieux Colombier
75006 Paris
Tel. (0)1 45 48 31 81 – Fax (0)1 45 48 35 16
M. Éric Azhar

Category ★★ **Rooms** 34 with soundproofing, bath or shower, WC, telephone, TV satellite, hairdryer, safe. **Price** Single and double 450-585F. **Meals** Breakfast 35F, served 6:30-10:30. **Credit cards** Visa, Eurocard, MasterCard, Amex. **Pets** Dogs not allowed. **Facilities** Elevator. **Parking** At place Saint-Sulpice. **How to get there** (Map 1): Bus: 39, 48, 63, 70, 86, 87, 95, 96 - Metro: Saint-Sulpice. **Open** All year.

On the corner of the Place Saint-Sulpice, this fine building is signalled out by its window-boxes and carefully maintained interior. The rooms ending with the number '1' are large and we recommend them as a priority. Giving onto the street but with double-glazing, they have a simple but attractive decor: bedspreads in white piqué, papered walls most often in pale blue, elegant curtains and white lacquered furniture. They have superb white bathrooms enhanced by a frieze in blue tileware. The other rooms are very much smaller but always well maintained, while those at the back enjoy an unobstructed view on the green and charming courtyards of the other buildings. On the ground floor you will be delighted by the really charming lounge with its deep leather armchairs and water-color paintings of Brittany. A desk is available if you want to do your mail, unless you prefer a game of chess or a drink. Breakfast is served close by in the dining room, with the tick-tock of a clock from earlier times.

Au Manoir Saint-Germain-des-Prés

153, boulevard Saint-Germain
75006 Paris
Tel. (0)1 42 22 21 65 - Fax (0)1 45 48 22 25
M. Claude Teil

Category ★★★★ **Rooms** 32 with air-conditioning, soundproofing, telephone, bath or shower, WC, TV satellite, minibar, hairdryer, safe. **Price** Single 790-950F, double 990-1300F, triple 1090-1400F. **Meals** Breakfast (buffet) 40F, served 6:30-10:30. **Credit cards** All major. **Pets** Dogs not allowed. **Facilities** Elevator, laundry service, bar. **Parking** In front of the hotel. **How to get there** (Map 1): Bus: 39, 48, 63, 86, 87, 95 - Metro: Saint-Germain-des-Prés. **Open** All year.

A neighbor of the famous Brasserie Lipp and facing the two ultra-famous cafés, La Flore and Les Deux Magots, the Manoir Saint-Germain-des-Prés has one of the best sites in the capital. Recently taken over and magnificently restored, it should have a lasting and well-earned success. How can you not be charmed by its small lounges with their green lime worked wood with dark set-offs, polished in the old way, the pale pink silks of the chairs, the genuinely antique furniture pieces, the old gilt mouldings of the mirrors and prints? This same timeless refinement, with beautiful 'Toiles de Jouy ', you find in all the recently renovated rooms. The other rooms have kept their contemporary decor. The whole effect is handsome, comfortable, perfectly maintained and well sound-proofed. The breakfast is good and the welcome attentive and pleasant.

Hôtel d'Aubusson

33, rue Dauphine
75006 Paris
Tel. (0)1 43 29 43 43 - Fax (0)1 43 29 12 62
M. Nicolas Caron

Category ★★★★ **Rooms** 49 with air-conditioning, soundproofing, telephone, bath or shower, WC, hairdryer, TV satellite, minibar, safe - 2 for disabled persons. **Price** Single 1200-1400F, double 1400-1900F, triple 1900F. **Meals** Breakfast (buffet) 80F, served 7:00-12:00. **Credit cards** All major. **Pets** Dogs allowed. **Facilities** Elevator, laundry service, bar, patio, room-service: menus 150-200F. **Parking** Privated under the hotel (100F per night). **How to get there** (Map 1): Bus: 58, 70 - Metro: Odéon, Pont-Neuf. **Open** All year.

The Hôtel d'Aubusson has only been open since November 1996. The entry hall and bar in acajou enhanced by gilded bronze define the space layout, from which you can walk onto the patio with its noble 17th-century facade, fountain and a few tables for drinks. You can also go directly into the finest room of the hotel, a lounge with high ceiling beams, stone fireplace and Louis XV furniture. With their Directory-style furniture the rooms are beyond criticism in layout and comfort, and beat all the standards for sound-proofing. The carpeting is in perfect harmony with the superb fabrics from the best houses, and while the rooms in the building on the courtyard often add beautiful ceiling beams to their decor, all are very pleasant and have irresistible 1930's-style bathrooms. Breakfast is served on the patio or in a superb dining room just behind the lounge, and dominated by a large, green Aubusson in the purest 18th century-style.

Hôtel Buci Latin

34, rue de Buci
75006 Paris
Tel. (0)1 43 29 07 20 – Fax (0)1 43 29 67 44
Mme Laurence Raymond

Category ★★★ **Rooms** 27 and 1 junior-suite (with balcon and whirlpool) with air-conditioning, soundproofing, bath or shower, WC, telephone, cable TV, hairdryer, minibar - 2 for disabled persons. **Price** Single and double 970-1250F, duplex 1590F, junior-suite 1750F. **Meals** Breakfast included, served from 6:30. Snacks available (brunchs, Chef's special, salad) and tea room 12:00-18:00 except Monday. **Credit cards** All major. **Facilities** Elevator, laundry service, safes at reception, bar. **Parking** Opposite 169, boulevard Saint-Germain. **How to get there** (Map 1): Bus: 39, 48, 63, 70, 86, 87, 95, 96 - Metro: Mabillon. **Open** All year.

Decorated by a designer, this is probably one of the most beautiful hotels in the neighborhood. Graceful and artistic, its unique decor includes sienna patina on the walls, soft lighting, pale wood furniture embellished with handsome wrought iron, sumptuous bathrooms, cleverly concealed closets, and an exotic wardrobe in every bedroom. Even lovelier are the duplex and the suite, which has a balcony and whirlpool bathtub; but the least expensive bedrooms (with shower) are just as charming. Whether your room is on the street or the courtyard, there is no noise problem because the rooms are air conditioned and the windows double-glazed. Works of young artists are displayed on the doors and in the elevator. Photographs of their works are also exhibited in the lobby and can be enjoyed from the adjacent lounge. In the basement, there is a charming coffee shop where you will be served breakfast on the house; light meals can be ordered until 6 PM.

Hôtel Le Clément

6, rue Clément
75006 Paris
Tel. (0)1 43 26 53 60 - Fax (0)1 44 07 06 83
M. and Mme Charrade

Category ★★ **Rooms** 31 with bath, WC, telephone, hairdryer, TV satellite. **Price** Double 490-610F, triple 675-715F. **Meals** Breakfast 50F, served 7:00-11:00. **Credit cards** All major. **Pets** Dogs not allowed. **Facilities** Elevator, bar. **Parking** Marché Saint-Germain. **How to get there** (Map 1): Bus: 39, 48, 58, 63, 70, 84, 86, 87, 95, 96 - Metro: Saint-Germain-des-Prés, Mabillon. **Open** All year.

You can only be seduced by this family hotel, very central and lovingly cared for by Mme Charrade. The small rooms are both simple and attractive with their bedcovers in white 'piqué', their wall-hangings coordinated with the Persian-style curtains signed 'Souléïado', and their furniture in rattan cane. The higher up you choose your room, the more of the Saint-Sulpice church you see rising above the roofs of the Saint-Germain market. It was here, right under your windows, that between the years 1482 and 1811 a motley crowd came to buy and sell their wares, take part in the street spectacles, and drink in the numerous bars. Today, things have all quietened down and any action is found rather closer to the Mabillon and the Rue de Buci, just a few minutes from the hotel. The bar is right alongside the elegant, small welcoming lounge with its worked wood and basket chairs.

Le Clos Médicis

56, rue Monsieur-le-Prince – 75006 Paris
Tel. (0)1 43 29 10 80 – Fax (0)1 43 54 26 90
e-mail: clos-medicis@compuserve.com
M. Beherec

Category ★★★ **Rooms** 38 with air-conditioning, soundproofing, bath or shower, WC, telephone, cable TV, hairdryer, safe, minibar - 1 for disabled persons. **Price** Single 790F, double 890-990F, duplex 1206F. **Meals** Breakfast 60F, served 7:00-11:00. **Credit cards** All major. **Pets** Dogs allowed (+60F). **Facilities** Elevator, patio. **Parking** At rue Soufflot. **How to get there** (Map 1): Bus: 21, 27, 38, 58, 82, 84, 85, 89 - Metro: Odéon - RER: Luxembourg. **Open** All year.

The Clos Médicis, like many hotels in this neighborrhood, is named after the Medici Palace which was built in the Luxembourg Gardens for Marie de Medicis. At Number 54 next door, Blaise Pascal wrote a large part of *Les Provinciales* and *Les Pensées*. The hotel, which has just been entirely renovated, has a beautiful and inviting reception area brightened by a cheerful fireplace in winter. With the first fine days of spring, breakfasts are served in the leafy courtyard which is just off the breakfast room. The bedrooms are generally spacious, and very comfortable, with modern conveniences and well-designed bathrooms; double windows and air-conditioning ensure that they are quiet. The walls are a pretty yellow, and the draperies and bedspreads are coordinated with lovely prints. The staff is very courteous.

Crystal Hôtel

24, rue Saint-Benoît
75006 Paris
Tel. (0)1 45 48 85 14 – Fax (0)1 45 49 16 45
Mme Choukroun and Mme Adda

Category ★★★ **Rooms** 26 (some with air-conditioning) with bath or shower, WC, telephone, minibar, safe, TV satellite. **Price** Single 606F, double 712-988F, triple 1094F, suite 1200F. **Meals** Breakfast 45F. **Credit cards** All major. **Pets** Dogs allowed. **Facilities** Elevator, laundry service. **Parking** Opposite 169, boulevard Saint-Germain. **How to get there** (Map 1): Bus: 39, 48, 63, 70, 86, 87, 95, 96 - Metro: Saint-Germain-des-Prés. **Open** All year.

At the end of the 17th-century the "road of the cows" that ran alongside the moats of the Saint-Germain Abbey was renamed the Saint-Benoît. In the 1950's its bistros were frequented by Juliette Gréco and Boris Vian, and they were a major feature of this quarter. The entrance of the Crystal Hôtel does not seem to have changed since that era: framed by two lanterns, it leads into a very welcoming British lounge with its old Chesterfields and Chippendale armchairs. You find this classical and comfortable charm again in the very cozy rooms. Often large, they have a pleasant decor with wall-hangings and bedspreads happily matched, while the antique or style furniture adds a touch of character. Some give onto the street but efficient sound-proofing ensures a welcome quiet. The bathrooms are recently renovated and very attractive. Breakfast is served under the barrel vaults of a friendly little basement dining room, and is excellent.

Hôtel Danemark

21, rue Vavin
75006 Paris
Tel. (0)1 43 26 93 78 - Fax (0)1 46 34 66 06
M. Nurit

Category ★★★ **Rooms** 15 with soundproofing, bath, WC, telephone, TV satellite, hairdryer, minibar. **Price** Single 620, 790F (with whirlpool), double 790, 890F (with whirlpool). In August 490F (without whirlpool). **Meals** Breakfast 55F. **Credit cards** All major. **Pets** Dogs allowed. **Facilities** Elevator. **Parking** At 116, boulevard du Montparnasse. **How to get there** (Map 10): Bus: 58, 68, 75, 82, 83, 91 - Metro: Vavin, Notre-Dame-des-Champs - RER Port-Royal - Rail station (TGV): gare Montparnasse. **Open** All year.

Near to the Luxembourg Gardens and the large Brasseries of Montparnasse, the Hôtel du Danemark faces the curious "House of Sporting Grades" (Maison à Gradins Sportives) built in 1912 by Henri Sauvage; some rooms enjoy this view in full. It may be due to this influence, or to recall the Danish taste for design, that the management has opted for a modern decor. The reception area and corner lounges have preserved their stone walls but are in bright and very contrasting colors. In the rooms they have opted for softer-toned materials and furniture inspired by the 1930's. They are few in number and rather small, but comfortable and well sound-proofed, while those with a jacuzzi are much larger, as are the top-floor rooms. The welcome is friendly and attentive.

Hôtel du Danube

58, rue Jacob
75006 Paris
Tel. (0)1 42 60 34 70 - Fax (0)1 42 60 81 18

Category ★★★ **Rooms** 40 with bath or shower, telephone, cable TV, 30 with WC. **Price** Double 450-850F, suite 1100F (2-4 pers.). **Meals** Breakfast 45F, served 7:00-10:30. **Credit cards** Visa, Eurocard, MasterCard, Amex. **Pets** Dogs allowed (+30F). **Facilities** Elevator, garden. **Parking** At Saint-Germain-des-Prés. **How to get there** (Map 1): Bus: 39, 48, 95 - Metro: Saint-Germain-des-Prés. **Open** All year.

In the heart of Saint Germain des Prés, the Danube is one of our favorite hotels. It is a beautiful Napoléon III building with a discrete oak window behind which you can glimpse an inviting reception lounge with antique furniture, bronze lamps, and deep sofas, all beautifully set off by the pink, green, and gray floral chintz wall fabrics and drapes. A charming patio with garden furniture and palm trees leads to the bedrooms, which overlook the courtyard or the street. On the courtyard, rooms are decorated with Japanese straw on the walls, antique and exotic furniture, decorative objects, and engravings. On the street side, the rooms are somewhat less quiet but they are more imaginatively decorated; with light streaming in from two windows (except on the top floors) and colorful wall fabrics, handsome mahogany pedestal tables, and lovely wing chairs forming a delightful corner sitting area. Breakfast is served in a room with pale, smooth, wood paneling on which small Chinese porcelains are displayed. The room opens onto a patio, where tables are set out in good weather. This is truly a hotel of great character and charm.

Hôtel Dauphine Saint-Germain

36, rue Dauphine - 75006 Paris
Tel. (0)1 43 26 74 34 - Fax (0)1 43 26 49 09
web: http://www.webscapades.com/france/paris/dauphine.htm
M. Noël Janvier

Category ★★★ Rooms 29 and 1 suite with air-conditioning, soundproofing, bath or shower, WC, telephone, plug for fax, cable TV, radio, hairdryer, safe. **Price** Single and double 865F, suite 1080F (1-2 pers.), 1240 F (3-4 pers.). **Meals** Breakfast (american buffet): 65F, served 7:00-13:00. **Credit cards** All major. **Pets** Dogs allowed. **Facilities** Elevator, laundry service, bar, Tea room. **Parking** At 27, rue Mazarine. **How to get there** (Map 1): Bus: 24, 27, 58, 70 - Metro: Odéon, Pont-Neuf - RER: Cluny-Saint-Michel. **Open** All year.

Both classical and cosy, the Hôtel Dauphine Saint-Germain is in a building from the 17th-century but totally refurbished in 1996, but its venerable age can still be seen in certain places as with the superb beamed ceilings in the rooms, the walls and the stone vaulting. Having crossed an entry hall lined in pale oak you come to a very attractive little bar and tearoom. This room is very light and gives straight onto the outside, and is one of the delights of the hotel. In the mornings the breakfast buffet is set out here, and guests may sit and read their newspapers or just watch the street as it starts to liven up. The rooms are pleasant, comfortable and very classical but those with numbers ending in a "5" are impeccable. This is really a fine Parisian address.

Hôtel Delavigne

1, rue Casimir Delavigne
75006 Paris
Tel. (0)1 43 29 31 50 – Fax (0)1 43 29 78 56
M. Fraioli

Category ★★★ **Rooms** 34 with bath or shower, WC, telephone, safe, TV satellite. **Price** Single 500-580F, double 580-650F, triple 750F; in July – Aug single 450-530F, double 530-600F, triple 680F. **Meals** Breakfast 45F, served 7:30-10:30. **Credit cards** Visa, Eurocard, MasterCard. **Pets** Dogs not allowed. **Facilities** Elevator, bar. **Parking** At rue de l'École-de-Médecine. **How to get there** (Map 1): Bus: 21, 27, 38, 58, 63, 82, 85, 86, 87, 89 - Metro: Odéon - RER: Luxembourg. **Open** All year.

Quietly situated right in the center of the Saint-Germain/ Saint-Michel/Luxembourg triangle, the Hôtel Delavigne offers pretty rooms with walls covered with Japanese wickerwork enhanced by a small frieze, or well draped in fabrics, with elegant bedspreads in raw cotton (or sometimes printed), and always with a small picture. The furniture is very varied; in some rooms you will find colored cane types, in others interesting bedheads in wood or wrought iron, while again in others - but less often - some elegant antique pieces. Room sizes vary but you should note that those on the corner are attractively sized. The bathrooms are a little outdated but still provide all the comforts. A pretty series of prints of Paris monuments add interest to the corridors, and a very attractive corner lounge is on the ground floor. This is a friendly hotel where the small details such as a bottle of mineral water and sweets in every room give you the pleasant impression of being expected.

Hôtel des Deux Continents

25, rue Jacob
75006 Paris
Tel. (0)1 43 26 72 46 – Fax (0)1 43 25 67 80
M. Helnneveux

Category ★★★ **Rooms** 41 (10 with air-conditioning) with bath or shower, WC, telephone, hairdryer, TV satellite. **Price** Single 695F, double 695-815F, triple 1020F. **Meals** Breakfast 45F, served at any time. **Credit cards** Visa, Eurocard, MasterCard. **Facilities** Elevator, safes at reception, laundry service. **Parking** Opposite 169, boulevard Saint-Germain. **How to get there** (Map 1): Bus: 38, 39, 48, 58, 63, 84, 85, 86, 87, 96 - Metro: Saint-Germain-des-Prés, Mabillon. **Open** All year.

The "two continents" means Europe and the New World, the latter illustrated by a large fresco of 19th-century New York on a wall in the breakfast room. The atmosphere here is restful and quiet, and the soft decor includes a thick green carpet, paintings, wall upholstery, and decorated ceilings. The comfortable bedrooms are in three buildings. If the noise of the street doesn't bother you, ask for a room in front or one in the second building (slightly less spacious, but quieter), as these are the largest. The smallest rooms are in the third building and are just as charming, with the additional advantages of air-conditioning and silence. Most rooms have just been tastefully renovated with elegant wall fabrics and coordinated drapes (from the designers in the neighborhood), patinated furniture in some rooms, more classic styles in others, and marble bathrooms.

July 6 → July 21   805   Name & Credit card

Hôtel Ferrandi

92, rue du Cherche-Midi
75006 Paris
Tel. (0)1 42 22 97 40 - Fax (0)1 45 44 89 97
Mme Lafond

Category ★★★ **Rooms** 41 and 1 suite with air-conditioning, soundproofing, bath or shower, WC, telephone, TV satellite, hairdryer. **Price** Single and double 485-1280F, suite 1380F. Speciale rates on request. **Meals** Breakfast 45-65F; snacks available on request. **Credit cards** All major. **Pets** Dogs allowed. **Parking** Garage at hotel (140F per day) and at Bon Marché. **How to get there** (Map 1): Bus: 39, 48, 84, 89, 94, 95, 96 - Metro: Saint-Placide, Sèvres-Babylone. **Open** All year.

The Hôtel Ferrandi is a classic of the quarter, just midway between Montparnasse and Saint-Germain-des-Prés. The reception areas are vast and fitted out in the Restoration-style, with acajou furniture, wide draped fabrics and numerous small corner lounges. The rooms look out onto the street side, but for this reason all have been air-conditioned and have efficient double glazing. Often spacious, not one is similar to the next: in each case a pretty decor has ben arranged around a different bed. This makes for a 'bourgeois' and cosseted whole, with very pretty wallpapers (sometimes in 'Toile de Jouy' fabrics) in the recently renovated rooms. The bathrooms going with them are impeccable while the suites are most attractive. The Hôtel Ferrandi directly faces the Hôtel de Montmorency which now houses the works of Ernest Hébert, thus giving an opportunity to discover this French artist much in fashion in the 19th-century.

Hôtel de Fleurie

32, rue Grégoire-de-Tours
75006 Paris
Tel. (0)1 53 73 70 00 and (0)1 53 73 70 10 - Fax (0)1 53 73 70 20
Family Marolleau

Category ∗∗∗ **Rooms** 29 air-conditioning, soundproofing, bath or shower, WC, telephone, plug for modem, TV satellite, hairdryer, safe, minibar. **Price** Single 680-880F, double 880F (780F in low season), "luxe room" 1200F, Familie room (3-4 pers.) 1560F (1460F in low season). **Meals** Breakfast (buffet) 50F. Snacks available. **Credit cards** All major. **Pets** Dogs not allowed. **Facilities** Elevator, laundry service. **Parking** At rue de l'École-de-Médecine, marché Saint-Germain. **How to get there** (Map 1): Bus: 58, 63, 70, 86, 87, 96 - Metro: Odéon, Mabillon - RER: Cluny-Saint-Michel. **Open** All year.

At a few paces from the Odéon crossroads and on both sides of the Boulevard Saint-Germain, the small Rue Grégoire-de-Tours enjoys a very quiet and central location. The white facade of the Hôtel de Fleurie, with a small niche on each story to shelter a small statuette, attracts the eye immediately. Light tones are found in the interior and the white stones and certain elements from the very beautiful architecture have been preserved to recreate an 18th-century atmosphere. The wood pieces, pictures and other objects mix well with the cane or tapestried chairs and the furniture in the lounge and the breakfast room. The same softness is found in the rooms, which are not large; those ending with a '4' are bigger. They are classically decorated with both care and taste and have comfortable bathrooms. Run by a welcoming and highly motivated family, this hotel has managed to create the atmosphere of a 'house' but with service that is all attention and energy.

Hôtel du Globe et des 4 Vents

15, rue des Quatre-Vents
75006 Paris
Tel. (0)1 46 33 62 69 and (0)1 43 26 35 50 - Fax (0)1 46 33 17 29
Mme Simone Ressier

Category ★★ Rooms 15 with soundproofing, bath or shower, WC, telephone, TV. **Price** Single with washstand 255F, double 390-495F. **Meals** Breakfast 45F, served 7:00-11:00. **Credit cards** Visa, Eurocard, MasterCard. **Pets** Dogs allowed. **Parking** At place Saint-Sulpice. **How to get there** (Map 1): Bus: 63, 70, 86, 87, 96 - Metro: Odéon - RER: Cluny-Saint-Michel. **Open** Sept 1 – Aug 4.

One finds it hard to believe that there are still small hotels right in the heart of Paris that offer real quality for some FRF 400 per room. This is however the case with the Globe, which as well as being economical also offers the luxury of being entirely filled with antique furniture. Situated on a narrow street among venerable houses with their superb ironwork, the hotel is happy to remain hidden away. To the right of the entrance area is a tiny room with two magnificent Louis XV wing chairs enhanced in green, an 18th-century mirror in gilded wood and a cupboard and small fountain. Then you climb a narrow staircase to reach the loggia, which serves as reception area. Alongside and upstairs are the very small rooms, none the same as its neighbor. Certainly you find everywhere the wooden beams and very often some beautiful 18th-century wardrobe doors serving as bedheads, but the rest of the decoration is varied: fabric wall drapes, amusing prints, an aged cupboard or stately armchair, lace bedspreads and other objects. There is a lot of personality with a touch of exuberance and of the 'Bohemian', and this is a rare type of hotel to be discovered but only by booking well in advance.

Grand Hôtel des Balcons

3, rue Casimir-Delavigne - 75006 Paris
Tel. (0)1 46 34 78 50 - Fax (0)1 46 34 06 27
web: http://www.paris-hotel.tm.fr/balcons
M. and Mme Corroyer

Category ★★ **Rooms** 55 with soundproofing, bath or shower, WC, telephone, TV. **Price** Single 365-515F, double 465-515F, triple 580F (free for children under 10 years). **Meals** Breakfast (buffet) 55F, served 7:30-10:00 (offered the day of your birthday). **Credit cards** Visa, Eurocard, MasterCard. **Pets** Dogs allowed. **Facilities** Elevator, safe at reception. **Parking** At rue de l'École de Médecine. **How to get there** (Map 1): Bus: 21, 27, 38, 82, 85, 86, 87, 89 - Metro: Odéon - RER: Luxembourg. **Open** All year.

Quietly situated at a couple of paces from the Luxembourg in a small street linking the Place de l'Odéon to the more lively districts of the Boulevards Saint-Germain and Saint-Michel, the hotel displays its beautiful facade and its rows of small flowered balconies. The lower-floor rooms have kept their Art Nouveau character which gives the hotel its originality: a very pretty breakfast room in bistro style with its straw-bottomed chairs in convoluted forms in the style of the period, a beautiful reception area, corner-lounge, and all with green plants. 1900's worked wood and stained glass pieces are found on the staircase. The rooms vary in size but all are classically modern, and despite their rather standardized format one feels at home in them. They have attractive little bathrooms and all is generally very well maintained with frequent renovations; this year it'sthe turn of the carpeting which is now elegant and soft under foot. The bill still remains reasonable especially when taking count of the quality of the breakfast in self-service style, and the welcome is most friendly.

81

Grand Hôtel de l'Univers

6, rue Grégoire-de-Tours - 75006 Paris
Tel. (0)1 43 29 37 00 - Fax (0)1 40 51 06 45
web: http://www.webscapades.com/france/paris/univers.htm
M. Nouvel

1998

Category ★★★ **Rooms** 34 with air-conditioning, soundproofing, bath, WC, telephone, TV satellite, hairdryer, safe, minibar. **Price** Single 680-750F, double 750-990F, triple 950F. In August: –10%. **Meals** Breakfast 40F, served 7:30-11:00. **Credit cards** All major. **Pets** Dogs allowed. **Facilities** Elevator, laundry service, bar, room-service. **Parking** Mazarine, rue de l'École-de-Médecine. **How to get there** (Map 1): Bus: 58, 63, 70, 86, 87, 96 - Metro: Odéon - RER: Cluny-Saint-Michel. **Open** All year.

Tradition goes back to the 15th-century about the origins of this building in one of the most charming corners of Saint-Germain-des-Prés, and so it is no surprise that a classical ambiance has been chosen for the decor of the Grand Hôtel de l'Univers, in full harmony with the bare stonework and ceiling beams found in a good number of the rooms. The reception area, lounge and corner-bar thus display alternating worked wood of cerused oak and stone facing, while the furniture, notably copies of the 18th century-style , and a few personal objects give the flavor of a 'house'. Always comfortable, the rooms are of two kinds with those on the upper floors at the same time both rustic and refined, while lower down they have more standard characters with their light wood furniture in the 1930's style along with pastel, pink or pale green fabrics. Breakfast is served in the basement in a vaulted room with a Louis XIII decor, and the welcome is friendly.

L'Hôtel

13, rue des Beaux-Arts
75006 Paris
Tel. (0)1 44 41 99 00 - Fax (0)1 43 25 64 81
M. Alain-Philippe Feutré

Category ★★★★ **Rooms** 27 with air-conditioning, bath or shower, WC, telephone, minibar, safe, TV satellite. **Price** Double 1000-2500F (600-1500F in low season), suite (1-2 pers.) 2800-3600F (1700-2200F in low season). **Meals** Breakfast 100F, served 7:00-12:00. **Credit cards** All major. **Pets** Dogs allowed. **Facilities** Elevator, laundry service, bar, room-service. **Parking** At rue Mazarine. **How to get there** (Map 1): Bus: 24, 39, 48, 95 - Metro: Saint-Germain-des-Prés. **Open** All year.

L'Hôtel is a real institution having succeeded in remaining private with no pushy publicity apart from a discreet 'word-of-mouth', which ensures that nowadays as in earlier times, the personalities of the day come here to get a taste of the older Paris with the certainty of not being too disturbed. In 1900, Oscar Wilde stayed here before "dying beyond his means" in room 16, now renovated just as it then was. Later on Mistinguett was a regular visitor to room 36 with its Domergue-signed furniture, with so many others down to Robert de Niro, who likes apartment 25 with its large flowery terrace. Entirely furnished with antiques, each room has its own style with their wall-hangings, curtains, various objects, pictures, furniture pieces and so on. Their size, often very small, and rather dated air will not appeal to everybody, especially taking count of their price-but then do places of legend have a price? On the ground floor the former courtyard is covered by honeycomb vaulting, and used as bar or breakfast room depending on the time of day. Both service and welcome are of high quality.

Hôtel-Jardin Le Bréa

14, rue Bréa – 75006 Paris
Tel. (0)1 43 25 44 41 – Fax (0)1 44 07 19 25
web: http://www.webscapades.com/france/paris/brea.htm
Mme Elguermaï

Category ★★★ **Rooms** 23 with air-conditioning, soundproofing, telephone, bath or shower, WC, TV, safe, 4 with minibar. **Price** Single 620F, double 690-800F, triple 800F. Extra bed 100F. Special rates in low season. **Meals** Breakfast 50F, served 7:30-10:30. **Credit cards** All major. **Pets** Dogs not allowed. **Facilities** Elevator, laundry service, bar. **Parking** At Montparnasse, Raspail. **How to get there** (Map 10): Bus: 83, 91 - Metro: Vavin, Notre-Dame-des-Champs - RER: Port-Royal. **Open** All year.

The Hôtel-Jardin Le Bréa is ideally placed for those wanting to stay in the heart of Montparnasse and enjoy all the life of this quarter, and also to visit the Luxembourg Gardens. The hotel has just been fully renovated wth Jean-Philippe called on to do the decoration, and he has created a cosseted and warm atmosphere in today's style. The South inspired the garden layout now converted into a winter garden, along with the lounge and the breakfast room, all now particularly attractive. The pretty rooms are split between two small buildings, one giving onto a quiet street, the other onto the interior courtyard, and the largest rooms are in the latter. Everywhere the colors are warm, the fabrics heavy and nothing is lacking for comfort, while the white bathrooms enhanced with russet marble have received the same attention. The Hôtel-Jardin Le Bréa is now a member of that new generation of hotels which are all recommendable.

Left Bank Saint-Germain Hôtel

9, rue de l'Ancienne-Comédie
75006 Paris
Tel. (0)1 43 54 01 70 - Fax (0)1 43 26 17 14
M. Teil

Category ★★★ **Rooms** 30 and 1 suite with air-conditioning, soundproofing, bath, WC, telephone, cable TV, safe, hairdryer, minibar. **Price** Single and double 895-990F, suite 1400F. **Meals** Breakfast (buffet) 50F. **Credit cards** All major. **Pets** Dogs not allowed. **Facilities** Elevator, laundry service. **Parking** Opposite 21, rue de l'Ecole-de-Médecine and 27, rue Mazarine. **How to get there** (Map 1): Bus: 58, 63, 70, 86, 87, 96 - Metro: Odéon - RER: Cluny-Saint-Michel. **Open** All year.

The Left Bank is in the heart of Saint-Germain-des-Prés, a neighbor of the Procope café with all its memories of the revolutionaries, the *Encyclopédistes* and the romantic movement. The small reception area opens on to a pretty lounge that already sets the tone of the house. Indeed various worked wood pieces in oak and walnut were made for the hotel, and they well match the few antique furniture pieces and Aubusson tapestries. The same solid walnut style furniture is in the bedrooms, recently renovated with their walls hung with silk damasks or 'Toile de Jouy' (our favorites), coordinated with double curtains. All adds to the warm and very comfortable ambiance of the hotel. Room sizes vary and those with a number ending in a '4' or '6' are largest. However, we also like those with numbers ending with a '3', which are square and very pleasantly proportioned with their two windows. All have beautiful bathrooms where nothing has been forgotten. Breakfast is self-service buffet-style, both good and large.

Hôtel Libertel Montparnasse

126, rue du Cherche-Midi
75006 Paris
Tel. (0)1 45 48 37 48 - Fax. (0)1 45 49 94 49
Mme Elfriede Leutwyler

Category *** **Rooms** 27 with soundproofing, telephone, bath or shower, WC, cable TV, hairdryer, safe, minibar - 1 for disabled persons. **Price** Single 650-780F, double 700-860F. **Meals** Breakfast (buffet) 75F, served 7:00-10:30. **Credit cards** All major. **Pets** Dogs allowed. **Facilities** Elevator, laundry service, room-service. **How to get there** (Map 1): Bus: 28, 39, 70, 82, 89, 92 - Metro: Duroc - Rail station (TGV): gare Montparnasse. **Open** All year.

The Libertel Montparnasse is a refined hotel with modern comforts and the yellow of the small lounge is also found in some of the rooms, unless they are in greys or raspberry. Recently renovated, all are very well equipped with furniture designed for the hotel, and even the smaller rooms have a small corner for writing and a hanging cupboard. The bathrooms are light and carefully thought-out, while their small 'designer' basins are covered with welcoming products. There are old prints on the walls while the breakfast room, cleverly lit by a glass roof, is quite as attractive as the rest of the establishment. Both the French and foreign papers can be found every morning. Just a few steps from the Boulevard de Montparnasse, the hotel is well-placed for those wanting an address close to the station, the Bon Marché store and this district much loved by window-shoppers. It is also an occasion to visit the two Hébert and Bourdelle museums situated close by. The welcome is friendly and competent.

Hôtel Libertel Prince de Condé

39, rue de Seine
75006 Paris
Tel. (0)1 43 26 71 56 – Fax (0)1 46 34 27 95
M. Philippe Roye

Category ★★★ **Rooms** 12 with air-conditioning, soundproofing, telephone, bath, WC, hairdryer, minibar, safe, cable TV - 1 for disabled persons. **Price** Single 910F, double 975F, suite 1700F. Extra bed 150F. **Meals** Breakfast (buffet) 75F, served 7:30-10:30. **Credit cards** All major. **Pets** Dogs allowed. **Facilities** Elevator, laundry service, room-service. **Parking** At rue Mazarine. **How to get there** (Map 1): Bus: 24, 58, 70 - Metro: Odéon. **Open** All year.

With a very impressive sense for detail, the interior decor of this small hotel is based on a classical style, half Napoleon III and half English, with the furniture pieces, wall drapings and other materials all top quality. Each room enjoys the same level of quality, and the soundproofing is excellent both internally and externally. Sizes are always adequate and satisfactory but with some advantage to rooms with numbers ending with a '2'. We must also stress the excellent price deal of the suite and the pleasant breakfast room. It is well designed from two small rooms and lets you overlook the rather austere and venerable vaulted basement, thanks to its range of small sofas and low armchairs in brightly colored fabrics, and always ranged around a low table. There are only twelve rooms in this small hotel in one of the most charming districts of the capital, which is the real guarantee of genuine privacy and an attentive welcome.

Hôtel Libertel Prince de Conti

8, rue Guénégaud
75006 Paris
Tel. (0)1 44 07 30 40 - Fax (0)1 44 07 36 34
M. Philippe Roye

Category ★★★ **Rooms** 26 with air-conditioning, soundproofing, bath or shower, WC, telephone, hairdryer, TV satellite, safe, minibar. **Price** Single 800-910F, double 975F, duplex 1350F, suite 1300F. **Meals** Breakfast (buffet) 75F, served 7:00-10:30. **Credit cards** All major. **Pets** Dogs allowed. **Facilities** Elevator, laundry service, room-service. **Parking** At rue Mazarine. **How to get there** (Map 1): Bus: 27, 58, 63, 70, 87, 96 - Metro: Odéon,Saint-Michel - RER: Cluny-Saint-Michel. **Open** All year.

A few meters from the Seine and the 'bouquinistes' and in the heart of the art galleries quarter of Saint-Germain-des-Prés, the Hôtel Prince de Conti is lodged in an 18th-century building of the Rue Guénégaud. Renovation of the house has created twenty-six rooms but it should be said straight away that they are not always large while adding that they are truly ravishing. The choice of the various coordinated colors is superb, there is quality furniture and the details are always carefully handled so that you feel really at home. On the comfort side, nothing is lacking and all the rooms are double-glazed along with air-conditioning and pretty, functional and well-equipped bathrooms. The duplex suites are also all charming and much larger, with a lounge and a room on a higher floor. You should also note one huge room (No. 1) and two singles giving onto the ground floor flowery courtyard. There is a roomy and very attractive area in the semi-basement with its lounge, bar and breakfast corner, and a very British and refined atmosphere, with the welcome both professional and friendly.

Hôtel Louis II

2, rue Saint-Sulpice
75006 Paris
Tel. (0)1 46 33 13 80 – Fax (0)1 46 33 17 29
Mme Brigitte Siozade-David

Category ★★★ **Rooms** 22 with soundproofing, bath or shower, WC, TV, minibar, hairdryer.
Price Single or double 560-790F, triple 950F. **Meals** Breakfast 48F. **Credit cards** All major.
Pets Dogs allowed. **Facilities** Elevator. **Parking** At Saint-Sulpice and École-de-Médecine
How to get there (Map 1): Bus: 58, 63, 70, 86, 87, 96 – Metro: Odéon, Saint-Michel – RER:
Luxembourg, Cluny-Saint-Michel. **Open** All year.

Between the Saint-Sulpice church and the Odéon, this is a charming hotel with cosseted comfort. From the entrance you have the impression of a private house, above all when you see the lounge with its antique furniture and notably the ravishing 18th-century wing chairs and the Empire mirror topped with its gilded bas-relief mantel. You can take breakfast here unless you prefer it in your room. These latter are on narrow landings and all overlook the street. All differently decorated, they do have common features: all are small but welcoming and decorated with flowered fabrics (a little bit stuffy for some people), with beautiful ceiling beams. Lace bedcovers give a charming grandmotherly ambiance, an oak wardrobe and a small antique armchair give an air of intimacy. As for the two rooms on the top floor, they are spacious and particularly well done, ideal for a family or those wanting an extended stay. This is a most charming place where you will receive a smiling welcome.

Hôtel Luxembourg

4, rue de Vaugirard - 75006 Paris
Tel. (0)1 43 25 35 90 - Fax (0)1 43 26 60 84
web: http://www.grolier.fr/luxembourg/
M. and Mme J. Mandin

Category ★★★ Rooms 33 with bath or shower, WC, telephone, safe, TV satellite, minibar, fan, hairdryer. **Price** Single 706-816F, double 732-822F, triple 998F; in low season, single 646-746F, double 672-752F, triple 918F. **Meals** Breakfast (buffet) 60F, including in low season, served 7:00-10:30. **Credit cards** All major. **Pets** Small dogs allowed. **Facilities** Elevator, laundry service, bar, patio. **Parking** At rue Soufflot. **How to get there** (Map 1): Bus: 21, 27, 38, 58, 82, 84, 85, 89 - Metro: Odéon - RER: Luxembourg. **Open** All year.

The building formerly served to lodge the post-horse riders of Louis XIV but has today become one of the prettiest hotels of the Luxembourg - Odéon perimeter. The tone is set right from the entry : elegant fabrics with their warm tones and furniture in the 18th century-style form the corner lounges, and the whole opens onto a ravishing flowered patio where one can take a drink. The same care and comfort are found in the rooms: of a good size with the smaller units let as singles, they have all just been renovated along with their bathrooms. A lot of shining furniture here also, some pretty armchairs, the bedheads in the form of antique pediments, and always the taste for beautiful fabrics. About half of them look onto the patio while the others understandably been double-glazed to keep out the street noise. Breakfast is served in a vaulted room in this refined hotel.

Hôtel du Lys

23, rue Serpente
75006 Paris
Tel. (0)1 43 26 97 57 - Fax (0)1 44 07 34 90
Mme Decharne

Category ** **Rooms** 22 with bath or shower, WC, telephone, TV satellite, hairdryer, safe. **Price** Single 380-470F, double 500F, triple 600F. **Meals** Breakfast included. **Credit cards** Not accepted. **Pets** Dogs allowed. **Parking** Square in front of Notre-Dame, École-de-Médecine. **How to get there** (Map 2): Bus: 21, 27, 38, 63, 85, 86, 87, 96 - Metro: Saint-Michel, Odéon - RER: Cluny-Saint-Michel. **Open** All year.

Right in the Latin Quarter, this small hotel offers you a room at a quite unexpected price in a beautiful town house from the 17th-century, still rich in memories from that era. This explains the rather varied nature of the rooms that will enchant all those nostalgic for the 'Old Paris'. There is no elevator to the rooms but the wooden staircase, just as old as the building, works out the legs. Some rooms are no bigger than a 'pocket handkerchief' while others are more generous in size. There's wooden beamed ceilings and some leaning walls, while one is often charmed by the decoration chosen by Mme Decharne with wallpapers and fabrics in real harmony, small antique furniture pieces here and there, sometimes a pretty pair of prints, and so on. On the sanitation side, here also the amenities are very variable and one has to admit that seeing some of the bathrooms just renovated the others do seem rather out-of-date. Each morning the elegant entry hall is transformed into the breakfast room, while lacking space many breakfasts are also served in the rooms. You get a warm welcome with a clientele often of artists and intellectuals.

Hôtel Madison

143, boulevard Saint-Germain
75006 Paris
Tel. (0)1 40 51 60 00 – Fax (0)1 40 51 60 01
Mme Maryse Burkard

Category ★★★ Rooms 55 with air-conditioning, soundproofing, telephone, bath or shower, WC, TV satellite, minibar, hairdryer, safe. **Price** Single 800-1000F, doubles 1100-2250F. Special rates in August, January and February. **Meals** Breakfast (buffet) included, served 6:30-11:00. **Credit cards** All major. **Pets** Dogs allowed. **Facilities** Elevator. **Parking** At Saint-Germain, Saint Sulpice. **How to get there** (Map 1): Bus: 39, 48, 63, 86, 87, 95 - Metro: Saint-Germain-des-Prés. **Open** All year.

This is the hotel Albert Camus opted for when visiting Paris and where he finished the manuscript of his "Stranger". Sited slightly back from the boulevard on a little square with its trees, it directly faces the church of Saint-Germain-des-Prés . You can choose a room with this view while the higher you are, the more the view widens over the roofs of the area. The rooms are large, classical and irresistibly elegant, and you will find the same comfort throughout: beautiful fabrics from 'Chez Lelièvre', deep printed carpeting, large cupboards with drawers in the English style, bathrooms with Italian tiles, and often antique furniture. All the corridors have received the same care while the lounge has just been completely redone in 18th-century style: wood carvings, Aubusson greeneries, fireplace and a studded floor. For breakfast you can choose the continental type in your room or the 'brunch' buffet in the dining room. This is a superb hotel offering an attentive and smiling welcome.

Hôtel Les Marronniers

21, rue Jacob
75006 Paris
Tel. (0)1 43 25 30 60 – Fax (0)1 40 46 83 56
M. Henneveux

Category ★★★ **Rooms** 37 with air-conditioning, bath or shower, WC, TV satellite. **Price** Single 540F, double 735-835F, triple 1060F. **Meals** Breakfast 45F, served 7:30-11:00. **Credit cards** Visa, Eurocard, MasterCard. **Pets** Dogs not allowed. **Facilities** Elevator, safe at reception, garden. **Parking** Opposite 169, boulevard Saint-Germain and at rue Mazarine. **How to get there** (Map 1): Bus: 39, 48, 63, 68, 69, 86, 87, 95 - Metro: Saint-Germain-des-Prés. **Open** All year.

The Rue Jacob conceals an incalculable number of tapestry dealers, decorators, antique sellers and the Hôtel Les Marronniers, which seems most content among such neighbors. This very pretty address also offers the luxury of a genuine little garden right in the center of Paris, and has managed a most happy interior transformation. There is first the small but warm entry area with its warm tones and a few antique pieces. Then follows the veranda in Napoleon III–style, used as a tearoom and also the breakfast room, with the whole having a rather "Empress Eugénie" ambiance with white wrought iron garden furniture against a background of flowery carpeting and billowing curtains. Lastly, the rooms and their bathrooms are all recently renovated and well equipped. From the third floor, those with a number ending with a '1' or '2' look onto the garden, while those on the fifth and sixth floors look onto the courtyard and with a pretty view over the roofs of the district. The welcome is friendly and prices are quite reasonable for the location.

Millésime Hôtel

15, rue Jacob
75006 Paris
Tel. (0)1 44 07 97 97 – Fax (0)1 46 34 55 97
Laurence and Robert Leclercq

Category ★★★ Rooms 21 air-conditioning, soundproofing, telephone, bath, WC, hairdryer, TV satellite, minibar, safe - 1 for disabled persons. **Price** Single 650-750F, double 750-900F. **Meals** Breakfast 55F, served 7:30-12:00. **Credit cards** Visa, Eurocard, MasterCard, Amex. **Pets** Small dogs allowed. **Facilities** Elevator, laundry service. **Parking** Opposite 169, boulevard Saint-Germain. **How to get there** (Map 1): Bus: 39, 48, 63, 68, 69, 86, 87, 95 - Metro: Saint-Germain-des-Prés, Mabillon. **Open** All year.

From the outside you can see the small welcome lounge of the Millésime, the foretaste of a classical style and fashion well matching the tone of this street so rich in boutiques and antique shops. Like us, you will delight to cross the threshold with its light wood tones and orange–ocre colorings seen from the front, and will soon note that the rest of the hotel does not disappoint your first impressions. The rooms are large and have comfortable beds standing against Directory-style pediments and covered with rich mixed piqué fabrics matching the dominant colorway. The walls are covered in beige tones and topped with a frieze, and you find a half-moon picture in each one, the reproduction of an Italian villa. The bathrooms are elegant, in white with grey touches, with smart chromed taps, new editions of older models. You should note the "Millésime" room with its double sloped ceiling and a very pretty view. Breakfasts are served in the vast basement in a huge room centered around an impressive pillar dating from the Middle Ages. This is one of the most successful renovations in this quarter.

Hôtel Normandie Mayet

3, rue Mayet
75006 Paris
Tel. (0)1 47 83 21 35 – Fax (0)1 40 65 95 78
Mme Atmoun

Category ★★★ **Rooms** 23 with bath or shower, WC, telephone, safe, TV satellite. **Price** Single 450F (395F for readers of this guide), double 650F (450F for readers of this guide). In low season single 360F, double 400F. **Meals** Breakfast 36F, served 7:30-10:00. **Credit cards** All major. **Pets** Dogs allowed. **Facilities** Elevator, bar. **Parking** Montparnasse. **How to get there** (Map 1): Metro: Duroc - Bus: 28, 39, 70, 82, 89, 92 and Air France bus. **Open** All year.

Close to the lively area but in total quiet, the small Rue Mayet is an ideal spot for relaxation without isolation. To decorate the reception area of this discreet little hotel, Italian artists came to complete the foliated frescoes as well as the peacocks decorating the walls, and the superb assembly of worked woods linking the bar and reception areas. This very "winter garden" atmosphere is further accentuated by the small open area at the end of the reception, with a stone fountain flanked by two basins with green plants, all out in the bright daylight. The small rooms are simple and comfortable, decorated with sponge-painted paper and flowered fabrics. Their bathrooms give onto a small courtyard and thus enjoy much welcome natural light. We would recommend the rooms on the street as the others only look out onto a blank wall, and should only be taken in an emergency. There is no restaurant but La Cadolle is just next door.

Hôtel Novanox

155, boulevard du Montparnasse
75006 Paris
Tel. (0)1 46 33 63 60 - Fax (0)1 43 26 61 72
M. Bertrand Plasmans

Category *** **Rooms** 27 with soundproofing, telephone, bath or shower, WC, minibar, hairdryer, safe. **Price** Single 550-680F, double 580-680F. From July 15 to August 30 490F (1 pers.), 550F (2 pers.). **Meals** Breakfast 50F, served 7:00-12:00. Snacks available. **Credit cards** All major. **Pets** Dogs allowed. **Facilities** Elevator, bar, terrace. **Parking** At Montparnasse-Raspail **How to get there** (Map 10): Bus: 38, 83, 91 - Metro: Vavin, Raspail - RER: Port-Royal. **Open** All year.

Hidden by a small hedge behind which several teak chairs and tables are set out, the Novanox strikes you with its originality. Designer fabrics and pale-wood furniture especially designed for the hotel create a contemporary atmosphere that is both sophisticated and pleasant. With their smart desk/dressing tables, elegant wardrobes, and handsomely upholstered chairs, the bedrooms are individually furnished. The bathrooms are well-equipped but they are much less remarkable. If you're concerned about noise from the boulevard (despite the double-glazed windows), ask for a room on the Rue Notre-Dame-des-Champs side. Breakfast is served in the lounge/bar. There's a vast choice of famous, late-night restaurants and *brasseries* here in Montparnasse.

Hôtel de l'Odéon

13, rue Saint-Sulpice
75006 Paris
Tel. (0)1 43 25 70 11 - Fax (0)1 43 29 97 34
M. and Mme Pilfert

Category ★★★ **Rooms** 30 with air-conditioning, soundproofing, bath or shower, WC, telephone, cable TV, hairdryer, safe. **Price** Single 680F, double 780-970F, triple 1180-1250F. **Meals** Breakfast 55F, orange juice 20F, snacks available. **Credit cards** All major. **Pets** Dogs allowed. **Facilities** Elevator, patio, bar. **Parking** At place Saint-Sulpice and rue de l'École-de-Médecine. **How to get there** (Map 1): Bus: 58, 63, 70, 86, 87, 96 - Metro: Odéon, Saint-Sulpice - RER: Cluny-Saint-Michel. **Open** All year.

In this ideally situated 16th-century building, all the styles have been happily mingled with the Louis-Philippe winged chairs and pedestal tables of the tiny lounge alongside a church pew, a few Oriental carpets, flowered English carpeting and so on. If you add in a telephone box that seems to have come directly from Trafalgar Square in London, some splendid old stained glass pieces delicately lightened, then you create a particularly warm atmosphere quite able to make you overlook the smallness of the place and some of the rooms. With these originality has also been shown and there is not one that resembles the next. Some are 'haute-époque' with a canopied bed, others are romantic style with a copper bedstead or twinned Sicilian beds of painted wrought iron with mother-of-pearl effects, while yet others offer integrated painted and polished furniture in the old style. All have a small corner area for writing or just relaxation. This is an astonishing place with the decor applied so as to make you forget you are even in a hotel.

Hotel La Perle

14, rue des Canettes
75006 Paris
Tel. (0)1 43 29 10 10 - Fax (0)1 46 34 51 04
Mme Spowe - M. Laterner

Category ★★★ **Rooms** 38 with air-conditioning, soundproofing, bath or shower, WC, telephone, minibar, safe, hairdryer, TV satellite - 2 for disabled persons. **Price** Single 900F, doubles 950-1400F. **Meals** Breakfast (buffet) 70F, served from 7:00. **Credit cards** All major. **Pets** Dogs allowed. **Facilities** Elevator, laundry service, bar, patio. **Parking** At Saint-Germain and Saint-Sulpice. **How to get there** (Map 1): Bus: 58, 63, 70, 86, 87, 96 - Metro: Saint-Germain-des-Prés, Saint-Sulpice, Mabillon. **Open** All year.

Lively with its many small restaurants, the narrow Rue des Canettes dates back to the 13th-century and is one of the most picturesque streets of the Left Bank. La Perle recently opened in an 18th-century house here, which is decorated in a beautiful combination of contemporary and classic styles. Old beams, pillars, and exposed-stone walls are used to handsome advantage in the reception areas. There is a pleasant bar that is designed somewhat like a boat, with exotic wood paneling and copper portholes. Adjacent to it is the bright breakfast room, which is in the old, almost entirely glassed-in interior courtyard. The comfortable, immaculately kept bedrooms, whose predominant colors vary with each floor, are air-conditioned and sound-proofed with effective double-glazing. They have beautiful beamed ceilings, but the decor, although tasteful, is somewhat conventional.

Hôtel Le Régent

61, rue Dauphine
75006 Paris
Tel. (0)1 46 34 59 80 – Fax (0)1 40 51 05 07
Mme Danièle Martin

Category ★★★ Rooms 25 with air-conditioning, soundproofing, bath or shower, WC, telephone, TV satellite, radio, hairdryer, safe, minibar. **Price** Single and double 750-1000F. Special rates in low season. Between December 1 and February 28 you pay 2 nights for a weekend with 3 nights. **Meals** Breakfast 55F, served 7:00-11:00. **Credit cards** All major. **Pets** Dogs not allowed. **Facilities** Elevator, laundry service. **Parking** At 27, rue Mazarine. **How to get there** (Map 1): Bus: 25, 27, 58, 63, 70, 86, 87, 96 - Metro: Odéon - RER: Cluny-Saint-Michel. **Open** All year.

Fully renovated, the Hôtel le Régent is in an old 18th-century building between the Boulevard Saint-Germain and the quays of the Seine. In the entry hall a wall mirror reflects the painted beams and ancient stonework of the house, and the classical lounge continues in similar style. The rooms are a success with a very beautiful harmony of coral, cream or lime-green shades and materials, with more contrasted colors on the top floor and superb enamel faiences in the bathrooms. All are light, furnished with elegance, extremely comfortable and in perfect taste. Converted into the breakfast room, the vaulted basement is very warm but there is some risk of crowding when the hotel is full and it may be better to take breakfast in your own room. The hotel owners also own the legendary Café des Deux Magots where you can take your meals at leisure.

Hôtel Relais Christine

3, rue Christine
75006 Paris
Tel. (0)1 40 51 60 80 – Fax (0)1 40 51 60 81
M. Yves Monnin

Category ★★★★ **Rooms** 35 and 16 duplex, with air-conditioning, soundproofing, bath, WC, telephone (fax with extra charge), cable TV, hairdryer, minibar. **Price** Single 1750F, double 1850F (from July 15 to August 31 1800F with breakfast (buffet) and a museum-pass for 1 day), room with lounge 2700F, duplex 2400-3300F. **Meals** Breakfast 110F, buffet 135F, served at any time. Snacks available. **Credit cards** All major. **Pets** Dogs allowed. **Facilities** Elevator, laundry service, bar, garden. **Parking** Free private parking. **How to get there** (Map 1): Bus: 24, 27, 58, 63, 70, 86, 87, 96 - Metro: Odéon, Saint-Michel - RER: Cluny-Saint-Michel. **Open** All year.

This hotel from the early 17th-century occupies a part of the former Augustins Convent, and is reached via a paved green courtyard. The interior has nothing nun-like about it, quite the contrary. A full range of warm colors has been chosen for the decoration, whether in the wainscotted lounge with its pretty collection of antique furniture pieces and portraits, or in the very pleasant rooms, with some facing onto a real treed garden. Small or somewhat larger, all are extremely comfortable and decorated in a classical and bright style. You should also note the duplexes, much appreciated by families and perfect for longer stays if the means allow. The breakfast room is in a superb vaulted room set around an imposing central pillar. This was the former kitchen area dating from the early 13th-century, whose fireplace and well can still be seen. Offering a very attentive, discreet and efficient welcome, the Relais Christine has become a classic among the Parisian hotels of charm.

Le Relais Médicis

23, rue Racine
75006 Paris
Tel. (0)1 43 26 00 60 – Fax (0)1 40 46 83 39
M. Chérel

Category ★★★ **Rooms** 16 with air-conditioning, soundproofing, bath, WC, telephone, cable TV, hairdryer, safe, minibar. **Price** Single 930F, double 995-1495F. **Meals** Breakfast included. **Credit cards** All major. **Pets** Dogs allowed. **Facilities** Laundry service. **Parking** At place Saint-Sulpice and opposite 21, rue de l'Ecole-de-Médecine. **How to get there** (Map 1): Bus: 58, 63, 70, 86, 87, 96 - Metro: Odéon - RER: Cluny-Saint-Michel. **Open** All year.

The Relais Médicis appropriately defines itself as a hotel with the colors of Provence and the scent of Italy. This is very much the atmosphere inside. Waxed beamed ceilings, garden furniture, antique paintings, and photos decorate the reception rooms downstairs. The bedrooms are fresh and cheerful with bathrooms as pretty as they are comfortable. The largest rooms overlook the street. The breakfast room has checked tablecloths and a vacation atmosphere. This is a hotel you'll look forward to returning to in the evening.

Le Relais Saint-Germain

9, carrefour de l'Odéon
75006 Paris
Tel. (0)1 43 29 12 05 – Fax (0)1 46 33 45 30
M. Laipsker

Category ★★★★ Rooms 22 with air-conditioning, soundproofing, bath, WC, telephone, cable TV, hairdryer, safe, minibar. **Price** Single 1290F, double 1550-1750F, suite 2000F, duplex (4-5 pers.) 3300F. **Meals** Breakfast included; snacks available. **Credit cards** All major. **Pets** Dogs allowed. **Facilities** Room-service. **Parking** At place Saint-Sulpice, opposite 21, rue de l'Ecole-de-Médecine. **How to get there** (Map 1): Bus: 58, 63, 70, 86, 87, 96 - Metro: Odéon - RER: Cluny-Saint-Michel. **Open** All year.

Pleasantly situated, this small and charming luxury hotel wants for nothing in comparsion with the very largest types, and the tone is set right from the reception area and neighboring lounge. Some beautiful 18th–century paintings in the style of Joseph Vernet set off a Louis XIV commode, various refined objects and shimmering fabrics, and we are here very far removed from some anonymous and standardized hotel. The exception proves the rule but the Relais Saint-Germain has only twenty-two rooms, all very successful thanks to the owners' taste and sense of comfort. Spacious or more cozy, all have beautiful printed or striped fabrics blending with the dominant color, plus antique furniture pieces. Some rooms have a certain flare and luxury that might surprise. The suites are superb and their prices seem entirely justified . There are open views from everywhere with the hotel giving onto the very typical Place de l'Odéon. The welcome and service are naturally faultless.

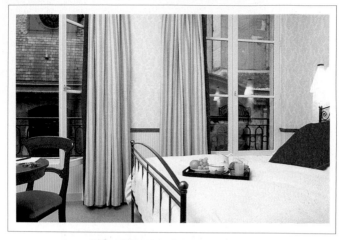

Hôtel Relais Saint-Sulpice

3, rue Garancière
75006 Paris
Tel. (0)1 46 33 99 00 – Fax (0)1 46 33 00 10
Mme Touber

Category ★★★ **Rooms** 26 with air-conditioning, soundproofing, bath, WC, telephone, TV satellite, hairdryer, minibar, safe - 2 for disabled persons. **Price** Single and double 920-1250F. **Meals** Breakfast (buffet) 50F, served 7:00-11:00. **Credit cards** All major. **Pets** Elevator, bar, laundry service. **Parking** In the hotel (150F per day) and at place Saint-Sulpice. **How to get there** (Map 1): Bus: 58, 63, 70, 86, 87, 96 - Metro: Saint-Sulpice, Mabillon. **Open** All year.

Very much in fashion, the Saint-Sulpice district is attracting more and more fashion boutiques and luxuriously decorated renovations. With the opening of the Relais Saint-Sulpice the hotel business has not lagged behind in this trend and we are sure that this new hotel will soon find its clientele. The entry area is in the form of a lounge-library. The rooms are often small but extremely comfortable with superb beds made irresistible by generous quilts and four pillows. The bathrooms are ravishing while the whole effect testifies to a real concern for details both in the quality of materials and forms and colors, very representative of modern trends. Taken over by a large greenhouse full of plants and flowers, the central courtyard which you can see, but not enter, lights a vast dining room in the basement. Breakfast is served in a winter garden atmosphere, with teak and wrought iron furniture, warmed by the dominant colors of yellow-orange and elegant prints. This is a fine and welcoming address.

Relais Hôtel Vieux Paris

9, rue Gît-le-Cœur - 75006 Paris
Tel. (0)1 44 32 15 90 - Fax (0)1 43 26 00 15
e-mail: vieuxparis@sollers.fr
Mme Claude Odillard

Category ★★★★ **Rooms** 13 and 7 suites with air-conditioning, soundproofing, bath (whirlpool in suites), WC, telephone, cable TV, plug for fax, safe, hairdryer, minibar. **Price** Single and double 990-1650F. **Meals** Breakfast 70F, served 8:00-11:30; snacks available. **Credit cards** All major. **Pets** Dogs not allowed. **Facilities** Elevator, laundry service, terrace. **Parking** At Palais de Justice, Marché aux fleurs. **How to get there** (Map 2): Bus: 21, 24, 27, 38, 85, 96 - Metro and RER: Saint-Michel. **Open** All major.

This is the very heart of the old Paris with Notre-Dame and the flower market. The building was built in 1480 and has conserved numerous traces of its past, such as the huge stone pillar in the small yellow dining room, bays and ceilings *á la française* and amusing volumes. In short, the place does not lack for style and four years ago Mme. Odillard ordered a complete renovation of the hotel and every room was warmly decorated with as much care for detail as if it were her own home: very fine coordinated fabrics, always well-designed furniture, even a little bell on the door of each room. A lot of comfort with a 'cozy' style, along with superb bathrooms with heating lamps and bath robes. All the suites have jacuzzis while those on the top floor have a lounge with mezzanine ceiling. Breakfasts are refined and lack for nothing including squeezed orange juice and tea made from the leaf. The welcome is very attentive.

Hôtel de Saint-Germain

50, rue du Four
75006 Paris
Tel. (0)1 45 48 91 64 – Fax (0)1 45 48 46 22
M. Lassalle

Category ★★ Rooms 30 with bath or shower, WC, telephone, cable TV, minibar, safe (+10F per day), 15 with hairdryer. **Price** Single 415-585F, double 520-695F. Special rates in low season. Extra bed +120F (free for children under 12). **Meals** Breakfast 45F, Englisch 60F, served 7:00-11:30. **Credit cards** All major. **Pets** Dogs allowed. **Facilities** Elevator, laundry service. **Parking** Saint-Sulpice, Bon Marché, Saint-Germain. **How to get there** (Map 1): Bus: 39, 48, 63, 70, 87, 94, 95, 96 - Metro: Saint-Sulpice, Sèvres-Babylone. **Open** All year.

A pretty reception area with a lounge in green cane, flowers, a small desk, and all is in place. At the Hôtel de Saint-Germain, space is in short supply but it has been made welcoming and warm, and although the rooms are also not very large, their white pine furniture with a small desk or cupboard fits them perfectly. Depending on floor, some have been kept in natural wood, while others, the more recent, have seen their furniture changed into green, blue or red, along with madras fabrics in stripes and squares. They are bright and have pocket-sized bathrooms with all the comforts. Those with a number ending in a '5' are slightly larger, while those with a '1' are at the back and quiet, but a bit dark. Number 11 also enjoys a tiny little courtyard with a table and chairs. Most however give onto the street with a lot of activity and, despite the double-glazing, there is never complete silence. The dining room is on the ground floor and decorated in the same spirit, and an English breakfast is served.

Hôtel Saint-Germain-des-Prés

36, rue Bonaparte
75006 Paris
Tel. (0)1 43 26 00 19 – Fax (0)1 43 25 74 39
M. Nouvel

Category ★★★ **Rooms** 28 and 2 suites with soundproofing (15 with air-conditioning), bath or shower, WC, telephone, TV, minibar, safe, hairdryer. **Price** Single 750-950F, double 750-1300F, suite 1600F (2 pers.) - In August: −10%. **Meals** Breakfast 50F, served 7:30-10:30. **Credit cards** Visa, Eurocard, MasterCard, Amex. **Pets** Small dogs allowed. **Facilities** Elevator, laundry service. **Parking** Saint-Germain-des-Prés. **How to get there** (Map 1): Bus: 39, 48, 63, 86, 87, 95 - Metro: Saint-Germain-des-Prés. **Open** All year.

Two steps off the Place Saint-Germain-des-Prés, this hotel reflects the beauty and sophistication of the famous neighborhood for which it is named. The handsome, antique oak doorway, set slightly back from the street, opens into an elegant lobby, with noble marble walls in trompe l'œil, Haute Epoque furniture, an Aubusson tapestry, and antiques. In the lounge, with its immense glass wall and floral fresco, you can have breakfast (somewhat disappointing) or a drink. Many bedrooms are small, but they are charming, with exposed beams and classic decor. The largest have beautiful antique or waxed oak furniture. The sound-proofing is not the best, and the Rue Bonaparte is very busy: It's best to ask for a room overlooking the courtyard.

Hôtel Le Saint-Grégoire

43, rue de l'Abbé-Grégoire
75006 Paris
Tel. (0)1 45 48 23 23 - Fax (0)1 45 48 33 95
Mme Agaud - M. Bouvier - M. de Bené

Category ★★★ **Rooms** 20 with air-conditioning, soundproofing, bath (1 with shower), WC, telephone, TV satellite, hairdryer. **Price** Double 690-990F, suites and rooms with terrace: 1390F. Extra bed 100F. **Meals** Breakfast 60F; snacks available. **Credit cards** All major. **Pets** Small dogs allowed (+70F). **Facilities** Elevator. **Parking** At rue de l'Abbé-Grégoire, rue de Rennes. **How to get there** (Map 1): Bus: 48, 89, 94, 95, 96 - Metro: Saint-Placide, Sèvres-Babylone. **Open** All year.

Midway between Montparnasse and Saint-Germain, the Saint-Grégoire is in a small 18th-century building whose intimate decor is both chic and successfully done. In the lounge there is often an open fire burning and play has been made with a range of warm colors subtly marrying orange and plum tones. The rooms ally the delicacy of yellow or pink walls with beautiful wall-hangings. Elegant and well fitted out, they are large (more or less) and always personalized by attractive furniture pieces and little 'kilims', to form a really comfortable overall ambiance. The very functional bathrooms meet the same standard. Some rooms, particularly appreciated in fine weather, even have a flowery terrace where breakfast can be served. An attractive address where you will enjoy an attentive and smiling welcome, while you should note that the owners also run the La Marlotte restaurant, some fifty meters distant, where you can sample market cuisine in a friendly atmosphere.

Hôtel Saint-Paul - Rive Gauche

43, rue Monsieur-le-Prince - 75006 Paris
Tel. (0)1 43 26 98 64 - Fax (0)1 46 34 58 60
web: http://www.webscapades.com/france/paris/stpaul.htm
Mlle Marianne Hawkins

Category ★★★ **Rooms** 30 (8 with air-conditioning) and 1 duplex (4 pers.) with bath or shower, WC, telephone, TV satellite, minibar, safe, hairdryer. **Price** Single 585-785F, double 685-985F, duplex (4 pers.) 1285F. Extra bed +180F. **Meals** Breakfast 55F, served 7:00-11:00. **Credit cards** All major. **Pets** Dogs allowed. **Facilities** Elevator, room-service. **Parking** At rue Soufflot, rue de l'École-de-Médecine. **How to get there** (Map 1): Bus: 21, 27, 38, 58, 63, 82, 84, 85, 86, 87, 89 - Metro: Odéon - RER: Luxembourg. **Open** All year.

This hotel has belonged to the same family for four generations and the present young owner takes care of her hotel the way she does her home. There are even several pieces of her own furniture in the bedrooms. Many rooms have a pretty flower box in the window, and if you're lucky enough to be in the rear of the hotel, you'll have a lovely view of a large tree in the tiny patio near the reception area. The bedrooms have beautiful beamed ceilings, oak doors and closets, and marble baths. There are many pieces of Haute Epoque furniture, except in the recently renovated rooms; those on the top floor, which are especially beautiful, are furnished in a more contemporary style. The duplex is perfect for families. Breakfast (the croissants are delicious) is served in a 17th-century barrel-vaulted cellar with a well, where you're likely to be greeted by Perkin, the house cat. Or you might find him snoozing on the sofa in the lovely small lounge.

Hôtel Sainte-Beuve

9, rue Sainte-Beuve
75006 Paris
Tel. (0)1 45 48 20 07 - Fax (0)1 45 48 67 52
Mme Compagnon

Category ★★★ **Rooms** 22 (some with air-conditioning) with bath, WC, telephone, TV satellite, safe, minibar. **Price** Single and double 760-1400F, suite 1600F, apartment 1810F. **Meals** Breakfast 90F, served from 7:00. Snacks available. **Credit cards** Amex, Visa, Eurocard, MasterCard. **Pets** Dogs not allowed. **Facilities** Elevator, bar. **Parking** At 116, boulevard du Montparnasse. **How to get there** (Map 1 and 10): Bus: 68, 82, 83, 91 - Metro: Vavin, Notre-Dame-des-Champs - RER: Port-Royal. **Open** All year.

The Sainte-Beuve is a model hotel of charm decorated by the Paris workshop of David Hicks, and you find here all the touches of the master with its non-fussy and comfortable luxury. All is very refined via a subtle harmony of colors and materials animating the new architecture of the lounge. Fully renovated in 1996, comfortable sofas and armchairs have been placed facing the fireplace, with a fire lit as soon as the weather turns cold. Everything has been refurbished in the bright and spacious rooms, with a delicate celadon green with the ivory walls showing off the fine antique furniture, prints, superb wall curtains alongside the small 'bonne-femme' taffeta curtains, and all those charming details that make the Sainte-Beuve such a refined house. The bathrooms are beautiful and sober. Breakfasts are particularly well prepared and delicious. Both service and attention are irreproachable and can only confirm that this really is a very fine address.

Hôtel des Saints-Pères

65, rue des Saints-Pères – 75006 Paris
Tel. (0)1 45 44 50 00 – Fax (0)1 45 44 90 83
e-mail: espfran@micronet.fr
Mme Salmon

Category ★★★ **Rooms** 39 and 3 suites with air-conditioning, soundproofing, bath or shower, WC, telephone, TV satellite, safe, minibar. **Price** Single and double 550-1650F, suite 1650F. **Meals** Breakfast 55F; snacks available. **Credit cards** Amex, Visa, Eurocard, MasterCard. **Pets** Dogs not allowed. **Facilities** Elevator, patio, bar. **Parking** Opposite 169, boulevard Saint-Germain. **How to get there** (Map 1): Bus: 39, 48, 63, 70, 84, 86, 87, 95 - Metro: Saint-Germain-des-Prés, Sèvres-Babylone. **Open** All year.

Built in the 17th-century by an architect of Louis XIV, the Hôtel des Saints-Pères is one of our favorites in Paris. Very cool and airy, its interior layout is set around a flowery and peaceful patio onto which most of the rooms give. It leads through to a warm lounge with comfortable leather furniture, a bar and dining room. Comfortable, quiet and very well equipped, all the rooms are decorated with antique furniture pieces, often in acajou, all matching with the prints or pictures from the 18th and 19th centuries, the chintz of the curtains, the colored carpeting and so on. A unique room and worthy of the major palaces, the so-called 'Frescoes Room' with its magnificent allegorical ceiling, boasts all the splendors of the 'Grand Siècle' in tones of deepest blue. On fine days a few tables are set on the patio and it is a real pleasure to start your day with a fresh-air breakfast surrounded by the small shrubs and flowers.

Hôtel de Seine

52, rue de Seine
75006 Paris
Tel. (0)1 46 34 22 80 – Fax (0)1 46 34 04 74
M. Henneveux

Category ★★★ **Rooms** 30 with soundproofing, bath, WC, hairdryer, telephone, TV satellite, safe. **Price** Single 695F, double 820-890F, triple 1090F. **Meals** Breakfast 45F. **Credit cards** Visa, Eurocard, MasterCard. **Pets** Dogs not allowed. **Facilities** Elevator. **Parking** At 27, rue Mazarine. **How to get there** (Map 1): Bus: 38, 39, 58, 63, 70, 84, 85, 86, 87, 96 – Metro: Mabillon, Saint-Germain-des-Prés – RER: Cluny-Saint-Michel. **Open** All year.

Known for its art galleries, the Rue de Seine links the Odéon district to the Institut de France, which is just separated from the Louvre by the Seine crossed by the charming Pont des Arts. Subject to a full renovation, the Hôtel de Seine is now a particularly recommendable hotel with the provincial charm of the lounge open on the street. Its panelling and wooden fireplace are brightened by a pretty colored and flowery tapestry, while all the rooms are just as pleasantly decorated with provincial fabrics and polished painted furniture. Bathroom comfort has also been improved and they are now all marble-covered. You should note there is one ground floor bedroom, with a bathroom in duplex, that gives directly onto the lounge. Both service and welcome are lively, with the hotel under the same management as the Hôtel des Marronniers and the Hôtel des Deux Continents.

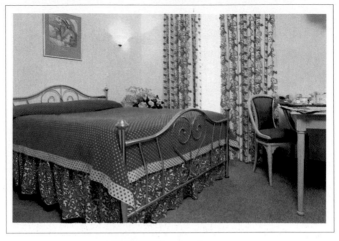

Hôtel Sèvres-Azur

22, rue de l'abbé-Grégoire
75006 Paris
Tel. (0)1 45 48 84 07 - Fax (0)1 42 84 01 55
M. and Mme Baguès

Category ★★ Rooms 31 with soundproofing, bath or shower, telephone, TV, hairdryer - 1 for disabled persons. **Price** Single and double 430-480F, triple 620F. Extra bed 90F. **Meals** Breakfast 38F, served 7:15-10:00. **Credit cards** All major. **Pets** Dogs allowed. **Facilities** Elevator, safe at reception. **Parking** At Boucicaut, rue de Sévres **How to get there** (Map 1): Bus: 28, 39, 75, 84, 85, 93, 95, 96 - Metro: Sèvres-Babylone, Saint-Sulpice. **Open** All year.

Very well situated in the triangle between Montparnasse, Saint-Germain-des-Prés , and Le Bon Marché, the Rue de l'Abbé-Grégoire is one of the quieter streets where the Hôtel Sèvres-Azur is found. Fully renovated in summer 1995, the rooms are comfortable and very attractive: egg-shell walls, elegant curtains, assorted bedspreads and divan bases, all mixing the warm shades of yellow and raspberry. The furniture is in light cerused wood, but whenever possible the bedsteads in copper or wrought iron-now once again sought after by the 'brocanteurs'-have been conserved. Whether facing street or courtyard, all the rooms are highly recommended with their impeccable bathrooms. The ground floor is shared by the reception area, a lounge with its black leather sofas, and the breakfast room which also serves as bar. All give onto a tiny little patio all in green with its small bench seat. One has a real 'affair of the heart' with this small hotel offering one of the best price-quality deals in Paris, along with one of the most friendly of welcomes.

La Villa

29, rue Jacob
75006 Paris
Tel. (0)1 43 26 60 00 - Fax (0)1 46 34 63 63
M. Colombier

Category ★★★★ Rooms 32 with air-conditioning, soundproofing, bath or shower, WC, telephone, minibar, safe, TV satellite. **Price** Single and double 900-1800F, suite 2000-3000F. Extra bed 400F. **Meals** Breakfast 80F, served 7:00-12:00; snacks available: salmon, foie gras, ham, fruits. **Credit cards** Visa, Eurocard, MasterCard, Amex. **Pets** Dogs not allowed. **Facilities** Elevator, bar. **Parking** At 400 m. **How to get there** (Map 1): Bus 39, 48, 95 - Metro: Saint-Germain-des-Prés. **Open** All year.

When the owners took over La Villa, they aimed at making it a unique and contemporary hotel. The decor was created by a young designer, Marie Christine Dorner. The result is a very pleasant, small jewel of a hotel. The reception area is sober and spare, brightened with a large Japanese-inspired floral spray. The room numbers are shown in lighted figures on each door. Inside, the decor is truly magical, with sleek, specially designed furniture, much of which is leather-upholstered and cheerfully coordinated with the predominant color scheme; extra-wide beds surmounted by low-tension lamps in the ceiling; and sublime bathrooms whose dark-gray, green-veined marble reflects the chrome basins, silver mirrors, and opaque, frosted-glass shelves. Breakfasts are served in a modern bar. In the basement, jazz groups perform regularly.

Hôtel de l'Académie

32, rue des Saints-Pères
75007 Paris
Tel. (0)1 45 49 80 00 – Fax (0)1 45 49 80 10
M. Chekroun

Category ★★★ **Rooms** 34 with soundproofing (22 with air-conditioning), telephone, bath or shower, hairdryer, WC, TV satellite, safe. **Price** Single 490-790F, double 690-890F, suite 990-1290F. **Meals** Breakfast 60F, served 7:00-11:00. Snacks available. **Credit cards** All major. **Pets** Dogs allowed. **Facilities** Elevator, bar, laundry service. **Parking** Private, opposite at the hotel (4 places: 150F per day) and public parking opposite 169, boulevard Saint-Germain. **how to get there** (Map 1): Bus: 39, 48, 63, 70, 84, 86, 87, 95 - Metro: Saint-Germain-des-Prés, Rue-du-Bac. **Open** All year.

At the heart of the Faubourg Saint-Germain-des-Prés, this hotel has started on a successful renovation and space has been well used to isolate the reception area, bar, warm lounge and a particularly attractive breakfast room. Here ceiling beams and fine stone work accent the 18th-century and Directory furniture, along with some fine fabrics with dominant reds and greens. The rooms are classical with their pastel cameos and have well equipped bathrooms. The quietest are on the courtyard side, but the air-conditioning in more than half the rooms and very effective sound-proofing allow one to sleep peacefully even in summer.

Hôtel de Beaune

29, rue de Beaune
75007 Paris
Tel. (0)1 42 61 24 89 – Fax (0)1 45 27 02 12
Mme Chelali

Category ★★ **Rooms** 19 with telephone, bath or shower, WC, TV cable, hairdryer, safe, minibar. **Price** Single and double 400-500F, suite 700F (2-3 pers.). **Meals** Breakfast 38F. **Credit cards** All major. **Pets** Dogs allowed. **Facilities** Elevator, bar, room-service. **Parking** At 9, rue Montalembert. **How to get there** (Map 1): Bus: 24, 27, 39, 48, 63, 68, 69, 70, 87, 95 - Metro: Rue-du-Bac - RER: Gare-d'Orsay. **Open** All year.

In a street where the majority of shopfronts are devoted to furniture and antiques, the Hôtel de Beaune is an exception. In the prettily renovated entry, Mme. Chelali has hung a few well-lit pictures on the red walls; in the background you'll notice the warm breakfast room. This is a simple hotel where the small rooms are all identical, some blue and others in raspberry. The copper bedsteads are covered with white cotton fabrics, and bistro chairs and tables form the essential decor. As for the bathrooms, they are simple and offer adequate comfort. The whole package has the advantage of being economical for the heart of Paris, beside the Seine and the Musée d'Orsay. However, it is now becoming urgent to renovate some of the rooms, notably the 'James Dean'. The hotel accepts this fact and numerous improvements are programmed for 1998.

Hôtel Bersoly's Saint-Germain

28, rue de Lille
75007 Paris
Tel. (0)1 42 60 73 79 – Fax (0)1 49 27 05 55
Mme Carbonnaux

Category ★★★ **Rooms** 16 with soundproofing, air-conditioning, telephone, bath or shower, WC, cable TV, hairdryer, safe. **Price** Single and double 600-700F. **Meals** Breakfast 50F. Snacks available. **Credit cards** Visa, Eurocard, MasterCard. **Pets** Dogs allowed on request. **Facilities** Bar. **Parking** Private; public parking 9, rue Montalembert. **How to get there** (Map 1): Bus: 24, 27, 39, 48, 63, 68, 69, 86, 87, 95 - Metro: Rue-du-Bac, Saint-Germain-des-Prés - RER: Musée-d'Orsay - Les Invalides Air Terminal. **Open** All year except 3 weeks in August.

There reigns in this small Hôtel Bersoly's an intimate and charming atmosphere due as much to the decor as to the numerous little details for the clientele. To harmonize with the rustic architecture of the house, the reception area and its small corner-lounge mix Louis XIII furniture pieces and sofas with flowered fabrics. For their part, the rooms are each given the name of a painter, and have a colorful decor both bright and very refined, with the largest rooms on the ground floor. They are comfortable and faultlessly maintained, and each has an electric kettle with a couple of cups, a much appreciated initiative on return from a walk or the Musée d'Orsay. Breakfast is served in the basement in a vaulted room decorated in a rather exotic style, while the welcome is one of the most friendly.

Hôtel Bourgogne et Montana

3, rue de Bourgogne – 75007 Paris
Tel. (0)1 45 51 20 22 – Fax (0)1 45 56 11 98
web: http://www.paris.tourisme/bourgogne
Mme Martine Monney

Category ★★★ **Rooms** 28 and 6 suites with bath, WC, telephone, minibar, cable TV. **Price** Single 760-1200F, double 900-1200F, Junior-suite 1500-1800F. Extra bed +300F. Special rates in low season (July, August, November, December). **Meals** Breakfast included, served 6:30-12:00. **Credit cards** All major. **Pets** Dogs allowed. **Facilities** Elevator, room for safes. **Parking** Invalides. **How to get there** (Map 1): Bus: 24, 63, 69, 73, 84, 93, 94 - Metro: Invalides, Assemblée-Nationale - RER: Invalides - Les Invalides Air Terminal. **Open** All year.

Acquired in 1919 by an ancestor of the present owners, the Bourgogne et Montana is one of the most beautiful hotels in this neighborhood. A cosmopolitan clientele comes here for the beautiful location and the smart, refined hotel itself. On the ground floor are the rotunda, the bar/lounge with its gleaming mahogany and dark-green carpet, and the beautiful breakfast room with Third Republic caricatures. Freshly refurbished, the most luxurious bedrooms on four of the six floors are handsomely decorated with Empire furniture, blue or salmon English wall fabrics, and exceptionally beautiful bathrooms. On the *sixième étage,* rooms 60 and 67 have a panoramic view over the National Assembly. The other bedrooms are also beautiful, with beige walls and decorative trim matching the curtains and bedspreads, tasteful furniture, and immaculate bathrooms. Many guests prefer the *premier étage* courtyard rooms for their low ceilings and small windows overlooking the roof of the rotunda, covered with ivy and impatiens. This very beautiful hotel offers a delicious breakfast buffet, which is included in the room rate.

Hôtel du Champ-de-Mars

7, rue du Champ–de–Mars
75007 Paris
Tel. (0)1 45 51 52 30 – Fax (0)1 45 51 64 36
M. and Mme Gourdal

Category ✶✶ Rooms 25 with bath or shower, WC, telephone, TV satellite. **Price** Single 355F, double 390-420F. **Meals** Breakfast 35F, served 7:00-10:00. **Credit cards** Visa, Eurocard, MasterCard, Amex. **Pets** Dogs not allowed. **Facilities** Elevator. **Parking** Joffre (École-Militaire). **How to get there** (Map 6): Bus: 28, 49, 80, 82, 87, 92 - Metro: École-Militaire - RER: Pont-de-l'Alma, Invalides. **Open** All year.

Acquired recently by a young and charming couple, this small hotel has been entirely renovated with the rooms given beautiful blue carpeting with small yellow motifs. These two colors are repeated on the wallpapers, blue with a yellow frieze on the street side, and the reverse on the courtyard; the frieze motifs are also repeated on both curtains and bedspreads. The small white bathrooms are new and the whole effect, sustained by the numerous details, is one of brightness and careful maintenance. The lounge, breakfast room and corridors have not been forgotten, having received the same care and 'meridional'-style as found throughout the house. The courtyard is charming with its recessed walls covered with ivy, small trees and zinc roofs, which all remind us that we are here in the midst of the 7th *arrondissement*, full of life and with many little shops. Close by is the Rue Cler whose market is known to all Parisians. Add to this the proximity of the Eiffel Tower and the Invalides, and you then realize just how well sited the Hôtel du Champ-de-Mars really is. However, its excellent quality/price package means you must always reserve well in advance.

Hôtel Chomel

15, rue Chomel
75007 Paris
Tel. (0)1 45 48 55 52 – Fax (0)1 45 48 89 76
M. and Mme Oularbi

Category ★★★ **Rooms** 23 with soundproofing, telephone, bath or shower, WC, cable TV, hairdryer, minibar. **Price** Single and double 595-880F. In low season (July, August, and November – March): 450-700F. **Meals** Breakfast 50F, served 7:00-10:00. **Credit cards** All major. **Pets** Dogs not allowed. **Facilities** Elevator, laundry service. **Parking** Boucicault (Bon Marché). **How to get there** (Map 1): Bus: 39, 63, 68, 70, 83, 84 - Metro: Sèvres-Babylone. **Open** All year.

On a very quiet street, this hotel is just a stone's throw from the Bon Marché department store. The small bedrooms have pleasant furniture and printed fabrics in soft colors, full modern amenities, and are well-kept. If you want a bit more space, ask for the twin-bed rooms whose numbers end in 1, or the junior suites whose numbers end in 4–they are ideal for families. The brightest rooms are those on the upper floors. A handsome lounge adjoins the breakfast room.

Hôtel Derby Eiffel

5, avenue Duquesne
75007 Paris
Tel. (0)1 47 05 12 05 – Fax (0)1 47 05 43 43
M. El Bawab

Category ★★★ **Rooms** 42 and 1 suite with bath or shower, WC, telephone, TV satellite, safe, minibar. **Price** Single and double 690-750F, suite 900F. **Meals** Breakfast (buffet) 65F, served 7:00-10:30. **Ccredit cards** All major. **Pets** Dogs allowed. **Facilities** Elevator, patio, laundry service. **Parking** École-Militaire. **How to get there** (Map 1 and 6): Bus: 49, 82, 92 - Metro: École-Militaire. **Open** All year.

This beautiful building of pale freestones faces the Ecole Militaire where, in the morning, you can watch riders practicing dressage or hurdle-jumping in the middle of the sumptuous Court of Honor, designed by the architect Gabriel in 1751. The equestrian theme is continued inside the hotel with English engravings in the bar-lounge depicting the racing world and the fox hunt. The lounge is furnished with handsome brown-leather armchairs and sofas. The bedrooms are tasteful, comfortable, and classic, with beige walls, functional but elegant mahogany furniture, thick beige and pink bedspreads with coordinated curtains, and small English engravings with lovely gilt-bronze sconces on either side. Breakfasts are served in the basement with its exposed-stone walls, where the decor, unfortunately, is not terribly imaginative. You can enjoy a drink in the delightful tiny patio planted with hydrangeas, impatiens, and geraniums.

Hôtel Duc de Saint-Simon

14, rue de Saint-Simon
75007 Paris
Tel. (0)1 44 39 20 20. – Fax (0)1 45 48 68 25
M. Lindquist

Category ★★★ **Rooms** 29 and 5 suites (some with air-conditioning) with bath (1 with shower), WC, telephone, TV on request, safe. **Price** Single and double 1050-1450F, suite 1825-1875F (2 pers.). **Meals** Breakfast 70F, served from 7:30; snacks available. **Credit cards** All major. **Pets** Dogs not allowed. **Facilities** Elevator, bar, patio. **Parking** Garage de l'Abbaye: 30, boulevard Raspail. **How to get there** (Map 1): Bus: 63, 68, 69, 83, 84, 94 - Metro: Rue-du-Bac. **Open** All year.

The Duc de Saint-Simon is without doubt one of the prettiest hotels in Paris. Once through the porch, you cross the paved courtyard with its wisteria and a few tables, and enter the warm interior recreating the atmosphere of those beautiful residences of earlier days. The bright colors of the polished worked wood and the superb fabrics mix with the paintings and other objects found throughout the house. Lounges, rooms and suites are entirely furnished with antiques of infallible taste. Whatever their size the rooms are all extremely comfortable, cosseted, and with superb bathrooms covered with Salerno tiling. Some even have terraces. The vaulted basement now shelters the breakfast room, bar and numerous little corners fitted out as small lounges. The whole effect is of total refinement with guaranteed peace and quiet at a premium, even though the Boulevard Saint-Germain is at the end of the street. As for the welcome, it is courteous and most friendly.

Grand Hôtel Lévêque

29, rue Cler
75007 Paris
Tel. (0)1 47 05 49 15 – Fax (0)1 45 50 49 36
M. Tourneur

Category ★ **Rooms** 50 (soundproofing for the rooms on the street) with telephone, TV satellite, safe, hairdryer, 45 with shower and WC, 5 with washstand (private WC outside the room). **Price** Single 250F, double 350-420F, triple 515F. **Meals** Breakfast 30F, served 7:00-10:30. **Credit cards** Visa, Eurocard, MasterCard, Amex. **Pets** Dogs allowed. **Facilities** Elevator. **Parking** Joffre (École-Militaire). **How to get there** (Map 6): Bus: 28, 49, 80, 82, 87, 92 - Metro: École-Militaire - RER: Pont-de-l'Alma, Invalides. **Open** All year.

The new owners of the Grand Hôtel Lévêque were guided by one original idea: a "one-star luxury hotel". Certainly the rooms are not large, as so often in Paris, but all the comforts are here: new bedding, small but impeccable shower rooms, hairdryer, safe, satellite TV and so on. The hotel was fully renovated in 1997 and all the rooms designed to the same model; walls flecked in yellow, light carpeting and printed fabrics. The rooms on the street (pedestrians only) are attractive with their two windows. If you book them in time you can also enjoy all the life of the market in the Rue Cler, very picturesque and popular with Parisians, but if you are afraid of being disturbed by noise, the other rooms at the back are quiet, but do avoid the singles. Breakfast is served in a bistro-style ambiance. This is a good location for a low price.

Hôtel de La Bourdonnais

111-113, avenue de La Bourdonnais - 75007 Paris
Tel. (0)1 47 05 45 42 - Fax (0)1 45 55 75 54
web: http://www.webscapades.com/france/paris/bourdonn.htm
M. Champetier

Category ★★★ **Rooms** 60 with bath or shower, WC, telephone, TV satellite, 20 with minibar.
Price Single 550F, double 720F, suite (3-4 pers.) 1100F. **Meals** Breakfast 50F, served 6:00-
11:00. **Credit cards** All major. **Pets** Dogs allowed. **Facilities** Elevator, patio, laundry service.
Restaurant Gastronomic; Menu: 240-420F. **Parking** Joffre (École-Militaire). **How to get
there** (Map 6): Bus: 28, 49, 69, 80, 82, 87, 92 - Metro: École-Militaire. **Open** All year.

Parallel to the Champ-de-Mars, the Avenue de la Bourdonnais is a line of stately buildings, and this hotel is no exception. Some small pointed trees form a guard of honor under the canopy of the entryway and shield the intimacy of the lounge windows. Inside there is one of the best tables of the capital where gourmets meet to thrill their taste buds in total privacy. Marvellously filled plates, top-quality products whose precious flavors are always respected, and a little bit of Provence in the decor; one leaves feeling at ease, but conquered. The 'bourgeois'-style hotel sports a host of squat armchairs in brown leather and antique furniture pieces in the lounge and very classical rooms. These are often large with a cosseted ambiance, although sometimes a little sad, while the smallest do not justify their price. The breakfast room is much more appealing and its wallpapers play on a trompe-l'oeil-theme with the veranda, which opens onto a small garden planted with ivy, ocuba and rhododendrons.

Hôtel Latour - Maubourg

150, rue de Grenelle – 75007 Paris
Tel. (0)1 47 05 16 16 – Fax (0)1 47 05 16 14
e-mail: victor@worldnet.fr
Victor and Maria Orsenne

Category ✶✶✶ **Rooms** 9 and 1 suite with soundproofing, bath or shower, WC, hairdryer, telephone, TV satellite, minibar. **Price** Single 550-660F, double 795-865F, suite 950F (1 pers.), 1150F (2 pers.), 1500F (4 pers.). Extra bed 180F. **Meals** Breakfast included, served 7:00-19:00. Between August 1 – 23: single 500F, double 600F. **Credit cards** Visa, Eurocard, MasterCard. **Pets** Dogs allowed (+50F). **Facilities** Laundry service, patio, room-service. **Parking** Invalides. **How to get there** (Map 1 and 6): Bus: 28, 49, 69 - Metro: Latour-Maubourg - RER: Invalides. **Open** All year.

A square with huge chestnut trees, a tiny little private hotel, and a grill all make this place one of our most charming discoveries of the year. The interior reminds you of a private house, with a very cozy lounge with old pictures, comfortable chairs and small tables where at any hour you can take breakfast. Just as successful, the rooms all display their elegant yellow-orange fabrics. They are all of a good size, while the suite is immense and a very good deal. The rooms open onto the trees and give a direct view, when the leaves have fallen, onto the noble facade of the Invalides under its famous glistening dome. With a cosseted comfort, they usually have one or two antique furniture pieces in tune with the quality prints and pictures. This is a very fine address run with much flare by M. and Mme. Orsenne, who live on the premises and give the place its inimitable feel of home.

Hôtel Lenox - Saint-Germain

9, rue de l'Université
75007 Paris
Tel. (0)1 42 96 10 95 - Fax (0)1 42 61 52 83
M. Grenet

Category ★★★ **Rooms** 34 (5 duplex) with soundproofing, bath or shower, WC, telephone, TV. **Price** Double 650-1100F, duplex 1500F. **Meals** Breakfast 45F; snacks available. **Credit cards** All major. **Pets** Dogs not allowed. **Facilities** Elevator, bar. **Parking** At 9, rue Montalembert and opposite 169, boulevard Saint-Germain. **How to get there** (Map 1): Bus: 24, 27, 39, 48, 63, 68, 69, 70, 87, 95 - Metro: Rue-du-Bac, Saint-Germain-des-Prés - RER: Musée-d'Orsay. **Open** All year.

Well situated at the angle of the Rue du Pré-aux-Clercs, known for its fashion boutiques, and the Rue de l'Université, the Lénox has for a long time kept a loyal clientele among the young and the chic. Open till late at night, the hotel bar with its rosewood and 1930's-style plays a big part in the ambiance. The rooms are sometimes rather small but most of them were renovated this year, losing in charm what they have gained in comfort. Many are more sober with attractive furniture designed for the hotel. The bathrooms were also modernized and are a great success. In general it is better to take a room on the upper floors. Some of them, particularly the suites are larger less noisy. The place could do with air-conditioning, but the Lénox remains a comfortable address with carefully thought out prices, and the welcome is friendly.

Hôtel Libertel Bellechasse

8, rue Bellechasse
75007 Paris
Tel. (0)1 45 50 22 31 - Fax (0)1 45 51 52 36
Mme Elfriede Leutwyler

Category ✶✶✶ **Rooms** 41 with telephone, bath or shower, WC, TV cable, minibar - 1 for disabled persons. **Price** Single 860-910F, double 920-975F. **Meals** Breakfast 75F, served 7:00-11:00. **Credit cards** All major. **Pets** Dogs allowed. **Facilities** Elevator, safe at reception, patio, room-service. **Parking** At rue du Bac. **How to get there** (Map 1): Bus: 24, 63, 73, 83, 84, 94 - Metro: Solférino - RER: Musée-d'Orsay. **Open** All year.

Recently opened just a few steps from the Musée d'Orsay and the Legion of Honor Museum, the Bellechasse is a hotel of great character and charm. The interior decor is influenced by the Empire style: the huge lobby with a black marble floor floor; beautiful striped fabrics in the exquisite dining room, corridors and bedrooms; sculpted armchairs in the Napoleonic style; pale-wood or antique bronze furniture with the famous cross-bars of the Empire epoch. Lovely bathrooms, pretty lamps, and a collection of old engravings further add to the allure of the Bellechasse. Ask for a bedroom with a view of the trees around the town houses in front. Those who love greenery will also enjoy the interior courtyard of the hotel, which has been transformed into a flower garden with chairs. Or you can take a seat in a deep armchair in the lounge and enjoy a pleasant view of the garden through the bay windows.

Hôtel Libertel Sèvres-Vaneau

86, rue Vaneau
75007 Paris
Tel. (0)1 45 48 73 11 - Fax (0)1 45 49 27 74
Mme Elfriede Leutwyler

Category ★★★ **Rooms** 39 with soundproofing, telephone, bath or shower, WC, cable TV, hairdryer, minibar. **Price** Single and double 825-890F, suite 970F. **Meals** Breakfast (buffet) 75F, served 7:00-10:30; snaks available, served 10:30-22:45. **Credit cards** All major. **Pets** Dogs allowed. **Facilities** Elevator, laundry service. **Parking** Opposite at the Bon Marché. **How to get there** (Map 1): Bus: 39, 70, 89 - Metro: Vaneau. **Open** All year.

The Sèvres-Vaneau is comfortable, elegant, and well located. Quite spacious, the bedrooms have white lacquered rattan furniture set off by refined fabrics and wallpaper. Many still have their original marble fireplace and beautiful stained glass. Statuettes and old engravings lend them the air of a guest room in a private home. The all-white bathrooms, with navy, burgundy or bottle-green friezes, are also very pleasant and well stocked with toiletries. The corridors are tastefully decorated with English oak-leaf wallpaper, and framed lithographs. Downstairs, near the reception area, you will find a cozy, rather British-style lounge. The generous breakfasts are served on this floor amid a bistro decor, which is somewhat less remarkable than the rest of the hotel.

Hôtel de Lille

40, rue de Lille
75007 Paris
Tel. (0)1 42 61 29 09 - Fax (0)1 42 61 53 97
M. Margouilla

Category ★★ **Rooms** 20 with sounproofing for the rooms on the street, telephone, bath or shower, WC, cable TV, safe. **Price** Single 490-520F, double 580-760F. Extra pers. 90F. **Meals** Breakfast included, served 7:30-11:00. **Credit cards** All major. **Pets** Dogs not allowed. **Facilities** Elevator, laundry service, bar. **Parking** At 9, rue Montalembert, Orsay. **How to get there** (Map 1): Bus: 39, 48, 68, 69, 83, 95 - Metro: Rue-du-Bac - RER: Musée-d'Orsay. **Open** All year.

We were enchanted at first sight with this small hotel on the Rue de l'Université and its smart yellow walls, 1930s-inspired furniture, lovely green-leather armchairs, mushroom lamps, and the adorable small bar. Beautiful engravings found in antique shops add a classic note to some bedrooms, while many others are much simpler, with colored bamboo furniture in the smallest, or 'burred-wood' furniture in the others. Some have a small folding desk. Most fabrics are bright and especially lovely are those in the rooms whose numbers end in 1. Rooms with numbers ending in 2, however, are our favorites. Lastly, Room No. 1 (on the ground floor overlooking a fountain) and the rooms on the top floor are the largest and thus the most expensive. The prices nevertheless are very reasonable for this neighborhood, particularly as breakfast is included. The basement is occupied by a huge barrel-vaulted room with an impressive pillar.

Hôtel Montalembert

3, rue Montalembert
75007 Paris
Tel. (0)1 45 49 68 68 – Fax (0)1 45 49 69 49
M. Hubert Bonnier

Category ★★★★ Rooms 51 and 5 suites with air-conditioning, soundproofing, bath, WC, telephone, mobile phone, TV satellite, video, hairdryer, safe, minibar. **Price** Single 1695F, double 1960-2200F, suite 2750-3800F. **Meals** Breakfast 100F, served 7:00-10:30. **Credit cards** All major. **Pets** Dogs allowed on request. **Facilities** Elevator, laundry service, video library, room-service, bar, restaurant. **Parking** At 9, rue Montalembert. **How to get there** (Map 1): Bus: 24, 63, 68, 69, 83, 84, 94 - Metro: Rue-du-Bac - RER: Gare-d'Orsay. **Open** All year.

The Montalembert is one of the best Parisian examples of the new generation of Grand Hotels adapting themselves to the needs of the times. Modernity has been exploited well with discreet luxury that should be approved by all. The sobriety of the entry hall enhances the internal layout, and the decoration of the lounge, both chic and welcoming, is organized around a reading room with open fire. All the rooms offer a very high standard of comfort and aesthetics. Some of them are in 'retro'-style with their furniture in burr wood marquetry, enhanced by delicate gilded bronzes, but others are contemporary, with their smooth dark brown wood panneling perfectly matching the fabrics and carpeting in dark blue, black and fawn tones. They are however often small, notably those with a number '5' at the end, but this is fully accounted for in their price. Happily the care for details and the high quality of facilities, service and welcome compensate for any such inconvenience.

Hôtel Muguet

11, rue Chevert
75007 Paris
Tel. (0)1 47 05 05 93 – Fax (0)1 45 50 25 37
Mme Pelletier

Category ★★ **Rooms** 45 with *6ème étage* air-conditioned, bath or shower, WC, telephone, TV satellite, safe, hairdryer - 3 for disabled persons. **Price** Single 460F, double 480-530F, triple 690F. **Meals** Breakfast 47F, served 7:00-11:00. **Credit cards** Visa, Eurocard, MasterCard, Amex. **Pets** Dogs allowed. **Facilities** Elevator, patio. **Parking** Invalides (300m.). **How to get there** (Map 1 and 6): Bus: 28, 49, 69, 80, 82, 87, 92 - Metro: École-Militaire. **Open** All year.

How one would like to be able to offer you more establishments like this one. This little hotel is a real joy for all those who know how to appreciate the simplicity of things made with devotion. The impeccable bedrooms are renovated and prettily decorated with a fine choice of fabrics and furniture pieces. Each has a charming bathroom tiled right up to the ceiling, to enhance an elegant frieze in enamelled terra-cotta. Among those giving onto the street, numbers 52, 53, 61 and 62 all have a view of the Eiffel Tower, while on the other side you look out onto the Invalides with its shining dome, from numbers 63 and 54. Whatever their view, all are very quiet and when it is fine you can only hear the canaries singing in their cage on the sunny patio. On fine days tables are set out on this patio for some bucolic breakfasts, next to the ferns, pansies and magnolias. When the weather is disappointing the small dining room then takes over, and it is very homey with its rustic cherrywood buffet and Chinese pottery.

Hôtel du Palais Bourbon

49, rue de Bourgogne – 75007 Paris
Tel. (0)1 44 11 30 70 – Fax (0)1 45 55 20 21
e-mail: htlbourbon@aol.com
M. Claudon

Category ★★ Rooms 32 with bath or shower, WC, telephone, minibar, TV satellite. **Price** Single 277-478F, double 322-550F, triple 672F, 4 pers. 740F. Special rates in low season. **Meals** Breakfast included, served 7:00-10:00. **Credit cards** Visa, Eurocard, MasterCard. **Facilities** Elevator. **Parking** Invalides. **How to get there** (Map 1): Bus: 28, 49, 63, 69, 82, 83, 84 - Metro: Varenne, Invalides - RER: Invalides - Les Invalides Air Terminal. **Open** All year.

In this part of the city where the finest Parisian houses are to be found (formerly the homes of the top aristocracy but now ministry buildings or embassies), one is surprised and delighted to find a small hotel both simple and economical. The Hôtel du Palais Bourbon is an establishment in a state of change, with many real qualities and some undeniable faults. Thus the entry area and small corner lounge have really no charm at all, but a new decor is planned for 1998. The rooms in contrast have just been renovated and are a welcome surprise. Most often fitted out with comfortable furniture specially made by a Breton cabinet maker, the rooms are very large and on elegant corridors. The bathrooms are also very well done except in a few single rooms. Naturally we are only recommending the new rooms, even if in some cases they have kept their rather sad wallpaper or some walls speckled with white patches that are a bit too obvious. However, in the older rooms renovations are continuing gradually and some fine fabrics are now beginning to liven up some of the rooms. This is a small and attractive hotel which has not yet completed its present conversion plans.

Hôtel Relais Bosquet - Tour Eiffel

19, rue de Champ-de-Mars
75007 Paris
Tel. (0)1 47 05 25 45 - Fax (0)1 45 55 08 24
M. and Mme Hervois

Category ★★★ **Rooms** 40 with sounproofing, telephone, bath, WC, TV satellite, safe, minibar - 1 for disabled persons. **Price** Single 535-800F, double 635-850F, triple 785F. Extra bed 100F. **Meals** Breakfast 53F, served 7:00-12:00. **Credit cards** All major. **Pets** Dogs allowed. **Facilities** Elevator, patio. **Parking** Some places reserved in the lot of École-militaire (85F/day). **How to get there** (Map 6): Bus: 28, 49, 80, 82, 92 - Metro: École-Militaire. **Open** All year.

Near the Avenue Bosquet, this hotel doesn't look like much from the street, but you'll be pleasantly surprised inside. Arranged somewhat like a living room in a private home, the reception area reflects the tasteful, imaginative decor throughout: A soft, green carpet, orange chintz-lined drapes, a skirted pedestal, a table, a Directoire-style desk, and armchairs all create a lovely setting. The bedrooms are spacious and handsome, with Directoire furniture, pretty prints, and charming white-tiled bathrooms with elegant double basins. Thoughtful touches include a selection of magazines, an iron and ironing board in the closets, and candies. Breakfasts are served in two ground-floor rooms (one is for non-smokers), which are illuminated by large bay windows and overlook a patio with bamboo and a magnolia tree.

Hôtel Saint-Dominique

62, rue Saint-Dominique
75007 Paris
Tel. (0)1 47 05 51 44 – Fax (0)1 47 05 81 28
Mme Petit and M. Tible

Category ★★ **Rooms** 34 with telephone, bath or shower, WC, TV, hairdryer, safe and minibar. **Price** Single 400-430F, double 480-520F, "Executive room" 610-710F. **Meals** Breakfast 40F. **Credit cards** All major. **Pets** Dogs allowed. **Facilities** Patio. **Parking** Esplanade des Invalides. **How to get there** (Map 1 and 6): Bus: 28, 42, 49, 69, 80, 92 - Metro: Latour-Maubourg, Invalides - RER: Invalides - Les Invalides Air Terminal. **Open** All year.

Its situation and very carefully thought out prices make the Saint-Dominique a much sought after address. The hotel is in a building on the very lively Rue Saint-Dominique, just close to Les Invalides. The tone is given right from the entry with its decor in Anglo–American style. The light pinewood furniture matches the soft color shades of the walls and the pink-beige fabrics. The rooms are fitted out in the same style and have a rural charm : most look onto the patio while those on the street are sound-proofed. They are pleasantly sized and their walls are all hung with carefully chosen fabrics: 'Toile de Jouy', flowery motifs, or even with a Persian look. Other larger rooms called 'executive rooms' have a corner-lounge. The bathrooms are very functional and all white with small colored friezes. You should not miss the pretty breakfast room recently renovated in a style just as refined as the whole building. These are so many qualities, which along with the charming and courteous welcome, make this one of our favorite hotels.

SEPTIEME

Hôtel Saint Germain

88, rue du Bac
75007 Paris
Tel. (0)1 49 54 70 00 – Fax (0)1 45 48 26 89
M. Michel Malric

Category ★★★ **Rooms** 29 with soundproofing, bath, 25 with WC (4 rooms with 2 shared WC outside the rooms), telephone, TV, safe, 20 with hairdryer. **Price** Single 450-700F, double 450-800F. Extra bed 150F. **Meals** Breakfast 50F, served 7:30-11:30. **Credit cards** Visa, Eurocard, MasterCard, Amex. **Pets** Dogs not allowed. **Facilities** Elevator, patio, room-service. **Parking** At 9, rue de Montalembert. **How to get there** (Map 1): Bus: 63, 68, 69, 83, 84, 94 - Metro: Rue-du-Bac, Sèvres-Babylone. **Open** All year.

Almost fully renovated, the Hôtel Saint-Germain has become one of the best addresses of the quarter and we particularly liked the library and the numerous little corner-lounges of the ground floor. They are decorated with Royal-blue armchairs, antique furniture and objects, modern pictures and so on. Such a diverse grouping gives the place the very attractive feel of someone's house. Alongside there is a green courtyard with its red-ocre tiles and its small fountain, which gives access to two rooms on this level, particularly attractive in summer. The others on the upper floors are also very attractive : small alcoves sheltering the beds, Empire or Louis-Philippe cupboards, fine double curtains often matched by a wallpaper frieze, bedcovers in cream piqué and so on. All can be recommended (except perhaps No. 53, not yet renovated), with special mention for No's. 15, 24, 34 and 44 which are large, with a very attractive view on the terrace-garden of the first floor.

Hôtel Saint-Thomas-d'Aquin

3, rue du Pré-aux-Clercs
75007 Paris
Tel. (0)1 42 61 01 22 - Fax (0)1 42 61 41 43
M. and Mme Carcanague

Category ★★ Rooms 21 with soundproofing, telephone, bath or shower, WC, cable TV, safe. **Price** Single 485-565F, double 570F. **Meals** Breakfast 40F, served 6:30-10:30. **Credit cards** All major. **Pets** Dogs allowed. **Facilities** Elevator, laundry service, bar. **Parking** At 9, rue Montalembert. **How to get there** (Map 1): Bus: 39, 48, 63, 68, 69, 73, 83, 94, 95 - Metro: Rue-du-Bac, Saint-Germain-des-Prés - RER: Musée-d'Orsay. **Open** All year.

The Rue du Pré-aux-Clercs is particularly quiet and well-situated between Saint-Germain-des-Prés and the Rue de Bac, with numerous fashion boutiques and the *Quais* of the Seine close by. The Saint-Thomas-d'Aquin is a very simple hotel, renovated regularly, well maintained and offering very fair prices for the district. Excepting their sizes, which do vary, the rooms are all laid out on the same mode; light wallpaper, standard furniture and a touch of brightness with the fabrics. The quilted bedspreads have been matched with the curtains, always with a dominant yellow, green or pink for the flowered motifs. They enjoy large windows, moulded ceilings and impeccable bathrooms. The twin rooms have a particularly attractive layout but are a little more expensive. On the ground floor, an L-shaped room is shared between a corner for breakfasts and a lounge with modern cherry furniture. The welcome is friendly.

Hôtel Solférino

91, rue de Lille - 75007 Paris
Tel. (0)1 47 05 85 54 - Fax (0)1 45 55 51 16
e-mail: espfran@micronet.fr
M. de Langlade

Category ★★ **Rooms** 32 with bath or shower, WC, telephone, TV. **Price** Single 350F, double 500-700F. **Meals** Breakfast 40F, served from 7:30. **Credit cards** Visa, Eurocard, MasterCard, Amex. **Pets** Dogs not allowed. **Facilities** Elevator, tea room. **Parking** Invalides and at 9, rue Montalembert. **How to get there** (Map 1): Bus: 63, 69, 73, 83, 84, 94 - Metro: Solférino, Assemblée-Nationale - RER: Musée-d'Orsay - Les Invalides Air Terminal. **Open** All major.

This fine building from the end of the 17th-century was formerly the property of the surgeon of Napoleon. In 1897 during the construction of the Gare d'Orsay, it was opened to the travelling public to become the Hôtel de la Nouvelle Gare (Hotel of the New Station). Today the Orsay station is a museum, the district has taken on a rather ministerial air, and the hotel is now named the Solférino, but it remains astonishingly affordable. It does not lack for charm with its small welcoming lounge furnished with Napoleon III causeuses (love seats) with a Persian decor, a pretty 18th-century commode and old pictures. With the rooms, the standard varies but major renovations are planned for 1998. In the meantime, we would recommend numbers 10, 17, 18, 24, 25 and 41. These are very large and have Mansard ceilings. The wallpapers have little-flowers, leafy designs, or are plain with friezes-some of them look rather 'tired', while others are in great shape. The furniture merits no particular comment and the sanitary facilities are always good, but the corridors continue to look rather sad. The rooms on the first floor looking over the street are double-glazed. This is a simple and attractive hotel where you will receive an excellent welcome.

Hôtel de Suède

31, rue Vaneau
75007 Paris
Tel. (0)1 47 05 00 08 - Fax (0)1 47 05 69 27
M. Chesnot

Category ★★★ Rooms 39 with bath or shower, WC, telephone, cable TV, hairdryer, safe. **Price** Single 590F, double 650F, triple 860F, suite (2 pers.) 1300F. **Meals** Breakfast included, served 6:30-11:00. Snacks available. **Credit cards** Amex, Visa, Eurocard, MasterCard. **Pets** Dogs not allowed. **Facilities** Elevator, patio. **Parking** At 30, boulevard Raspail, square Boucicaut. **How to get there** (Map 1): Bus: 82, 87, 92 - Metro: Saint-François-Xavier, Sèvres-Babylone. **Open** All year.

The Hôtel de Suède enjoys the peace and quiet found in this district of embassies, the Invalides and the Rodin Museum. Classical in its style, the reception area is very large and entirely wainscotted, as are the numerous corner-lounges with sofas, armchairs and other wing chairs allowing one to relax in full comfort. Breakfasts are served here but in fine weather you may prefer to eat on the flowery patio with a few tables. Some of the rooms need to be freshened up, but all are very 'Gustavian': grey-white and sky-blue monochromes, Directory-style furniture pieces painted in ivory, with bedspreads and curtains in the same shades. Rooms with a double bed usually have a shower, while the twin-bed rooms are the largest and there are more of them. If you reserve in good time, ask first for those giving onto the courtyard or those on the upper floors with a view over the Matignon gardens. The welcome is courteous.

Thoumieux

79, rue Saint-Dominique
75007 Paris
Tel. (0)1 47 05 49 75 - Fax (0)1 47 05 36 96
M. Bassalert

Category ★★★ **Rooms** 10 with bath, WC, telephone, TV. **Price** Single 550F, double 600F. **Meals** Breakfast 35F, served 7:00-11:00. **Credit cards** Visa, Eurocard, MasterCard, Amex. **Pets** Dogs allowed. **Facilities** Laundry service, bar service in bedroom. **Restaurant** Menu 82-160F, also à carte. **Parking** Invalides (200m.). **How to get there** (Map 1 and 6): Bus: 28, 49, 69. - Metro: Latour-Maubourg, Invalides - RER: Invalides - Les Invalides Air Terminal. **Open** All year.

In the shopping area of the Rue Saint-Dominique, the Thoumieux Restaurant is a veritable institution, frequented by people from the nearby embassies and ministries who enjoy the bistro atmosphere, and the excellent Corrèze specialties that have been popular for three generations. Eclipsed perhaps by this gastronomic reputation, and due to the fact that it doesn't advertise, the hotel is less well-known. And yet its bedrooms, many of which are very large, are comfortable, and the bathrooms are gorgeous. The decor is lovely: textured wallpaper, pretty print fabrics, pleasant carpets. We like all the rooms, but our favorites are Number 2, with autumnal Persian fabrics and two large windows overlooking the street; and the large Rooms 5 and 10, with a corner sitting area and windows overlooking the courtyard. You will be hospitably greeted but don't expect a great deal of service, as most of the staff is very busy in the restaurant.

Hôtel Le Tourville

16, avenue de Tourville
75007 Paris
Tel. (0)1 47 05 62 62 - Fax (0)1 47 05 43 90
M. Bouvier - Mme Agaud - Mlle Piel

Category ★★★★ Rooms 30 with air-conditioning (4 with terrace), bath, WC, telephone, TV satellite, hairdryer. **Price** Single and double 590-1090F, room with terrace 1190-1390F, junior-suite 1490-1990F (low season Nov 15 – Feb 28 and in Aug). Extra bed 100F. **Meals** Breakfast 60F. **Credit cards** All major. **Pets** Dogs allowed. **Facilities** Elevator. **Parking** At place de l'École-Militaire. **How to get there** (Map 1 and 6): Bus: 28, 49, 82, 87, 92 - Metro: École-Militaire - RER: Invalides - Les Invalides Air Terminal. **Open** All year.

A beautiful building situated between the Invalides Dome and the Rodin Museum shelters the Hôtel Le Tourville. The atmosphere is cosseted in the refined lounge whose decoration was carried out by the David Hicks studio. The subdued lighting and slightly sharp colors give a lot of charm to the elegant, comfortable rooms. Small or large, they are all personalized by kilims and antique furniture pieces and pictures. The bathrooms are also impeccable with beautiful white faience and grey-veined marble. Four of them open onto attractive flower-covered and well laid out terraces: Even if their prices are difficult to justify in the winter period, with the good weather they become particularly attractive as they serve as genuine living space thanks to their large area and quietness. This is a fine hotel with reasonable prices allowing you to appreciate the charms of the Left Bank; both welcome and service are very attentive.

Hôtel de la Tulipe

33, rue Malar
75007 Paris
Tel. (0)1 45 51 67 21 - Fax (0)1 47 53 96 37
M. Fortuit

Category ** **Rooms** 22 with soundproofing for the rooms on the street, bath or shower, WC, telephone, TV satellite, minibar - 1 for disabled persons. **Price** Single and double 500-650F. **Meals** Breakfast 45F. **Credit cards** Amex, Visa, Eurocard, MasterCard. **Pets** Dogs allowed. **Facilities** Small garden, laundry service, tea room. **Parking** At Esplanade des Invalides. **How to get there** (Map 6): Bus: 28, 49, 63, 69, 80, 83, 92 - Metro: Latour-Maubourg, Invalides - RER: Pont-de-l'Alma. Les Invalides Air Terminal. **Open** All year.

This small hotel is installed in an ancient convent but only a little paved courtyard now remains from the original structure, covered in greenery. This courtyard is the central feature of the hotel and from it several staircases lead off to the rooms. Naturally some tables have been placed here so that breakfasts and other meals can be served outside on finer days. Inside, the rural character of the building has been preserved with its wooden beams and stone walls, also found in some of the rooms. These are small but quiet (those looking onto the street, with few passers-by, are sound-proofed). They have cane furniture and are generally brightened with provincial fabrics, while all have attractive small bathrooms. If reserving in good time, ask for the largest and in particular for the two new rooms, fitted out at the same time as the very attractive breakfast room which is very popular. Lastly, a lively and welcoming management have created a relaxed and friendly atmosphere.

Hôtel de l'Université

22, rue de l'Université
75007 Paris
Tel. (0)1 42 61 09 39 - Fax (0)1 42 60 40 84
Mme Bergmann

Category ★★★ **Rooms** 27 with air-conditioning, bath or shower, WC, telephone, TV, safe. **Price** Single 650-700F, double 850-1300F, triple 1100-1500F. **Meals** Breakfast 45F; snacks available. **Credit cards** Visa, Eurocard, MasterCard, Amex. **Pets** Dogs not allowed. **Facilities** Elevator, bar. **Parking** At 9, rue de Montalembert and opposite 169, boulevard Saint-Germain. **How to get there** (Map 1): Bus: 24, 27, 39, 48, 63, 68, 69, 70, 87, 95 - Metro: Rue-du-Bac, Saint-Germain-des-Prés - RER: Musée-d'Orsay. **Open** All year.

The Hôtel de l'Université enjoys a privileged location with antique shops and art galleries in the neighboring streets and with the Louvre and Musée d'Orsay a few paces away, while Saint-Germain-des-Prés is also close by. In addition, this is a hotel of character which the management has insisted on personalizing to give it all the charm of a private house. The ancient vaulting with supporting pillars in oak, the staircase and fireplaces have all been conserved. Damask and velvet in an ocre coloring cover the sofas and armchairs of the small lounges, and the same tones are found in the rooms which are comfortable and decorated with antique furniture and small objects. Often large, they usually have bathrooms in marble. All are air-conditioned and well sound-proofed from any street noise, while some of them look over the back courtyard. The two suites with their Mansard roofs on the top floor also have small private terraces. The welcome is very attentive.

Hôtel de Varenne

44, rue de Bourgogne – 75007 Paris
Tel. (0)1 45 51 45 55 – Fax (0)1 45 51 86 63
web: http://www.webscapades.com/france/paris/varenne.htm
M. Janin

Category ✶✶✶ **Rooms** 24 with bath or shower, WC, telephone, hairdryer, TV. **Price** Single 590F, double 610-720F. Extra bed 120F. **Meals** Breakfast 48F, served at any time. **Credit cards** Visa, Eurocard, MasterCard, Amex. **Pets** Dogs allowed. **Facilities** Elevator, patio, laundry service. **Parking** Invalides. **How to get there** (Map 1): Bus: 28, 49, 63, 69, 82, 83, 84 - Metro: Varenne, Invalides - RER: Invalides - Les Invalides Air Terminal. **Open** All year.

The charming, small Hôtel de Varenne has a particularly appealing lush garden courtyard where you can enjoy breakfast or a drink. Adjoining the lobby, the dining room has a somewhat British feel, with its engravings, mahogany furniture, and pink wall fabrics. Most of the bedrooms (our favorites) overlook the garden, and they have soft colors, natural-wood or antiqued furniture, and functional, well-kept bathrooms with beige floor-to-ceiling tiles.

Hôtel Verneuil - Saint-Germain

8, rue de Verneuil
75007 Paris
Tel. (0)1 42 60 82 14 - Fax (0)1 42 61 40 38
Mme de Lattre

Category ★★★ **Rooms** 26 with soundproofing, telephone, bath or shower, WC, cable TV, hairdryer, safe, minibar. **Price** Single and double 650-950F. **Meals** Breakfast included, served 7:00-10:30. **Credit cards** All major. **Pets** Dogs not allowed. **Facilities** Elevator, laundry service, bar. **Parking** At boulevard Saint-Germain and 9, rue Montalembert (special rates). **How to get there** (Map 1): Bus: 39, 48, 63, 73, 95 - Metro: Saint-Germain-des-Prés, Rue-du-Bac. **Open** All year.

The Rue de Verneuil is marvellously situated in the quiet area between Saint-Germain-des-Prés and the Seine, right in the heart of the Left Bank *carré*. The Hôtel de Verneuil is in an old building that has conserved all its charm: French-style ceilings, stone walls and so on, but as so often with such older buildings the rooms are not always very large. This is why you find several room sizes, while those with a number ending in '3' are charming but really small and would prove difficult for any longer stay. Fitted with small but modern bathrooms in marble, they are however all very pleasant, comfortable and warmly decorated. Always different, they are hung with superb fabrics and fitted out with refinement, and one particularly notes the ravishing series of prints. The largest rooms often have a canopied bed. As for the lounges, they are in the image of the house: classical, well arranged with taste and skill, and one feels as if in a private home. An excellent welcome confirms this good impression on all counts; this is really a fine address.

Hôtel de l'Arcade

9, rue de l'Arcade
75008 Paris
Tel. (0)1 53 30 60 00 – Fax (0)1 40 07 03 07
Mme Chiesa

Category ★★★ **Rooms** 37 and 4 duplex with air-conditioning, soundproofing, telephone, bath, WC, hairdryer, TV satellite, minibar, safe. **Price** Single 780-880F, double 960F, triple and duplex 1150F. **Meals** Breakfast (buffet) 55F, served 7:00-10:30. **Credit cards** All major. **Pets** Small dogs allowed. **Facilities** Elevator, laundry service, tea room. **Parking** At place de la Madeleine. **How to get there** (Map 7): Bus: 24, 42, 43, 52, 84, 94 - Metro: Madeleine - RER: Auber - Rail station: gare Saint-Lazare. **Open** All year.

After a complete renovation the Hôtel de l'Arcade has just reopened its doors. The long lobby-lounge is a very open and airy place where benches, small sofas and armchairs create attractive little corners for relaxation and conversation. The soft colors predominate with a pinky beige for the seating, light green carpet and grey-blue for the cerused wall panelling, all adding to the peace and quiet. The small breakfast room next door has the same ambiance, while the bedrooms are just as elegant. They only differ in size with the singles naturally the smallest, although the bed is still a double. There is a lot of comfort in the very well equipped marble bathrooms (they even have a telephone). The welcome from the young ladies at reception is charming, and this very restful hotel is just a few paces away from the Madeleine church.

Hôtel Balzac

6, rue Balzac
75008 Paris
Tel. (0)1 44 35 18 00 - Fax (0)1 44 35 18 05
M. Christian Falcucci

Category ★★★★ Rooms 70 with air-conditioning, soundproofing, 2 telephones, bath, WC, hairdryer, cable TV, minibar. **Price** Single 1800F, double 1950-2200F, suite (2-3 pers.) 3200-6000F. **Meals** Breakfast 90F, served from 6:00. **Credit cards** All major. **Pets** Dogs allowed. **Facilities** Elevator, laundry service, room service (24h/24), restaurant. **Parking** Private garage and Champs-Elysées or Friedland. **How to get there** (Map 6): Bus: 22, 52, 72 - Metro: George-V, Charles-de-Gaulle-Étoile - RER: Charles-de -Gaulle-Étoile. **Open** All year.

The Hôtel Balzac is in a beautiful building near the Champs–Elysées, just off the Etoile. Several stairways lead to the revolving doors, where you'll be greeted by bellboys. The Italian-style decor includes large, gilt-wood baroque sconces and marble floors. You will find the same atmosphere in the lounge-veranda, lighted by a large skylight through which you can see the white ceramic walls of the building. The bedrooms are truly palatial, with immense beds, thick carpets, and marble bathrooms. The hospitality and service at the Balzac are outstanding, the atmosphere calm and distinguished. Lastly, all 'gastronomes' will delight in lunching or taking dinner in Pierre Gagnaire's restaurant inside the hotel.

Hôtel Beau Manoir

6, rue de l'Arcade
75008 Paris
Tel. (0)1 42 66 03 07 - Fax (0)1 42 68 03 00
Mme Teil - Mme Duhommet

Category ✴✴✴✴ **Rooms** 32 with air-conditioning, soundproofing, bath, WC, telephone, TV satellite, hairdryer, safe, minibar. **Price** Single 995-1100F, double 1155-1300F, suite 1465-1600F. **Meals** Breakfast (buffet) included. **Credit cards** All major. **Pets** Dogs allowed. **Facilities** Elevator, bar, laundry service. **Parking** At place de la Madeleine, rue Chauveau-Lagarde. **How to get there** (Map 7): Bus: 24, 42, 43, 52, 84, 94 - Metro: Madeleine - RER: Auber - Rail station: gare Saint-Lazare. **Open** All year.

Using their 'know-how' the owners have succeeded in creating a genuine small prestige hotel with the Beau Manoir, and once across the threshold you can admire the quality of the craftsmen who worked here. In the lounge old worked wood pieces enhance the greeneries of an 18th-century Aubusson, while damask-covered sofas and wing chairs also add to an atmosphere both luxurious and intimate. Polished walnut furniture in the Louis XIII-style has been chosen for the rooms, whose decor blends happily with a mix of coordinated prints. All are perfectly sound-proofed (as witnessed by the heavy doors and efficient double-glazing), spacious and comfortable; they often have a small corner lounge and a marble bathroom. Our favorites are those with a number ending with a '1'. This is a fine address just a few steps away from the Madeleine.

Hôtel Bedford

17, rue de l'Arcade – 75008 Paris
Tel. (0)1 44 94 77 77 – Fax (0)1 44 94 77 97
web: http://www.123france.com
M. Berrut

Category ✻✻✻ **Rooms** 135 and 11 appartments with air-conditioning, telephone, bath or shower, WC, hairdryer, TV satellite, minibar. **Price** Single 830-930F, double 930-1000F, triple 1200F, apartment (3-4 pers.) 1700F. **Meals** Breakfast 70F, served 7:00-10:30. **Credit cards** Amex, Visa, Eurocard, MasterCard. **Pets** Small dogs allowed. **Facilities** Elevator, laundry service, restaurant, bar-grill. **Parking** At place de la Madeleine. **How to get there** (Map 7): Bus: 24, 42, 43, 52, 84, 94 - Metro: Madeleine - RER: Auber - Rail station: gare Saint-Lazare. **Open** All year.

The Bedford has all the airs of a Grand Hôtel with its liveried personnel in the lobby and the vast hall with corner-lounges. These are both soberly furnished and combine the grey and beige tones which are also found in all the rooms. Classically modern and with a discreet elegance, the rooms have a cosseted comfort. However, the hotel is in the course of renovation and for the present we recommend those on the fifth floor (our favorites) and below, but avoid the sixth floor which have not yet been worked on. You should note that the hotel offers interesting deals for families as certain rooms can be linked together, and there are also apartments. The breakfast room is really astonishing as it has conserved its rich 'pastry decoration' in grey stucco, while the bar is more modern and an attractive place for relaxing or meetings. The service is stylish and friendly.

Hôtel Bradford-Élysées

10, rue Saint-Philippe-du-Roule
75008 Paris
Tel. (0)1 45 63 20 20 – Fax (0)1 45 63 20 07
M. Mathieu Clayeux

Category ★★★ **Rooms** 50 with air-conditioning, telephone, bath or shower, WC, hairdryer, TV satellite, safe, minibar. **Price** Single 650-890F, double 750-1090F, triple 990-1290F. **Meals** Breakfast 65F. Snacks available. **Credit cards** All major. **Pets** Dogs not allowed. **Facilities** Elevator, laundry service. **Parking** At 60, rue de Ponthieu. **How to get there** (Map 6): Bus: 52, 83, 92 - Metro: Saint-Philippe-du-Roule. **Open** All year.

As soon as you cross the threshold of the Bradford you knowl you are in an elegant hotel in a very fine building situated between the Champs-Elysées and Rue du Faubourg-Saint-Honoré. The lounge and dining room are on the ground floor and an beautiful flight of stairs leads up to the rooms. The recent renovation has until now only involved the top two floors but it has not reworked the internal layouts, as the rooms have kept their size and period furniture pieces. Excepting those with numbers ending with a '2', which are the 'singles', the rooms are really very comfortable and 'soigné', with impeccable bathrooms. Our preference is for those on Rue Saint-Philippe-du-Roule, very sunny in the morning. Some rooms can be used by families without feeling too crushed. The renovation work in progress will give Paris yet one more hotel of high quality where you will be assured of a pleasant stay.

Hôtel de L'Élysée

12, rue des Saussaies
75008 Paris
Tel. (0)1 42 65 29 25 - Fax (0)1 42 65 64 28
Mme Lafond

Category ★★★ **Rooms** 32 with air-conditioning, telephone, bath, WC, hairdryer, TV satellite. **Price** Single 620-720F, double 620F, 790F, 1280F; suite 1480F. Special rates the weekends and in low season, prices on request. **Meals** Breakfast 45-65F, served 7:00-11:00. **Credit cards** All major. **Pets** Dogs allowed (+40F). **Facilities** Elevator, laundry service, bar. **Parking** Hôtel Bristol. **How to get there** (Map 7): Bus: 49, 52 - Metro: Madeleine, Miromesnils. **Open** All year.

Ideally situated between the Faubourg-Saint-Honoré, the Madeleine church and the Champs-Elysées, the Hôtel de l'Elysée of course owes its name to the Presidential Palace close by. Its decor is very definitely Directory-style, with trompe l'oeil paintings on the stairs, and the lounge with its rounded tables and late-18th-century 'gendarme hat'-style chairs set around an open fireplace, topped by the traditional mirror framed with candle-sticks. The rooms are variable: some have an attractive and cozy air (beds topped by a canopy or quilting, stylish chairs and small furniture pieces), but others are rather disappointing. The bathrooms are well maintained but some could be freshened up. The major strength of this hotel remains the breakfast in the lounge, a real moment of enjoyment and refinement. This is a charming address, with both qualities and faults, and the prices in general are good value.

Hôtel Élysées-Mermoz

30, rue Jean-Mermoz
75008 Paris
Tel. (0)1 42 25 75 30 - Fax (0)1 45 62 87 10
M. Breuil

Category ★★★ **Rooms** 26 with air-conditioning, soundproofing, telephone, bath, WC, hairdryer,TV, safe - 1 for disabled persons. **Price** Single 720F, double 780-890F, suite (1-4 pers.) 1190F. **Meals** Breakfast 47F, served 7:00-10:30. **Credit cards** All major. **Pets** Small dogs allowed. **Facilities** Elevator, laundry service. **Parking** Rond-Point-des-Champs-Élysées, rue Rabelais. **How to get there** (Map 6): Bus: 28, 32, 49, 52, 73, 83, 93 - Metro: Franklin-Roosevelt, Saint-Philippe-du-Roule. **Open** All year.

The Hôtel Elysées Mermoz, which has just been entirely redone, is between the Rond Point des Champs-Elysées and the Rue du Faubourg Saint-Honoré, on a lively street lined with ministries, corporate headquarters, restaurants, and the famous Arcurial art gallery and bookshop. The entrance and veranda are charming, with a skylight, rattan furniture, and a colorful patchwork quilt in the reception area. The bedrooms are decorated in bright, sunny colors, with a predominance of yellow and blue, or yellow and red; rooms on the courtyard are brightened with lovely, Provençal-yellow walls: a ray of sunshine in a gray Paris day. There are handsome modern amenities, and the bathrooms, some of which are paneled, have beautiful white tiles with blue borders, and even heated towel racks. The bedrooms are fairly large, and the suites can accommodate four people. Noise is no problem, regardless of the season: All the bedrooms are sound-proofed and air-conditioned.

Hôtel Étoile-Friedland

177, rue du Faubourg-Saint-Honoré
75008 Paris
Tel. (0)1 45 63 64 65 - Fax (0)1 45 63 88 96
M. Jean-Bernard Denis

Category ★★★★ **Rooms** 40 with air-conditioning, soundproofing, telephone, bath or shower, WC, hairdryer, cable and satellite TV, minibar, safe - 2 for disabled persons. **Price** Single and double 850-1200F. **Meals** Breakfast 75F, served 6:45-12:00. **Credit cards** All major. **Pets** Dogs allowed. **Facilities** Elevator, laundry service, bar, room-service from 11:00 to 22:45. **Parking** At 163, boulevard Haussmann. **How to get there** (Map 3): Bus: 22, 43 - Metro and RER: Charles-de-Gaulle-Étoile. **Open** All year.

Very close to the Etoile, the hotel is in a building on the corner of Avenue de Friedland and Rue du Faubourg-Saint-Honoré. Recently renovated, the hotel has rediscovered a new and lively spirit perceptible from the entrance. At reception Bernard greets you with all due attention, and both room and bar service are just as efficient and smiling. This brightness is also seen in the light and colorful decor. The largest rooms are on the top floor and their Mansard ceilings give them extra charm. All are air-conditioned and sound-proofed and so you should not be disturbed by the heavy traffic of Avenue de Friedland, but to be on the safe side reserve the upper floors. This is a convivial hotel with a good, humorous atmosphere.

Hôtel Folkestone Opéra

9, rue de Castellane
75008 Paris
Tel. (0)1 42 65 73 09 – Fax (0)1 42 65 64 09
M. Michel Léger

Category ★★★ **Rooms** 50 with soundproofing, (45 with air-conditioning) telephone, bath, WC, TV satellite, hairdryer, safe, minibar. **Price** Single 715F, double 800F, triple 905F, 4 pers. 1020F. **Meals** Breakfast (buffet) 50F, served 7:00-11:00. **Credit cards** All major. **Pets** Dogs allowed. **Meals** Elevator, bar, laundry service. **Parking** At place de la Madeleine and rue des Mathurins. **How to get there** (Map 7): Bus: 24, 42, 52, 84, 94 - Metro: Madeleine, Havre-Caumartin - RER: Auber - Rail station: gare Saint-Lazare. **Open** All year.

No need to sing the praises of this quarter of the Madeleine, where Rue de Castellane runs into Rue Tronchet, an obligatory track for shopping fanatics. The Folkestone-Opéra is a pretty little hotel where the space has been very well utilized; by the time you reach reception you have already passed through two very cozy small lounges. Bordeaux red, green and yellow are the colors used in the printed fabrics decorating the rooms to create a comfortable and elegant atmosphere. A copious breakfast buffet with house gateaux is laid out in a ground-floor room, but if you are staying on the sixth floor you can also take it on your balcony.

Hôtel Franklin-Roosevelt

18, rue Clément-Marot
75008 Paris
Tel. (0)1 47 23 61 66 – Fax (0)1 47 20 44 30
M. and Mme Le Boudec

Category ★★★ **Rooms** 44, 2 junior-suites and 2 apartments with soundproofing, telephone, bath or shower, WC, TV, hairdryer - 1 for disabled persons. **Price** "Standard" 945F, "supérieures" 1200-1600F, apart. 2200F. **Meals** Breakfast 65F, buffet 80F. **Credit cards** Amex, Visa, Eurocard, MasterCard. **Pets** Dogs not allowed. **Facilities** Patio, bar, room-service until 20:00. **Parking** Opposite 4, avenue George-V, Rue François-Iᵉʳ. **How to get there** (Map 6): Bus: 32, 42, 63, 80, 92 - Metro: Franklin-Roosevelt, Alma-Marceau - RER: Pont-de-l'Alma, Charles-de-Gaulle-Étoile. **Open** All year.

A recent change of ownership has given the Franklin–Roosevelt the occasion to freshen itself up. The breakfast room has been enlarged, an English bar installed on the ground floor, and small and very cosy lounges opened in the basement. The fourth floor has been totally refurbished, and two large apartments opened on the sixth floor. The Franklin-Roosevelt has gained in standing and also in warmth. Naturally the prices have also gone up with the services but regular clients of the hotel should appreciate such changes, while the nostalgics will continue to reserve the first three floors, still just as charming with their romantic ambiance and panoramic wallpapers. This is a fine address to discover, or rediscover, close to the Grand Palais and the Petit Palais museum, and at easy distance from both sides of the Seine.

Hôtel La Galerie

16, rue de la Pépinière
75008 Paris
Tel. (0)1 40 08 06 08 – Fax (0)1 40 08 07 77
M. Michel Agid

Category ★★★ **Rooms** 49 with air-conditioning, soundproofing, telephone, bath or shower, WC, hairdryer, TV satellite, safe, minibar. **Price** Single 700F, double 850F. Extra bed 180F. Special rates in low season. **Meals** Breakfast 55F, buffet 70F, served 7:00-10:00. **Credit cards** All major. **Pets** Dogs allowed. **Facilities** Elevator, bar, laundry service, patio, room-service. **Restaurant** Menu: 90-110F. **Parking** At place Bergson. **How to get there** (Map 4): Metro: Saint-Augustin, Saint-Lazare - Rail station: gare Saint-Lazare - All bus for Saint-Lazare. **Open** All year.

The ambiance is chic and contemporary behind the walls of this fine 19th-century building in cut stone. The Hôtel La Galerie has just been refurbished, where the charm comes more the harmony of the materials and colors. First of all there is the ravishing patio with tables and parasols, ideal for breakfast, lunch or dinner. Then there is the small lounge bar and dining room on either side of the entry area, with their comfortable vivid red armchairs and the smooth and sombre panels in exotic woods, with pictures on them. Decorated very carefully in the same style, the rooms all have very sober and integrated furniture, while the bathrooms are covered in pretty faience-mosaics with small grey and white banding. Whatever their size (Number 708 is the largest) the comfort level is always excellent. This is a great address to discover and you can also dine very well here.

Hôtel Galileo

54, rue Galilée
75008 Paris
Tel. (0)1 47 20 66 06 - Fax (0)1 47 20 67 17
M. Buffat

Category ★★★ **Rooms** 27 with air-conditioning, telephone, bath, hairdryer, WC, plug for fax, safe, cable TV, minibar - 2 for disabled persons. **Price** Single 800F, double 950F. **Meals** Breakfast 50F, served 7:15-11:00. **Credit cards** Amex, Visa, Eurocard, MasterCard. **Pets** Dogs not allowed. **Facilities** Elevator, winter garden. **Parking** George-V (70-80F). **How to get there** (Map 6): Bus: 22, 30, 31, 52, 73 - Metro: George-V, Charles-de-Gaulle-Étoile - RER: Charles-de-Gaulle-Étoile. **Open** All year.

Well-situated between the Champs-Eluysées and avenue Georges V, the Galiléo is a charming hotel. Refinement and modernity have guided the recent changes. It was renovated to add modern touches to the rooms, such as air-conditioning, reading lamps, fax lines, and radios in the bathrooms. Certain rooms are more spacious: The two on the ground floor, and the two on the *cinquième étage* with adorable verandas are our favorites. Other areas of the hotel were refined, including the lounge, with its 18th-century chimney and its Aubusson tapestry. On the ground floor there's a breakfast room, with soft lighting and color-scheme, and a pretty view onto the cleverly laid-out garden.

Hôtel Lancaster

7, rue de Berri - 75008 Paris
Tel. (0)1 40 76 40 76 - Fax (0)1 40 76 40 00
e-mail: pippaona@hotel-lancaster.fr
M. Jean-Michel Desnos

Category ★★★★ **Rooms** 50 and 10 suites with air-condition, soundproofing, telephone, bath or shower, WC, hairdryer, cable TV, minibar, safe. **Price** Single 1650-1950F, double 2250-2650F, suite 3000-10000F. **Meals** Breakfast 120F, served from 7:00. **Credit cards** All major. **Pets** Dogs allowed on request. **Facilities** Elevator, bar, laundry service, garden, room-service (24 h/24). **Restaurant** For residents only. Plates from 150F, also à la carte. **Parking** At 5, rue de Berri. **How to get there** (Map 6): Bus: 73 - Metro: George-V - RER: Charles-de-Gaulle-Étoile. **Open** All year.

The Lancaster continues to be one of the leading examples of Parisian 'Grand Hôtels,' thanks to a remarkable restoration that has conserved more than one thousand antique articles and pieces accumulated by its founder, E. Wolf. In parallel, the reception area, restaurant and bathrooms were entrusted to the talents of Christian Liaigre, who has combined both elegance and modernity. The rooms are vast, the suites immense, and all are decorated with very beautiful fabrics, period furniture and pictures often of an exceptional quality. The bathrooms are in the modern style but have kept a noble sobriety. The main saloon and dining room have been rejuvenated with subtlety, notably by a choice of rather mat colors tending to give a more modern touch to the furniture, rugs and old pictures. The garden adds to all the refinement with its atmosphere of great calm; portions of the walls are covered by large brown reeds, and giant plants collected from all five continents, and the noise of splashing water.

Hôtel Lido

4, passage de la Madeleine
75008 Paris
Tel. (0)1 42 66 27 37 - Fax (0)1 42 66 61 23
Mme Teil

Category ★★★ **Rooms** 32 with air-conditioning, soundproofing, bath, WC, telephone, plug for modem, TV satellite, hairdryer, safe, minibar. **Price** Single 830-980F, double 930-1100F. **Meals** Breakfast (buffet) included. **Credit cards** Amex, Visa, Eurocard, MasterCard, JCB. **Pets** Dogs allowed. **Facilities** Laundry service, bar. **Parking** At place de la Madeleine, Rue Chauveau-Lagarde. **How to get there** (Map 7): Bus: 24, 42, 43, 52, 84, 94 - Metro: Madeleine - RER: Auber. **Open** All year.

The first hotel in a small group including the Beau Manoir next door, the Lido is a good example of personalized hotelry, and a lot of the atmosphere is due to Mme. Teil who personally looks after the well-being of her clients. Carpets, 18th-century Aubusson tapestry and Haute époque-style chairs furnish the warm reception area and lounge. The rooms have kept their ceiling beams and are recently been refurbished. The walls are usually draped with damask silks or 'Toile de Jouy', along with the double curtains. Their style mixes rusticity and refinement and is always well thought out, with functional cupboarding and comfortable bathrooms in marble offering numerous welcoming product lines. You should note that rooms with numbers ending with a '3' are the largest. A good breakfast is served in a vaulted room, with house pastries and home-made jams.

Hôtel-Résidence Lord Byron

5, rue de Chateaubriand
75008 Paris
Tel. (0)1 43 59 89 98 - Fax (0)1 42 89 46 04

Category ★★★ **Rooms** 31 with telephone, bath or shower, WC, hairdryer, TV satellite, minibar, safe. **Price** Single 660F, double 820-920F, junior-suite 1270F (2 pers.), 1420F (3-4 pers.). **Meals** Breakfast 50F, served 7:15-12:00. **Credit cards** All major. **Pets** Dogs not allowed. **Facilities** Elevator, laundry service, garden. **Parking** At 5, rue de Berri. **How to get there** (Map 6): Bus: 22, 31, 52, 73 - Metro: George-V - RER: Charles-de-Gaulle-Étoile. **Open** All year.

In a quiet street near the Etoile and between the Avenue de Friedland and the Champs-Elysées, the Résidence Lord Byron is an attractive hotel. A fine entryway in classical style with worked wood pieces, mouldings and corniches, antique furniture and English carpeting leads through to reception. The hotel splits its rooms between the main building with most of them, and a second building on the other side of the garden, which is abundant with flowers in the summer. Breakfast and drinks are seved in the garden in the fine weather. The rooms are pleasantly decorated, flowery, bright and very light on the garden side. You get either bathtub or shower depending on room category and size; the smallest is on the top floor but has the charm of Mansard ceilings. You are well received here but if it's full, you should know that the same management runs the hotel next door, the Mayflower, which is fully comparable with the Lord Byron except for the garden.

Résidence Monceau Hôtel

85, rue du Rocher
75008 Paris
Tel. (0)1 45 22 75 11 – Fax (0)1 45 22 30 88
Mme Touber – Mme Loreau

Category ★★★ **Rooms** 50 and 1 suite with soundproofing, telephone, bath or shower, WC, hairdryer, TV satellite, minibar - 2 for disabled persons. **Price** Single and double 720F, triple 870F. **Meals** Breakfast (buffet) 50F, served 7:00-11:00. **Credit cards** All major. **Pets** Dogs not allowed. **Facilities** Elevator, laundry service, bar, individual safes at reception, garden. **Parking** At boulevard des Batignolles, avenue de Villiers. **How to get there** (Map 4): Bus: 30 - Metro: Villiers - Rail station: gare Saint-Lazare. **Open** All year.

The lounge, reception area, and bar of the Résidence Monceau create a large, convivial area. Rattan window boxes and furniture brighten the lounge, while the bar, which opens onto a small courtyard, is more modern, with black and mahogany furniture. On the ground floor there is a spacious breakfast room, which also opens onto a lush garden, where breakfast is served in good weather. The bedrooms are more ordinary, with conventional furniture in burr walnut or oak veneer, and they are comfortable. It's preferable to ask for a quiet room overlooking the courtyard, especially in summer. Note that Room 117 is not spacious, but it does have a large terrace. The hotel is near two of the most popular monuments in Paris: the Arc de Triomphe and Sacré Coeur.

New Orient Hôtel

16, rue de Constantinople
75008 Paris
Tel. (0)1 45 22 21 64 – Fax (0)1 42 93 83 23
Mme Wehrle

Category ★★ **Rooms** 30 with soundproofing, telephone, bath or shower, WC, TV satellite. **Price** Single 390F, double 490F, triple 590F. In January, February and August, single 320F, double 420F, triple 500F. **Meals** Breakfast (buffet) 38F, served 7:00-12:00. **Credit cards** All major. **Pets** Dogs allowed. **Facilities** Elevator, bar. **Parking** Europe, avenue de Villiers. **How to get there** (Map 4): Bus: 30, 53 - Metro: Europe, Villiers, Saint-Lazare - Rail station: gare Saint-Lazare. **Open** All year.

This charming little hotel owes much of its personality to its owners as Catherine and Sepp Wehrle have chosen to fit it out with the same care as for a private house, and to this end spend part of their free time in acquiring and restoring 'retro' furniture pieces. All the results are here and each landing displays a fine antique cupboard, while in a good number of the rooms you find late-19th-century bedheads along with Napoleon III chairs and small furniture pieces. This creates a very personal overall effect, warm and bright, and even if the bathrooms could do with a bit more attention to details, they are nevertheless well maintained. All these qualities, the reasonable prices, and the friendly welcome, make the New Orient Hôtel a precious little address in this district.

Hôtel Newton Opéra

11 *bis*, rue de l'Arcade
75008 Paris
Tel. (0)1 42 65 32 13 - Fax (0)1 42 65 30 90
M. Simian

Category ★★★ **Rooms** 31 with air-conditioning, telephone, bath, WC, hairdryer, TV satellite, radio, minibar, safe. **Price** Single and double 700-830F - Special rates in Aug. **Meals** Breakfast (buffet) 50F, served 6:45-10:00. Snacks available. **Credit cards** All major. **Pets** Small dogs allowed. **Facilities** Elevator, laudry service, room-service. **Parking** At place de la Madeleine, rue Chauveau-Lagarde. **How to get there** (Map 7): Bus: 22, 24, 42, 43, 52, 84, 94 - Metro: Madeleine, Saint-Lazare - RER: Auber - Rail station: gare Saint-Lazare. **Open** All year.

Among the many hotels on the Rue de l'Arcade, the Newton Opéra is possibly the simplest, but offers excellent comfort at the best prices. You'll find a somewhat country atmosphere, with rustic painted furniture, and fabrics in bright, floral motifs. What's surprising about this small hotel are the services offered: air-conditioning, minibar, private safe, trouser-press, and room service with Hédiard tray-meals. In the bathrooms various accessories have been added such as make-up wipes'and a delicate scent of vanilla. On arrival a small carafe of mandarin juice awaits you. In the summer, if you reserve in good time, you may be able to get one of the two rooms with a terrace with table and deck chairs, which are ideal for any longer stay. In the lounge you find the daily press and various magazines. As for the vaulted room in the basement, you will find a generous breakfast buffet—all you can eat—served in the vaulted room in the basement. What's not surprising is that this family-run hotel has attracted many faithful customers over the years.

Hôtel Queen-Mary

9, rue Greffulhe – 75008 Paris
Tel. (0)1 42 66 40 50 – Fax (0)1 42 66 94 92
e.mail: hotelqueenmary@wanadoo.fr
M. Byrne – M. Tarron

Category ★★★ **Rooms** 36 with air-conditioning, soundproofing, telephone, bath, WC, hairdryer, cable TV, minibar, safe (extra charge). **Price** Single 755F, double 875-935F, suite 1300F. **Meals** English breakfast 75F, served 7:30-10:00. **Credit cards** Amex, Visa, Eurocard, MasterCard. **Pets** Dogs not allowed. **Facilities** Elevator, patio, room-service. **Parking** At place de la Madeleine. **How to get there** (Map 7): Bus: 22, 24, 28, 32, 49, 80, 84, 94 - Metro: Madeleine, Havre-Caumartin - RER: Auber - Rail station: gare Saint-Lazare. **Open** All year.

Close to the lively quarter of the Grands Magasins but sheltered from the traffic, the Queen Mary has opened again after a very successful renovation, and you will appreciate the elegance and very cozy comfort of the small lounge and bar, just as much as the ambiance of the bedrooms decorated in an English style. Youl notice the walls in beige tones, acajou furniture perfectly harmonizing with the striped chair fabrics, drapes and bedspreads, pretty gilt wall-lamps and impeccable white bathrooms. The comfort is perfect for the price and you will also appreciate the details such as the trouser-press and carafe of sherry wine awaiting your arrival. You should also note the very tiny patio where you can take a glass during the day, along with the basement breakfast room prettily decorated in green and yellow tones. This is a very agreeable small hotel with an attentive and available service.

Royat Park Hôtel

5, rue Castellane
75008 Paris
Tel. (0)1 42 66 14 44 – Fax (0)1 42 66 48 47
M. Michel Léger

Category ★★ **Rooms** 30 with soundproofing, telephone, bath or shower, WC, TV satellite, safe, minibar. **Price** Single 490F, double 520F, triple 630F. **Meals** Breakfast 30F, served 7:00-10:30. **Credit cards** All major. **Pets** Dogs allowed. **Facilities** Elevator, laundry service. **Parking** At place de la Madeleine and at rue des Mathurins. **How to get there** (Map 7): Bus: 24, 42, 52, 84, 94 - Metro: Madeleine, Havre-Caumartin - RER: Auber - Rail station: gare Saint-Lazare. **Open** All year.

Close to the Place de la Madeleine, the Opera and the large stores, this little hotel has the big advantage of offering a very good quality-price deal. We are not talking a lot of charm but the establishment has sought to add a little elegance to its "two-star" category standard. Thus the breakfast room has on its walls a fine series of architectural drawings of various Parisian monuments, while the rooms are simple, comfortable and perfectly maintained. Rare at this price level, each even has a small safe. Those with a number ending in '6' have just been renovated. A continental breakfast is served with house *pains au chocolat* and *croissants*.

Hôtel San Régis

12, rue Jean Goujon - 75008 Paris
Tel. (0)1 44 95 16 16 - Fax (0)1 45 61 05 48
e-mail: message@hotel-sanregis.fr
M. Joseph Georges

Category ★★★★ **Rooms** 41 and 3 suites (34 with air-conditioning) with telephone, bath or shower, WC, cable and satellite TV, minibar, hairdryer. **Price** Single 1700F, double 2300-2950F, triple 3350-3700F, suite (2 pers.) 5800F. **Meals** Breakfast 110F, served 7:00-10:30. **Credit cards** All major. **Pets** Dogs not allowed. **Facilities** Elevator, bar, laundry service, room-service. **Restaurant** À la carte **Parking** At rue François-Ier. **How to get there** (Map 6): Bus: 32, 42, 63, 80, 92 - Metro: Franklin-Roosevelt. **Open** All year.

Apart from the luxurious and celebrated Rue Montaigne and Rue François I, which lodge the really big names of 'Haute Couture,' the district also has its own charming small hotel in the San Régis. The welcome is spontaneous and very attentive as you are led through the large lounge or small dining room of the hotel restaurant. The cosseted ambiance, antique furniture and pictures, and abundance of fine motifed fabrics, all go to make a very 'British' atmosphere. This same feeling of comfort is in both the corridors and rooms, where the deep-pile carpeting kills any noise. The suites and rooms are all spacious and each has its own special decor, made by a very fine choice of well-coordinated fabrics. The singles, in another wing of the house, are more sober and smaller. They are all equally comfortable and could even suit a couple looking for a more reasonable price. The personnel is particularly attentive and on-hand at any moment to offer you all the establishment services.

Hôtel Sydney Opéra

50, rue des Mathurins
75008 Paris
Tel. (0)1 42 65 35 48 - Fax (0)1 42 65 03 07
M. Michel Léger - Mme Anne-Marie Gerbault

Category ★★★ **Rooms** 38 with soundproofing (34 with air-conditioning), telephone, bath or shower, WC, TV satellite, safe, minibar. **Price** Single 715F, double 800F, triple 905F, 4 pers. 1020F. **Meals** Breakfast (buffet) 50F, served 7:00-11:00. **Credit cards** All major. **Pets** Dogs allowed. **Facilities** Elevator, bar, laundry service. **Parking** Opposite at the hotel. **How to get there** (Map 4 and 7): Metro: Saint-Lazare - RER: Auber - Rail station: Saint-Lazare - All bus to Saint-Lazare. **Open** All year.

Golden yellow walls with green ribbon edging, 1930's-style armchairs and seats covered with very elegant fabrics, the rounded acajou style of the bar-the reception hall of the Hôtel Sydney Opéra well illustrates the quality of the recently completed renovation. Certainly some sacrifices have been made to today's tastes but the result is bright, warm and comfortable, and it is a great success. You will not be disappointed by the room fittings: thick red-wine carpeting with small motifs, yellow ocre walls to highlight the gilt wall-lamps and the dark browns of the smooth and modern furniture, pretty flowery or tartan fabrics, and with the same attention given to the all-white bathrooms with just a tiny yellow streaking. Lastly, because one cannot overestimate the importance of breakfast, we should give credit to the elegance and size of the dining room, lit by a glass roof and in an extension from the lounge, where a self-service buffet awaits the clientele.

Hôtel Vernet

25, rue Vernet - 75008 Paris
Tel. (0)1 44 31 98 00 - Fax (0)1 44 31 85 69
e-mail: hotelvernet@jetmultimédia.fr
M. Bruno Bazi

Category ★★★★ **Rooms** 54 and 3 suites with air-conditioning, soundproofing, telephone, bath with whirlpool, WC, hairdryer, cable TV, minibar, safe. **Price** Single 1700-1900F, double 2100-2500F, suite 3900F. **Meals** Continental breakfast 130F, served 7:00-10:30. **Credit cards** All major. **Pets** Small dogs allowed. **Facilities** Elevator, laundry service, bar, room-service (24h/24). **Restaurant** Gastronomic, menu 370 (lunch), 390-730F (diner), also à la carte. **Parking** Private. **How to get there** (Map 6): Bus: 24, 42, 43, 52, 84, 94 - Metro and RER: Charles-de-Gaulle-Étoile. **Open** All year.

The Etoile-Champs-Elysées area remains the most prestigious quarter of international Paris and most of the luxury hotels are found here. It is then difficult to make a choice as all offer the same services. What makes the difference is a welcome that does not finish with simple conventional courtesies, plus the close attention given to clients. This is the case with the Hôtel Vernet, located in a building from the 1920's, where a superb glass roof over the Les Elysées restaurant has been preserved along with the staircase cage seen from the transparent elevator. The restaurant chef is Bruno Cirino, with his Mediterranean-style cuisine awarded a two-star rating. An Italian-type gallery with an antique decor of false marble, columns and illuminated vases serves the lounges and bar. With the open fire and piano music, you are only too glad to linger here at tea-time or for a cocktail. The rooms are regularly renovated and all offer the latest comforts in a refined setting. This is a very good address where you are immediately given all that consideration due to a good client.

Westin Demeure Hôtel Marignan-Élysées

12, rue de Marignan
75008 Paris
Tel. (0)1 40 76 34 56 – Fax 01 40 76 34 34
M. Patrick Langlois

Category ★★★★ **Rooms** 56 and 17 suites with air-conditioning, bath, WC, hairdryer, cable TV, safe, minibar, 3 telephone and plug for fax. **Price** Double 1690-2300F, suite 2300-2950F. **Meals** Breakfast (buffet) 140F, served 6:30-11:00. **Credit cards** All major. **Pets** Dogs allowed. **Facilities** Elevator, laundry service, room-service 24h/24, bar. **Restaurant** "La Table du Marché": Specialties: Provençale cooking. Closed Sunday. Price: 250F. **Parking** At rue François-Ier. **How to get there** (Map 6): Bus: 42, 73, 80 - Metro: Franklin-Roosevelt - RER: Charles-de-Gaulle-Étoile. **Open** All year.

In a residential neighborhood, the Marignan-Elysées occupies a very beautiful, late-19th-century building, which has been well renovated in collaboration with the Historic French Buildings Association. It is now a luxurious hotel. The lounges are richly furnished with 17th-century chests of drawers with gilt bronze decoration, wall clocks and Aubusson tapestries. The hotel is bright, and the breakfast room, which serves as a very pleasant tea room in the afternoon, is illuminated by a large skylight. Simpler in style, the bedrooms—some of which have a view of the Eiffel Tower—are decorated with lovely yellow and blue floral motifs. The modern amenities and service are what you would expect of a four-star hotel. The hotel is teamed up with a Saint-Tropez restaurant, *La Table du Marché*. where, in a Mediterranean atmosphere, you can enjoy aromatic Provençal specialties prepared with great finesse.

Austin's Hôtel

26, rue d'Amsterdam
75009 Paris
Tel. (0)1 48 74 48 71 - Fax (0)1 48 74 39 79
M. Hamidi

Category ★★ **Rooms** 36 with soundproofing, telephone, bath or shower, WC, hairdryer, TV satellite. **Price** Single 380F, double 440F - Special rates Friday, Saturday and Sunday. **Meals** Breakfast (buffet) 30F, served 7:00-10:00. **Credit cards** All major. **Pets** Dogs not allowed. **Facilities** Elevator, bar. **Restaurant** Menu: 69-99F. Specialties: traditional cooking, couscous. **Parking** Gare Saint-Lazare. **How to get there** (Map 4): Metro and rail station: Gare Saint-Lazare - RER: Auber - All bus to Saint-Lazare. **Open** All year.

Here is a good example to prove that with a small budget you can still live well in Paris. In the very animated quarter of the Gare Saint-Lazare, Austin's Hôtel is in a small street running along one of the sides of the imposing building, and the hotel is equally close to the Grands Magasins of Boulevard Haussmann. The interior is however very quiet and the comfort offered is exemplary considering its price. Its very recent reopening now enables it to offer rooms that are not very large but prettily decorated with stripes or printed papers in dominant greens or blues. The bathrooms are impeccable and the service very professional with tray-meals on request. A very good breakfast is served for you in an attractive bistro-style room, and this is a good new recruit for our cheaper section of the guide.

Hôtel Chopin

10, boulevard Montmartre (46, passage Jouffroy)
75009 Paris
Tel. (0)1 47 70 58 10 – Fax (0)1 42 47 00 70
M. Philippe Bidal

Category ★★ **Rooms** 35 with telephone, bath or shower, TV and 34 with WC. **Price** Single 405-435F, double 450-490F, triple 565F. **Meals** Breakfast (buffet) 38F, served 7:15-9:45. **Credit cards** Visa, Eurocard, MasterCard. **Pets** Dogs allowed. **Facilities** Elevator. **Parking** At rue Chauchat. **How to get there** (Map 7): Bus: 20, 39, 48, 67, 74, 85 - Metro: Richelieu-Drouot. **Open** All year.

On the Boulevard Montmartre between the Musée Grévin and the Hard Rock Café, the glass roofing of Passage Jouffroy shelters numerous bookshops, including one to delight all movie fans, as well as the Hôtel Chopin. The hotel lobby has a piano and two portraits of the celebrated couple of Chopin and George Sand. It's up a few steps to the dining room, where breakfasts are served, and the elevator to the floors above. Some materials are perhaps a little faded and the rooms are not always very light, with a rather jaded comfort, but the atmosphere is warm. You should note that rooms on the two upper floors are the most comfortable and also the lightest.

Hotel du Léman

20, rue de Trévise
75009 Paris
Tel. (0)1 42 46 50 66 – Fax (0)1 48 24 27 59
M. Legrand

Category ★★★ **Rooms** 24 with soundproofing, telephone, bath or shower, WC, hairdryer, TV, minibar. **Price** Single 390-540F, double 450-660F. **Meals** Breakfast (buffet) 40F, served 7:00-10:45; snack availables. **Credit cards** All major. **Pets** Dogs allowed. **Facilities** Elevator, laundry service. **Parking** At rue Richer. **How to get there** (Map 4): Bus: 26, 42, 49, 74 - Metro: Cadet, Rue-Monmartre, Poissonnière. **Open** All year.

Between the Grands Boulevards, the popular Boulevard Montmartre and the world-famous Folies Bergères, the Rue de Trévise on which Le Léman stands is actually a very quiet street. The hotel reception area conserves some of the souvenirs of its globe-trotting owners such as the fine Italian marble marquetry panels surrounding the office. The rooms are very pleasant, light and airy, with their floral (or even better) white piqué bedspreads. Everything works to create that peaceful atmosphere sought by M. Legrand for his clientele. The rooms on the top floor have Mansard ceilings, notably No. 66, and are very popular. The welcome from M. Legrand is very attentive to all your requests and you can stay here without many constraints. Breakfast can be served outside normal hours, though it would be a pity to miss the copious buffet, and snacks are always available should you feel hungry.

Hôtel Libertel Franklin

19, rue Buffault
75009 Paris
Tel. (0)1 42 80 27 27 - Fax (0)1 48 78 13 04
Mme Esnault

Category ★★★ **Rooms** 68 and 9 suites with soundproofing, telephone, bath or shower, WC, hairdryer, minibar, cable TV - 2 for disabled persons. **Price** Single 825F, double 890F, suite 990F (3 pers.). **Meals** Breakfast (buffet) 75F, served 7:00-10:30. **Credit cards** All major. **Pets** Dogs allowed. **Facilities** Elevator, laundry service, safe at reception, garden, room-service. **Parking** At rue Buffault, square Montholon. **How to get there** (Map 4): Bus: 26, 32, 43, 49 - Metro: Cadet. **Open** All year.

Very welcoming, the large reception area of the Libertel Franklin has an unexpected and rather naive panorama on its walls, but the hotel itself is mainly inspired by the Napoleonic era. No richly decorated furniture pieces in acajou to recall the Empire, but rather wrought iron chairs and tables more typical of a military campaign. The rooms are papered in wide grey or dark red stripes, and soberly but elegantly fitted with cerused furniture and decorated with prints recalling chosen themes. They are very comfortable with perfect bathrooms. Very well organized, the hotel had adapted itself to clientele needs with non-smoking floors, and room-service to provide tray-meals for the exhausted business clientele, or those not wishing to miss the TV soccer match at any price.

Hôtel Libertel Lafayette

49-51, rue Lafayette
75009 Paris
Tel. (0)1 42 85 05 44 – Fax (0)1 49 95 06 60
Mme Dessors

Category ★★★ **Rooms** 103, (1 floor for non-smokers, 28 rooms with air-conditioning) with telephone, bath or shower, WC, hairdryer, TV satellite, minibar, safe, kettle, trouser-press - 2 for disabled persons. **Price** Single 910F, double 975F, suite 1700F. **Meals** Breakfast (buffet) 75F, served 6:30-10:30; snack availables. **Credit cards** All major. **Pets** Small dogs allowed. **Facilities** Elevator, laundry service. **Parking** At rue Buffault. **How to get there** Bus: 26, 42, 49, 74 - Metro: Le Peletier, Cadet. **Open** All year.

Close to the Opéra Garnier, the Grands Boulevards and the Grands Magasins you find the Libertel Lafayette, entirely renovated and now a real hotel of charm. The restructuring and decoration were directed by Anne-Marie de Ganay, who was inspired by the elegance and comfort of 'bourgeois' residences across the Channel. Thus on the facade two windows with cobalt-blue lacquered molding frame the entrance with its two large copper lanterns. The elegant lobby leads through to the bar and a smoking lounge lit by a skylight covered in clever tromp-l'oeil. The space is light and airy with a beige cameo. The floor is stone, with cerused furniture, the walls covered with linen fabrics printed with medaillons, and chairs in beige and white squares sit alongside acajou furniture pieces. The rooms are just as well done with blue, green or beige 'Toile de Jouy' depending on the floor, giving them a cosy country atmosphere. Nothing is lacking for comfort, including an electric kettle with tea or coffee for moments of relaxation in your room. Both welcome and service are attentive.

Hôtel Libertel Moulin

39, rue Fontaine
75009 Paris
Tel. (0)1 42 81 93 25 - Fax (0)1 40 16 09 90
Mme Frédérique Péchenart

Category ★★★ Rooms 48 and 2 junior-suites with soundproofing, telephone, bath or shower, WC, minibar, cable TV and 20 with hairdryer. **Price** Single 795F, double 860F, junior-suite 960F (2 pers.), triple 1010F. **Meals** Breakfast (buffet) 75F, served 7:00-10:30. **Credit cards** All major. **Pets** Dogs allowed (+50F). **Facilities** Elevator, laundry service, safe at reception, room-service: 11:00-14:00, 18:30-22:30. **Parking** At rue Mansart. **How to get there** (Map 4): Bus: 30, 54, 74 - Metro: Blanche.**Open** All year.

The Moulin Rouge district is certainly just what you would expect: popular, touristy, and noisy, but the Hôtel Libertel Moulin is set back from all the agitation. One must also add that you are close to all that gives this district its full charm (provided you have good legs) with the Rue Lepic market, the bistros in the Rue des Abbesses, and the Butte Montmartre and Sacré-Coeur church. The hotel interior is carefully maintained with a combined reception area and comfortable lounge, filled mainly with black leather 'club' armchairs. Most of the rooms have just been redone, and they are not large but are cosy, with their warm brick tones; all have comfortable bathrooms in bicolored travertin. Rooms on the street are very light but those on the courtyard are quieter. Both welcome and service are attentive, the breakfast-buffet is copious and the rates are attractive.

Hôtel de la Tour d'Auvergne

10, rue de la Tour d'Auvergne
75009 Paris
Tel. (0)1 48 78 61 60 - Fax (0)1 49 95 99 00
M. Duval

Category ★★★ **Rooms** 24 with telephone, bath, WC, hairdryer, TV. **Price** Single 450-600F, double 550-700F. **Meals** Breakfast (buffet) 52F, served 7:00-10:00. **Credit cards** All major. **Pets** Dogs allowed (+50F). **Facilities** Elevator, laundry service. **Parking** Square Montholon. **How to get there** (Map 4): Bus: 26, 32, 42, 43, 46, 49, 74, 85 - Metro: Cadet, Anvers. **Open** All year.

In a lively neighborhood not far from the top of Montmartre, with its theaters, and, of course, Sacré Coeur, the Tour d'Auvergne has just been extensively renovated. The decor is eclectic: bright or soft colors, Jouy or Indian fabrics, floral motifs or stripes, a country or a baroque atmosphere. All the rooms have comfortable bathrooms. As is always the case in Paris, you'll be sure to have a quiet room on the courtyard, but the view there is somewhat gray and gloomy. We prefer the rooms on the street side, particularly as there's not much traffic. The bar is pleasant, and the staff charming.

Hôtel William's du Pré

3, rue Mayran/square Montholon
75009 Paris
Tel. (0)1 48 78 68 35 - Fax (0)1 45 26 08 70
M. Dupré

Category ★★★ **Rooms** 30 with soundproofing, telephone, bath or shower, WC, hairdryer, TV. **Price** Single 425F, double 490-515F. **Meals** Breakfast (buffet) 50F (offered between November 15 and March 15), served 8:00-10:00. **Credit cards** All major. **Pets** Dogs allowed. **Facilities** Elevator. **Parking** Mayran. **How to get there** (Map 4): Bus: 32, 42, 43, 48, 49 - Metro: Cadet. **Open** All year.

The Square Montholon is a pleasant oasis of greenery and gardens in this neighborhood located half-way between the Opéra and Sacré-Coeur. All the bedrooms of the Hôtel William's du Pré enjoy a lovely view of the gardens. Decorated in shades of pink or blue, depending on the floor, the rooms have tinted furniture, with beds and drapes in coordinated, floral cotton-satin; the decor may not be remarkable, but the rooms are comfortable. Those on the *deuxième* and *cinquième étages* open onto a balcony, and the higher up you are, the better your view of the Square. The breakfast room in the basement is where you'll be served a delicious buffet. Note that there is a public parking lot just in front of the hotel, an added plus.

Hôtel Libertel Champagne Mulhouse

87, boulevard de Strasbourg
75010 Paris
Tel. (0)1 42 09 12 28 - Fax (0)1 42 09 48 12
M. Delahaye

Category ★★ **Rooms** 31 (1 floor for non-smokers) with soundproofing, telephone, bath or shower, WC, hairdryer, cable TV. **Price** Single 510F, double 570F. **Meals** Breakfast (buffet) 45F, served 7:00-10:30. **Credit cards** Amex, Visa, Eurocard, MasterCard. **Pets** Dogs allowed. **Facilities** Elevator, room-service. **Parking** Gare de l'Est. **How to get there** (Map 4): Bus: 31, 38, 39 - Metro and rail station: Gare de l'Est. **Open** All year.

On the forlorn Boulevard de Strasbourg in front of the Gare de l'Est train station (and métro stop), this hotel has a discrete entrance behind the terraces of the *brasseries* surrounding it. Several stairways, one with a beautiful sculptured-oak railing, lead to the reception area. Inside, every effort has been made to make you forget the drab street. In the small reception lounge, the carpet by the American designer Hilton McConnico, the sofa, and the armchairs are in bright shades of cherry red, carmine, vermillion, and orange, while the breakfast room is decorated in bold shades of green, lavender blue, and turquoise. The bedrooms are equally cheerful, with yellow or almond-green striped fabrics and bedspreads in floral chintz or tartan cotton; they are very comfortable for a two-star hotel, and have practical, pivoting reading lamps and cable television. The bathrooms are well-equiped with toiletries and come with hair dryers. The copious breakfast buffet and good value make this recently opened hotel an even more attractive place to stay.

Hôtel Libertel Terminus Nord

12, boulevard de Denain
75010 Paris
Tel. (0)1 42 80 20 00 - Fax (0)1 42 80 63 89
M. Picaud

Category ★★★ **Rooms** 236 (1 floor for non-smokers) with soundproofing, telephone, bath, WC, TV satellite, safe - 4 for disabled persons. **Price** Single 985F, double 1050F, "prestige room" 1600F. Extra bed 150F. **Meals** Breakfast (buffet): 75F, served 6:30-10:30. **Credit cards** All major. **Pets** Small dogs allowed. **Facilities** Elevator, Laundry service, secretariat, room service (24 h/24). **Parking** Gare du Nord. **How to get there** (Map 4): Bus: 26, 42, 43, 49 - Metro, RER and rail station: Gare du Nord. **Open** All year.

One of the most beautiful monuments in Paris, the Gare du Nord Train station has become the crossroads of northern Europe with the opening of the Channel Tunnel and the Eurostar Paris-London train. This undoubtedly explains the large numbers of English people who frequent the Terminus Nord, which is just in front of the station and next to the famous, glittering *Brasserie Terminus Nord* (oyster lovers shouldn't miss it). This is a hotel in the grand style, with porters and bellboys to greet you, and courteous, polyglot receptionists behind the large desk. The huge lobby is very Art Nouveau with its skylight, the original stained glass that was discovered when the hotel was last renovated, and large yuccas. It opens onto several lounges. The bar, the private lounges, and the breakfast room are on the *premier étage*. Employing an extraordinary variety of fabrics and colors which are artistically coordinated, the decor throughout is both sumptuous and comfortable. The bedrooms and suites are exquisite: quilted, floral chintz in shades of red, dark-wood furniture in some and painted furniture with white and blue fabrics in others. Our favorite rooms are those on the *quatrième étage* and up, with a view over the great neoclassical caryatids of the Gare du Nord. The bathrooms, which are still their original size, are all beautiful and comfortable.

Hôtel Beaumarchais

3, rue Oberkampf
75011 Paris
Tel. (0)1 53 36 86 86 - Fax (0)1 43 38 32 86
M. Alain Quintard

Category ★★ **Rooms** 33 with soundproofing (28 with air-conditioning), telephone, bath or shower, WC, hairdryer, TV satellite, safe. **Price** Single 290-350F, double 390-450F. **Meals** Breakfast 35F, served 7:00-11:00. **Credit cards** Amex, Visa, Eurocard, MasterCard. **Pets** Dogs allowed. **Facilities** Elevator, patio, room-service. **Parking** Private (30 m). **How to get there** (Map 8): Bus: 20, 96 - Metro: Oberkampf, Filles-du-Calvaire. **Open** All year.

Not far from the Cirque d'Hiver (Winter Circus), the small white facade of the Hôtel Beaumarchais conceals a very pleasant discovery. An architect recently converted into a hotelier, Alain Quintard wanted to maintain the extremely reasonable prices of the establishment but also to offer a good level of comfort and an attractive decor; and he did just that. The reception lounge and breakfast room open straight onto a flowery patio, and they show a pronounced taste for the South (coatings in red-ochre stucco, bright colors and so on) and contemporary art. The rooms retain a bit of this bright style and are well-maintained and always simple. However, they offer services rare for a 'two-star' hotel such as air-conditioning, private safes, hairdryers, etc. The shower rooms however, are sometimes poorly designed. No major faults however, and at these prices one would still excuse them, while the welcome is friendly and very attentive.

Home Plazza Saint-Antoine

289, rue du Faubourg Saint-Antoine
75011 Paris
Tel. (0)1 40 09 40 00 – Fax (0)1 40 09 11 55
Mme Valérie Thromat

Category ★★★ **Rooms** 89 with soundproofing, telephone, bath, WC, hairdryer (on request), cable TV, minibar, safe, kitchenette - 2 for disabled persons. **Price** Single 447-787F, double 454-894F, triples and 4-5 pers. 740-1508F. **Meals** Breakfast (buffet): 65F, served 7:00-10:00. **Credit cards** All major. **Pets** Dogs allowed (80F). **Facilities** Elevator, laundry service, patio. **Parking** On site (95F/day). **How to get there** Bus: 86 - Metro and RER: Nation. **Open** All year.

This is the perfect spot for those wishing to spend a long time in the capital, or for families as rooms can be transformed into private apartments for four to five people. Whatever their size, all are equipped with a kitchenette, refrigerator, hot plates, a microware, dishes, and a breakfast nook. The largest also have a small living room with a pull-out couch and bunk beds. All rooms are identically furnished and there is a delightful courtyard garden. The staff is always at your service, and will greet you in the large, light, reception area, furnished with chairs and decorated with engravings and a large painting by Bernard Buffet. The family-oriented Home Plazza is a practical place to stay.

Hôtel Libertel Croix de Malte

5, rue de Malte
75011 Paris
Tel. (0)1 48 05 09 36 – Fax (0)1 43 57 02 54
Mlle Stéphanie Biagini

Category ** **Rooms** 29 with soundproofing, telephone, bath or shower, WC, cable TV - 1 for disabled persons. **Price** Single 480F, double 540F. **Meals** Breakfast (buffet): 45F, served 7:00-10.30. **Credit cards** Amex, Visa, Eurocard, MasterCard. **Pets** Dogs not allowed. **Facilities** Elevator, bar, safe at reception. **Parking** At place de la République. **How to get there** (Map 8): Bus: 46, 56, 96 - Metro: Oberkampf, Filles-du-Calvaire. **Open** All year.

The hotel is sited on one of the three sections making up the Rue de Malte, between Rue Oberkampf and Boulevard Voltaire. The rooms are split between two small buildings, each facing a veranda framed by two small courtyards painted with an attractive decor of tropical forests in 'trompe l'oeil'. Drinks from the bar are served here along with breakfast, but do not leave it too late as the buffet is not always fully restocked. The whole hotel rather smacks of the exotic as shown by the colored reproductions by Wallace Ting. In the blue and white area with its elevator, the rooms are rather standard and not very large, but they are well thought-out and always come with a small desk and well-equipped bathrooms. In the other building, with two floors but no elevator, there is the same decor but in green and orange. In the rooms on the upper floor, the bathrooms are reached by a rather steep spiral staircase. They have mansard ceilings and charm, but one needs to be quite agile all the same. Rooms on the ground floor open onto the small courtyards. This is an attractive hotel with attractive prices as well.

Hôtel Belle Époque

66, rue de Charenton
75012 Paris
Tel. (0)1 43 44 06 66 - Fax (0)1 43 44 10 25
Mme Isabelle Frouin

Category ★★★ **Rooms** 30 with air-conditioning, soundproofing, telephone, bath, WC, hairdryer, TV satellite, safe, minibar. **Price** Single 576-766F, double 607-772F, triple 568-818F, junior-suite 812-1024F. **Meals** Breakfast (buffet) 70F, served 7:00-11:00. **Credit cards** All major. **Pets** Dogs allowed. **Facilities** Elevator, bar, patio. **Parking** At rue du Faubourg-Saint-Antoine. **How to get there** (Map 2 and 8): Bus: 28, 29, 63, 65, 91 - Metro: Ledru-Rollin, Bastille - RER and Rail station (TGV): gare de Lyon. **Open** All year.

Just five minutes from the Place de la Bastille, the Hôtel Belle Epoque is completely dedicated to the 'Art Deco' style. The reception area gives onto a small green courtyard with some tables in summertime for the breakfast brunch. The bar is just next door. The rooms are in a 1900s-style while the furniture is 1930's copies, with the best found in the *"chambre d'époque"* suite with a bed, wardrobe and chairs in the Printz style. The others are more sober and recall the furniture of Ruhlman. All are large enough and have marble bathrooms, while some also have small balconies. It is better to sleep on the courtyard side but the double-glazing and air-conditioning in the suites will cut out any noise from the street.

Hôtel Claret

44, boulevard de Bercy
75012 Paris
Tel. (0)1 46 28 41 31 - Fax (0)1 49 28 09 29
M. Le Marec

Category ★★★ **Rooms** 52 with telephone, bath or shower, WC, TV satellite. **Price** Single 390-550F, double 600-650F, triple 800F. **Meals** Breakfast 50F, served 7:00-10:00. **Credit cards** All major. **Pets** Dogs allowed. **Facilities** Elevator, laundry service, safe at reception, bar. **Restaurant** with terrace - Menu: 68-100F, also à la carte. **Parking** Private with 5 places (50F per day) and public parking at 100 m. **How to get there** (Map 11): Bus: 24, 87 - Metro: Bercy - RER and rail station (TGV): gare de Lyon (300 m). **Open** All year.

The Bercy quarter has been totally transformed but it should be stressed that the district does not make the Claret a hotel best-suited for tourists. But its very closeness to the Gare de Lyon, the All-Sports hall (Palais Omnisports) of Bercy and the new French National Library (Bibliothèque Nationale de France) could prove convenient. In earlier times Bercy welcomed many *'négociants en vin'*, which is why each hotel room has the name of a vineyard. All have water-color paintings and stencilled friezes on the cupboards representing grapes and vines. Their decor is all much the same, but the rooms are comfortable, with good beds and bedding and a corner for writing. On the top floor they are much larger but a little darker. Reserve a room at the back where you can enjoy some greenery, while those on the front just look over the railway lines. Breakfast is served in the hotel restaurant, La Villa Romaine, which offers Italian cuisine served on the terrace in summertime.

Nouvel Hôtel

24, avenue du Bel-Air
75012 Paris
Tel. (0)1 43 43 01 81 – Fax (0)1 43 44 64 13
M. and Mme Marillier

Category ** **Rooms** 28 with soundproofing, telephone, 4 with bath, 24 with shower, WC, TV. **Price** Single 370-390F, double 390-560F. **Meals** Breakfast 40F, served 7:00-10:30. **Credit cards** All major. **Pets** Dogs allowed. **Facilities** Garden, patio. **Parking** Garage Renault: 24, avenue de Saint-Mandé (100m). **How to get there** (Map 8): Bus: 29, 56, 86 and 351 for terminal Roissy-Charles-de-Gaulle - Metro and RER: Nation. **Open** All year.

From the very ordinary façade of this small hotel, you would never know just how charming it is. Near the reception area, there is a small, countrified lunch room with pretty table linens and floral wallpaper brightened by a beautiful freize with fruit motifs. A labyrinth of corridors with lovely pale-green cane chairs leads to the cheerful, cozy bedrooms, which are decorated with beautiful Laura Ashley fabrics. Some rooms overlook the street, but most overlook the garden and its climbing plants, or the rooftops. Our favorite is Number 109, where guests have direct access to the garden and almost total privacy once the breakfast service there is finished. This is also the room in the greatest demand, although all have their own charm. We should add that breakfast, which includes cheese, orange juice, and preserves, is delicious, which is not always the case in an inexpensive two-star hotel. The Nouvel Hôtel is on a broad, quiet avenue off the bustling Place de la Nation.

Hotel Paris Bastille

67, rue de Lyon
75012 Paris
Tel. (0)1 40 01 07 17 – Fax (0)1 40 01 07 27
Mme Frouin

Category ★★★ **Rooms** 36 with air-conditioning, soundproofing, telephone, bath, WC, hairdryer, TV satellite, minibar, safe - 2 for disabled persons. **Price** Single and double 576-772F, junior-suite (2-4 pers.) 950-1350F.**Meals** Breakfast 55F, buffet 70F, served 7:00-11:00. **Credit cards** All major. **Pets** Dogs allowed. **Facilities** Elevator, laundry service, bar, room-service until 22:00. **Parking** At 65, rue de Lyon. **How to get there** (Map 2): Bus: 20, 27, 28, 29, 63, 65, 87, 91 - Metro: Bastille - RER and rail station (TGV): gare de Lyon (300 m). **Open** All year.

Just like its neighbor next door, described on the previous page, the Paris Bastille is just in front of the Bastille Opera, one of the last of the Parisian *'Grands Travaux'*, with its controversial architecture; it has now become the capital's temple of all the lyric arts. The large reception area is very light and opens onto the street; it leads through to the lounge-bar where breakfast is also served. The decor is simple with Japanese panels, light wood furniture and colors declining in shades of grey. You find the same contemporary spirit and colors in the rooms. They are spacious and comfortable with their only fantasy shown in the flowery quilted bedspreads. Such elegant sobriety creates an atmosphere of well-being, while the welcome from the personnel is courteous and very professional.

Hôtel Le Pavillon Bastille

65, rue de Lyon
75012 Paris
Tel. (0)1 43 43 65 65 - Fax (0)1 43 43 96 52
M. and Mme Arnaud - Mme Dubost

Category ★★★ Rooms 25 with air-conditioning, soundproofing, telephone, bath, WC, hairdryer, TV satellite, minibar, safe - 1 for disabled persons. **Price** Single and double 650-955F, suite 1200F. **Meals** Breakfast (buffet) 65F, served at any time; snack availables. **Credit cards** All major. **Pets** Dogs allowed. **Facilities** Elevator, laundry service, courtyard-garden, room-service. **Parking** At 65, rue de Lyon. **How to get there** (Map 2): Bus: 28, 29, 63, 65, 91 - Metro: Bastille - RER and rail station (TGV): gare de Lyon (300m). **Open** All year.

Modernity and efficiency are the two words best qualifying Le Pavillon Bastille, even if the beautiful 17th-century fountain has been conserved in the pretty entry courtyard of the hotel. 'Baroque Modernity' describes the rather aggressive decor in the reception hall, all in contrasting colors, materials and lighting. The rooms are softer and offer all the fittings that you might wish for; international TV, minibar and so on. You find the same style in the bathrooms with very comfortable bath robes provided from the famous House of Porthault. The welcoming team is efficient and offers 24-hour room service. You can also ask the management to reserve your tickets for the Bastille Opera, and profit from all the evening-deals or weekend-deals offered by the hotel. The Bastille district is one of the 'trendy' areas of Paris with its 'avant-garde' galleries (Jousse-Seguin, Durand, and others), restaurants (Café de l'Industrie, Chez Paul) and late-closing cafés.

Résidence Les Gobelins

9, rue des Gobelins
75013 Paris
Tel. (0)1 47 07 26 90 – Fax (0)1 43 31 44 05
M. and Mme Poirier

Category ★★ **Rooms** 32 with bath or shower, WC, telephone, TV. **Price** Single 350-395F, double 395-455F, triple 545F. –10% in August. **Meals** Breakfast 37F. **Credit cards** All major. **Pets** Dogs not allowed. **Facilities** Patio. **Parking** At place d'Italie and rue Censier. **How to get there** (Map 10): Bus: 27, 47, 83, 91 - Metro: Gobelins - RER: Port-Royal. **Open** All year.

Close to the 'Manufacture Royale des Gobelins', the hotel is in a quiet area despite the lively and colorful district. The Rue Mouffetard and its market are close by as well as all the souks, 'hammam' cafés and restaurants surrounding the Paris Mosque. The decoration of the hotel is simple and lively, while the rooms are well maintained and furnished with colored bamboo furniture. The largest can easily take three people and the top-floor rooms have Mansard ceilings. Those facing the courtyard have a view of the garden from the upper floors. Thanks to its large windows the breakfast room looks directly onto the flowery patio covered by a luxurious honeysuckle. Well arranged with its teak furniture and parasols, this would be the ideal spot to relax and take a drink. This is an attractive address but very simple, with particularly carefully thought out rates and a very friendly welcome.

Hôtel Le Vert Galant

41, rue Croulebarbe
75013 Paris
Tel. (0)1 44 08 83 50 – Fax (0)1 44 08 83 69
Mme Laborde

Category ★★★ Rooms 15 with soundproofing, telephone, bath or shower, WC, hairdryer, minibar, cable TV, some with kitchenette - 1 for disabled persons. **Price** Single 400F, double 450-500F. **Meals** Breakfast 40F, served 6:30-11:00. **Credit cards** All major. **Pets** Dogs not allowed. **Facilities** Laundry service, bar, garden. **Restaurant** Menu 100F for readers of this guide; also à la carte. **Parking** Private. **Hout to get there** (Map 10): Bus: 27, 47, 83 - Metro: Gobelins, Corvisart. **Open** All year.

Facing the René Le Gall park and a few paces from the Manufacture des Gobelins, the hotel is next to the excellent Basque auberge, the "Etchegorry", under the same ownership. From the entrance one notes the pretty garden onto which all the rooms face from both ground and first floors. Of a pleasant size, all are comfortable and fitted out very elegantly. Decorated in the same style, they offer varying tones, but always very soft with the dominant color found even in the little knots attaching the pillow bolster ties. The most expensive have discreetly concealed small kitchenettes. All the colors have been chosen with care, with small carpets or rugs and reproductions of Impressionist works hanging almost everywhere in the house. Breakfasts are taken in the reception area which is fitted out as a winter garden with small bistro tables. A quiet atmosphere reigns here while the charm and excellent price-quality relationship make this address one of our favorites.

Hôtel Aiglon

232, boulevard Raspail
75014 Paris
Tel. (0)1 43 20 82 42 - Fax (0)1 43 20 98 72
M. Jacques Rols

Category ★★★ **Rooms** 47 and 9 suites (some with air-conditioning), with bath or shower, WC, telephone, TV satellite, hairdryer, minibar. **Price** Single and double 490-750F, suites 1030F (2 pers). Extra bed +120F. **Meals** Breakfast 35F, served 7:00- 11:00. **Credit cards** All major. **Pets** Dogs allowed. **Facilities** Elevator, individual safes at reception, bar, laundry service. **Parking** In the hotel (8-car - 80F/day) or boulevard Edgar-Quinet. **How to get there** (Map 10): Bus: 68, 91 - Metro: Raspail. **Open** All year.

In front of the Montparnasse Cemetery, on the corner of the Raspail and Edgar Quinet Boulevards, the Aiglon is a comfortable hotel near the great *brasseries* dating from this neighborhood's Golden Age. Empire style was chosen for the reception areas, with mahogany woodwork, green leather and gilt interlacing motifs, and period furniture. The lobby, lounge, library/bar, and beautiful dining room reflect the same style. Classic inspiration can also be seen in the bedroom decor, with custom-made cherrywood or burl furniture, headboards in the shape of an ancient pediment (in some rooms), and, in the most recent bedrooms (our favorites), a charming assortment of green and yellow fabrics. The rooms are bright and tasteful, and have the requisite double-glazing for this busy area; those on the cemetery side have a better view of trees and greenery. There are lovely suites, and the corner bedrooms are charmingly arranged. The prices are reasonable, and even the least expensive rooms are attractive.

Hôtel de Bretagne Montparnasse

33, rue Raymond Losserand
75014 Paris
Tel. (0)1 45 38 52 59 - Fax (0)1 45 38 50 39
Jean-Luc Houdré

Category ★★★ **Rooms** 44 with soundproofing, telephone, bath or shower, WC, hairdryer, cable TV, minibar. **Price** Single 500-650F, double 550-700F, triple 650-800F, suite 750-900F. **Meals** Breakfast (buffet) 45F, served 5:30-11:30. **Credit cards** All major. **Pets** Dogs allowed. **Facilities** Elevator, bar, laundry service, room-service (24h/24). **Parking** Gaîté. **How to get there** (Map 10): Bus: 28, 58 and Air France Montparnasse - Metro: Pernety, Gaîté - Rail station (TGV): gare Montparnasse. **Open** All year.

The Hôtel de Bretagne's modern, prim decor brightened with warm colors includes a small sienna lounge with Le Corbusier black leather sofas and armchairs, a honey-colored carpet. Elegant bedrooms come with yellow-, orange- and blue-striped fabrics, straw-yellow wall upholstery, and lovely colors in the modern baths. Most rooms are a good size, and the largest have a sofa bed. Avoid the ground-floor rooms, which are small and dark. Breakfasts are served in a barrel-vaulted basement room, with pretty oval tables and small, modern chairs. The hotel is near the Montparnasse TGV train station and the new business districts.

Hôtel Broussais - Bon Secours

3, rue Ledion
75014 Paris
Tel. (0)1 40 44 48 90 – Fax. (0)1 40 44 96 76
M. Michaël Robb

Category ★★ **Rooms** 25 and 1 suite, with soundproofing, shower, WC, telephone, TV. **Price** Single 240F (195F the weekend and 180F in August), double 280F (210F in August) suite (3-4 pers.) 480F. **Meals** Breakfast 30F, served 7:00-11:00. **Credit cards** All major. **Pets** Small dogs allowed. **Facilities** Safe at reception, patio. **Parking** Porte d'Orléans, 36, rue Friant. **How to get there** (Map 10): Bus: 58, 62, PC - Metro: Alésia, Plaisance. **Open** All year.

You cannot imagine our happy surprise when we discovered that the discreet Rue Ledion sheltered a small hotel just as confidential. Fully renovated from the bathrooms through to the sound-proofing, and also including the bedding, carpets and everything else needed to make a hotel clean and attractive, the Broussais has refound its youth. The small rooms with their light-colored walls now have very simple white furniture with little extras including prints, lighting and pretty duvets. All is young, fresh, without pretention and well maintained. The breakfast room has been decorated in bistro-style but in fine weather you can enjoy the pleasure of eating outside on the small patio-terrace. A little off the center, the hotel is however well served for Montparnasse, Saint-Germain-des-Prés and even the Porte de Versailles exhibition center. The welcome is friendly and this is one of our lowest price hotels in the capital.

Hôtel Delambre

35, rue Delambre
75014 Paris
Tel. (0)1 43 20 66 31 – Fax (0)1 45 38 91 76
M. Patrick Kalmy

Category ★★★ **Rooms** 30 and 1 suite with soundproofing, telephone, bath or shower, WC, hairdryer, TV satellite, safe - 1 for disabled persons. **Price** Single and double 440-490F, suite (4 pers.) 650F. **Meals** Breakfast (buffet) 38F, served 7:30-10:30. **Credit cards** Visa, Eurocard, Mastercard, Amex. **Pets** Dogs allowed. **Facilities** Elevator, laundry service, bar. **Parking** Tour Montparnasse, boulevard Edgar-Quinet. **How to get there** (Map 10): Bus: 28, 48, 58, 68, 82, 91, 92, 94, 95, 96 - Metro: Vavin, Edgar-Quinet, Montparnasse - Rail station (TGV): gare Montparnasse. **Open** All year.

Difficult not to be attracted by this small hotel entirely renovated in 1996 by the architect–decorator, Jean–Philippe Nuel. For each room he chose cerused beech furniture with curving lines wrought iron work enhancing the straw yellow of the walls, while the flecked carpeting and fabrics are mainly in the blues and in brick red. The bathrooms are clear and smooth and just as impeccable. All the rooms are pleasant but if you reserve in good time, you should ask for number 7 for its size and private terrace. Numbers 1 and 2 are recommended in the summer for their small, private, equipped courtyards. The hall-lounge and breakfast room are in the image of the rest of the house, which means comfortable, cosseted and warm. The fine overall effect thus once again proves to us that charming hotels really do exist in Paris at reasonable prices, well situated and well planned.

Hôtel Istria

29, rue Campagne-Première
75014 Paris
Tel. (0)1 43 20 91 82 - Fax (0)1 43 22 48 45
Danièle and Philippe Leroux

Category ★★ **Rooms** 26 with bath or shower, WC, telephone, TV, hairdryer, safe. **Price** Single 470F, double 540-580F. Special rates in low season. **Meals** Breakfast 40F, served 7:00-10:00. **Credit cards** All major. **Pets** Dogs allowed. **Facilities** Elevator, drink service. **Parking** Boulevard du Montparnasse (150 m). **How to get there** (Map 10): Bus: 68, 83, 91 - Metro: Raspail. **Open** All year.

On a quiet street just off crowded Montparnasse with its cinemas, theatres, and famous *brasseries,* this small, family-style hotel adjoins a beautiful building occupied by artists' ateliers. The hotel's lovely reception area and lounge area are furnished with deep, black-leather sofas, a handsome antique wardrobe, and several African statues. The bedrooms are quite sober, with Korean straw on the walls, rustic burl headboards, small desks and wardrobes, quilted bedspreads with colorful motifs, and Japanese lamps. Even though the bedrooms are rather small (those on the street are larger), you will be comfortable here, especially as the rooms are bright, very well kept, and have beautiful new bathrooms. Some rooms, located in a small house, open onto the patio at ground level; they are quiet but rather dark. Breakfasts are served in a barrel-vaulted room in the basement.

Hôtel de l'Orchidée

65, rue de l'Ouest
75014 Paris
Tel. (0)1 43 22 70 50 - Fax (0)1 42 79 97 46
M. and Mme Mollière

Category ★★★ Rooms 40 with soundproofing, telephone, bath or shower, WC, hairdryer on request, cable TV - 2 for disabled persons. **Price** Single 456-556F, double 502-602F, triple 608-708F. **Meals** Breakfast 35F, served 7:00-12:00. **Credit cards** All major. **Pets** Dogs not allowed. **Facilities** Elevator, laundry service, garden, safe at reception, bar, room-service, sauna, whirl-pool. **Parking** Private. **How to get there** (Map 10): Bus: 28, 58, 91 - Metro: Pernety. **Open** All year.

The "Orchid" hotel stands on a small, tree-lined square near the Montparnasse high-speed train (TGV) station. Red awnings brighten the facade and inside you will find a large, bright lounge and bar with many green plants, a luminous skylight, and bay windows overlooking the garden. There is a new exhibit of paintings here each month. In good weather, it's delightful to have breakfast in the garden. The bright bedrooms are decorated in the same style as the lounge, with salmon, green, or blue cerused bamboo furniture, lovely fabrics, and small, modern baths. Those with numbers ending in 5, 6, or 7 are at the rear, and overlook the garden. The hotel has the added bonuses of a relaxation bathtub and a sauna in the basement.

Hôtel du Parc-Montsouris

4, rue du Parc-Montsouris
75014 Paris
Tel. (0)1 45 89 09 72 - Fax (0)1 45 80 92 72
Mme Piguet - M. Grand

Category ★★ **Rooms** 35 with bath or shower, WC, telephone, TV (2 with TV satellite). **Price** Single and double 330-390F, twins (2-3 pers.) 440F, apartment (2-4 pers.) 500F. **Meals** Breakfast 35F. **Credit cards** Amex, Visa, Eurocard, MasterCard. **Pets** Dogs allowed. **Facilities** Elevator. **Parking** In private road. **How to get there** Bus: 28, 38, 68, PC - Metro: Porte-d'Orléans - RER: Cité Universitaire. Bus for Orly from Porte-d'Orléans. **Open** All year.

While staying in this part of the 16th *Arrondissement* you will discover another aspect of the capital; its quiet cul-de-sacs and 1930's villas, some fine examples from Sauvage, Le Corbusier and Lurçat, as well as two immense parks, the International University City and Parc Montsouris. The hotel has been opened in one of these villas and its columns and Art Deco pictures recall the earlier character of the house. Comfortable but soberly fitted out with standard furniture, the rooms are light and well maintained. Their light walls have numerous reproduction pictures adding to their pleasant atmosphere; we prefer those in the main building where most of them have a view onto Parc Montsouris. No. 633 has a fine panorama over Paris and its monuments. The rooms in the small house behind are bright enough in the summer but seemed rather sombre to us. You should also note the seven apartments with their two communicating rooms, much appreciated by families. This is a hotel where you can be assured of nice quiet nights.

Hôtel Raspail Montparnasse

203, boulevard Raspail – 75014 Paris
Tel. (0)1 43 20 62 86 – Fax (0)1 43 20 50 79
web: http://www.scapades.com/france/paris/raspail.htm
Mme Christiane Martinent

Category ★★★ **Rooms** 36 and 2 suites with air-conditioning, soundproofing, bath or shower, WC, telephone, hairdryer, cable TV, minibar, safe. **Price** Single 520F, double 740-890F, junior-suite 1160F. **Meals** Breakfast 50F. **Credit cards** All major. **Pets** Dogs not allowed. **Parking** At 116, boulevard du Montparnasse. **How to get there** (Map 10): Bus: 68, 82, 83, 91 - Metro: Vavin, Raspail - RER: Port-Royal. **Open** All year.

A little before his death the famous decorator Serge Pons was attracted by this Art Deco hotel and in 1992 he renovated the vast and airy vestibule, with its large rounded bay windows and ceilings lined with fine geometrical mouldings. He opened up the monumental staircase, renovated the corner lounge-bar, and had the superb coat of arms on the facade reworked. The rooms with pretty bathrooms have a studied decor, and their furniture is inspired by the 1930's. All have the name of and a fine reproduction by some painter who lived in Montparnasse, and each floor has its own color scheme. You move from blue, very successful, through sienna, very warm, while passing through the creams and greys; the third floor, recently renovated, displays an elegant harmony of green and beige. You should note the corner rooms which are particularly large with their three windows. Other qualities to be stressed are efficient sound-proofing and a professional and relaxed welcome in this very "Montparnasse" hotel.

Hôtel de l'Avre

21, rue de l'Avre
75015 Paris
Tel. (0)1 45 75 31 03 – Fax (0)1 45 75 63 26
M. Bernard Vialettes

Category ★★ **Rooms** 26 with soundproofing, telephone, bath or shower, WC, TV, hairdryer - 1 for disabled persons. **Price** Single 310F, double 380-430F, triple 450-490F. **Meals** Breakfast 35F (offered the weekend for readers of this guide), served 7:30-12:00. **Credit cards** All major. **Pets** Small dogs allowed. **Facilities** Elevator, laundry service, garden, safe at reception. **Parking** At 104, rue du Théâtre. **How to get there** (Map 6): Bus: 49, 80 - Metro: La Motte-Picquet-Grenelle. **Open** All year.

Bernard Vialettes bought the Hôtel de l'Avre recently and it is with an obvious pleasure that he receives his guests. He has redone the breakfast room, bought pretty crockery, laid out colored tablecloths and flowered his garden. In the rooms the renovations have also been completed and depending on the floor, the wallpapers are blue (very cheerful), yellow (very light) or even ivory (more classical) while the white piqué bedspreads go well with the pretty curtains. The furniture is sober, the bedding new, the bathrooms impeccable and the general impression very pleasant, and all is irreproachably maintained. The sound-proofed rooms ensure little noise, even in those on the street side. You should note that the garden is bathed in sunlight in the mornings and breakfast is served there in fine weather. This is a haven of peace at low prices, close to the center and the Porte de Versailles exhibition center.

Hôtel du Bailli de Suffren

149, avenue de Suffren – 75015 Paris
Tel. (0)1 47 34 58 61 – Fax (0)1 45 67 75 82
web: http://www.webscapades.com/france/paris/suffren.htm
Mme Tardif

Category ★★★ Rooms 25 with soundproofing, bath or shower, WC, hairdryer, telephone, TV satellite, minibar, safe. **Price** Single 545-670F, double 650-800F, triple 750-840F, apart. 1100-1300F. −15% for weekend (2 nights). **Meals** Breakfast 65F, served 7:00-11:00. Snack availables (75F). **Credit cards** All major. **Pets** Small dogs allowed (+50F). **Facilities** Elevator, laundry service, bar. **Parking** At rue François-Bonvin. **How to get there** (Map 1 and 6): Bus: 28, 39, 92 - Metro: Ségur, Sèvres-Lecourbe. **Open** All year.

In this district of UNESCO, on the boundary of the 15th and 7th *arrondissements*, the hotel has been tastefully renovated on the theme of the Bailli de Suffren. M. and Mme. Tardif opted first to improve comfort and thus renewed most of the bathrooms which are now very functional and well fitted, some having particularly large bathtubs. The rooms are all personalized, warm and comfortable. The new rooms, such as "Versailles" or the "Bailli" suite, have been successfully done, while the older rooms also have their charm and are being renovated as occasion arises. The quietest and brightest are on the courtyard side and certain rooms are convertible into two-room suites ideal for families. The lounge matches the rest of the house, both refined and prettily furnished. You find here all the newspapers and magazines and all the discreet attention of the owners, ready to make your stay as happy as possible. It is no surprise that both service and welcome are faultless.

Hôtel Charles Quinze

37, rue Saint-Charles / 36-38, rue Rouelle
75015 Paris
Tel. (0)1 45 79 64 15 - Fax (0)1 45 77 21 11
M. and Mme Fournerie

Category ★★ **Rooms** 30 with soundproofing, telephone, bath or shower, WC, hairdryer, cable TV, minibar. **Price** Single 425F, double 505-520F, triple 670F. **Meals** Breakfast 45F, served 7:00-10:30. **Credit cards** All major. **Pets** Dogs allowed. **Facilities** Elevator, laundry service, patio. **Parking** Beaugrenelle (rue Linois). **How to get there** (Map 6): Bus: 42 - Metro: Dupleix, Charles-Michels. **Open** All year.

A stone's throw from the Front de Seine business complex, the Charles Quinze is a lovely small, hotel. In the bedroom, you will find honey-colored English-pine furniture, and, depending on the floor, either yellow, blue, or pink fabrics, textured wallpaper and tiled friezes in the white bathrooms. Breakfasts are served in a basement room decorated in the same spirit, with Haitian primitive paintings on the walls; in good weather, the small patio with pretty plants is where breakfast is served. The lounge is charming, with beautiful blue sofas and armchairs. This comfortable, quiet, reasonably priced hotel is near the Eiffer Tower.

Hôtel Fondary

30, rue Fondary
75015
Tel. (0)1 45 75 14 75 – Fax (0)1 45 75 84 42
M. Bosson

Category ★★ **Rooms** 21 with telephone, bath or shower, WC, TV, minibar. **Price** Single and double 385-405F. –10% for the weekends and in July-August. **Meals** Breakfast 38F, served 7:00-10:00. **Credit cards** Amex, Visa, Eurocard, MasterCard. **Pets** Small dogs allowed. **Facilities** Elevator, laundry service, bar, patio, safe at reception. **Parking** Garage de la Poste (104, rue du théâtre). **How to get there** (Map 6): Bus: 80 - Metro: Émile-Zola, La Motte-Picquet-Grenelle. **Open** All year.

Behind La Motte-Picquet and not far from the Parc des Expositions at Porte de Versailles, the Fondary is a simple, economical hotel with small, beautifully kept bedrooms, many with rattan furniture; the bathrooms are pleasant. The bedrooms at the back overlook a small courtyard; those on the street (it's fairly quiet) are slightly larger. The large room downstairs is divided into a reception area, a small corner lounge, and the breakfast room/bar; a small flower-filled veranda opening onto the patio will be opened in the spring. The hotel is convenient to public transportation.

Hôtel Montcalm

50, avenue Félix-Faure
75015 Paris
Tel. (0)1 45 54 97 27 - Fax (0)1 45 54 15 05
Mme Taillère

Category ✴✴✴ **Rooms** 40 and 1 suite with bath or shower, WC, telephone, TV satellite, minibar, safe - 1 for disabled persons. **Price** Single 420-610F, double 490-710F, family-suite 860-1200F. **Meals** Breakfast (buffet) 52F. **Credit cards** All major. **Pets** Small dogs allowed. **Facilities** Elevator, garden, laundry service. **Parking** 50 meters. (80F/day). **How to get there** (Map 9): Bus 42, 62, 70 - Metro: Boucicaut - RER: Javel-André-Citroën. **Open** All year.

Not far from the Parc des Expositions at the Porte de Versailles, the Montcalm has a tasteful brick and stone facade. Beyond the small entrance hall and the comfortable lounge, is a lovely veranda with rattan furniture, and a ravishing garden, with hydrangeas, large basins overflowing with flowers, soft carpets of green plants, and a magnolia tree– the perfect spot to relax and enjoy a drink. The small house set in the garden is ideal for families. The sizeable bedrooms are identically decorated with old-pink fabric on the walls, printed navy curtains, and ash furniture and woodwork. We prefer the rooms overlooking the garden, particularly charming Room 4 on the ground floor. The bathrooms are lovely (though some of the ash shelves are difficult to keep clean), as is the wood-paneled cellar dining room looking onto the garden.

Hôtel Pasteur

33, rue du Docteur-Roux
75015
Tel. (0)1 47 83 53 17 - Fax (0)1 45 66 62 39
Mme Michelet

Category ★★ Rooms 19 with telephone, bath or shower, WC, hairdryer, cable TV, 16 with minibar, 12 with safe. **Price** Single 320-390F, double 320-450F, 4 pers. 660F. **Meals** Breakfast 40F, served 7:00-12:00. **Credit cards** Visa, Eurocard, MasterCard. **Pets** Dogs allowed (+20F). **Facilities** Elevator. **Parking** Rue Falguière. **How to get there** (Map 9 and 10): Bus: 39, 48, 70, 95 - Metro: Pasteur, Volontaires. **Open** All year except in Aug.

This small hotel is named after the Pasteur Institute on the same street. The bedrooms and baths are small and very simple but well-kept, and there are modern amenities. The decor is nothing to write home about, the tones are often autumnal and the rooms have all the necessary comforts, while number 22 is also very large. In good weather, you'll find the main attraction of the hotel outside in the garden, with its umbrellas and chaise longues, a delightful spot to read or enjoy a drink. The hotel is convenient if you want to be near the Porte de Versailles, and the prices are reasonable—something of a rarity in Paris. Don't miss a visit to the Pasteur Museum, which is in Louis Pasteur's apartment in the Pasteur Institute.

Hôtel Tour Eiffel - Dupleix

11, rue Juge
75015 Paris
Tel. (0)1 45 78 29 29 - Fax (0)1 45 78 60 00
M. Ruchaud

Category ★★ **Rooms** 40 with soundproofing, telephone, bath or shower, WC, hairdryer, cable TV. **Price** Single and double 480-670F. In low season: 390-580F. **Meals** Breakfast (buffet) 43F. **Credit cards** All major. **Pets** Dogs allowed (+50F). **Facilities** Elevator, laundry service, safe at reception, patio. **Parking** At hotel. **How to get there** (Map 6): Bus: 42 - Metro: Dupleix. **Open** All year.

This hotel has just opened its doors in a lively quarter close to the new "Front de Seine" buildings and UNESCO. Fully in the spirit of the times, everything is new, smooth and fitted out with an appreciable eye for details and natural materials. The breakfast room is pleasantly decorated in a bistro style with its yellow walls, light wood parquet floor and generously wide windows opening on to a patio, where tables and chairs are of course set out in good weather. The reception area has a small lounge alongside with its wicker-work chairs and little tables. As for the rooms, even if they have all been decorated in an identical way with ivory walls, fabrics in blue tones and polished wood furniture, they are not at all standardized or impersonal. Often small, with those on the sixth floor generally larger, they are bright, well maintained and comfortable. Prices are reasonable and the welcome and services professional.

Villa Toscane

36–38, rue des Volontaires
75015 Paris
Tel. (0)1 43 06 82 92 - Fax (0)1 40 56 33 23
Mlle Christelle Le Mentec

Rooms 7 with telephone, showed, WC, TV, hairdryer, safe. **Price** Single 380F, double 480F. **Meals** Breakfast 49F, served 7:30-10:30. **Credit cards** Visa, Eurocard, MasterCard. **Pets** Dogs allowed. **Restaurant** Italian - Menu 130F, also à la carte (around 200F). **Parking** François-Bonvin. **How to get there** (Map 9): Bus: 39, 70, 89 - Metro: Volontaires.**Open** All year.

The road still preserves its old paving stones, the street is quiet while its alignment of one- or two-story buildings gives it a very soothing atmosphere. La Villa Toscane is no exception to this rule and one enters the reception area via some small steps serving both hotel and restaurant. Making a virtue of the narrowness of the house, Christelle Le Mentec has made this a most intimate place and in the small dining rooms, tables and chairs are found in the smallest corners. Upstairs the seven rooms are in the same style, rather small but cosy and amply decorated with heavy-design fabrics. They all have a 1930's chest of drawers or dressing table, a copper bedstead covered by yellow or red quilts, and all their bathrooms are stylish. Sampling excellent Italian cuisine here is undeniably one more extra. What more to say but that the welcome is extremely friendly, while the very favorable prices make La Villa Toscane an address to discover.

Hôtel Alexander

102, avenue Victor Hugo
75116 Paris
Tel. (0)1 45 53 64 65 – Fax (0)1 45 53 12 51
M. Christian Cartier

Category ★★★★ **Rooms** 60 and 2 suites with bath or shower, WC, telephone, cable TV, minibar.
Price Single 840-1100F, double 1210-1320F, suite 1890F. Extra bed 200F. Special rates in
low season (December to February and August). –15% for the readers of this guide. **Meals**
Breakfast (buffet) 80F. Snack availables. **Credit cards** All major. **Pets** Dogs not allowed.
Facilities Elevator, small garden, laundry service, room-service. **Parking** Avenue Victor-
Hugo (50 m). **How to get there** (Map 6): Bus: 52, 82 - Metro: Victor-Hugo - RER: Charles-
de-Gaulle-Étoile - RER and bus for Airport Roissy. **Open** All year.

Supremely classic, the Alexandre is a small, four-star hotel that is
elegant without being ostentatious. The beautiful lobby is entirely
paneled in natural oak, a handsome reproduction of 18th-century
woodwork. The sitting areas are adorned with Louis XV chairs, crystal
wall sconces, mirrors, and soft carpets with floral motifs. They are
delicious places to enjoy a drink, as is the adjacent garden. Many
bedrooms are done in a beige-salmon color, offset with white moldings,
and have Louis XV and Louis XVI furniture (with one or two
contemporary exceptions). In some rooms, the seats and chairs are
covered in pink velvet, which is coordinated with the drapes and
bedspreads, while others are decorated with predominantly pink and
green chintz. All rooms are spacious, and many overlook several
neighboring gardens. (The loveliest rooms are Numbers 105, 123, 142,
152, 161, and 182.) Each morning, guests are pampered with a new
variation on the delicious breakfast.

Hôtel Ambassade

79, rue Lauriston
75116 Paris
Tel. (0)1 45 53 41 15 – Fax (0)1 45 53 30 80
M. Mullie

Category ★★ **Rooms** 38 with telephone, shower, WC, hairdryer, TV satellite. **Price** Single 405-480F, double 520-580F. Weekends: –10%. **Meals** Breakfast 45F, served 7:00-10:30. **Credit cards** All major. **Pets** Small dogs allowed. **Facilities** Elevator, laundry service, safe at reception. **Parking** Avenue Kléber. **How to get there** (Map 6): Bus: 22, 30, 52, 82 - Metro: Boissière, Victor-Hugo. **Open** All year.

Midway between the Place de l'Etoile and the Trocadero, you will find the Hôtel Ambassade, an attractive accommadation well run by a lively manageress wanting to prove that one can still find charm in a 'two-star' hotel. Certainly space is in rather short supply and the few tables in the reception area double for breakfast use. The rooms are not large and only have showers, but the decor is pleasant : the colors are soft, the prints discreet and the bedspreads well chosen. One tip, however; avoid the ground floor rooms as they are too close to the street, as a general rule reserve those on the courtyard. The welcome is both smiling and friendly.

Au Palais de Chaillot Hôtel

35, avenue Raymond-Poincaré
75116 Paris
Tel. (0)1 53 70 09 09 – Fax (0)1 53 70 09 08
Thierry and Cyrille Pien

Category ★★ **Rooms** 28 with soundproofing, telephone, bath or shower, WC, hairdryer, TV satellite. **Price** Single 450F, double 520-590F, triple 690F. **Meals** Breakfast 39F, served 7:00-11:00. **Credit cards** All major. **Pets** Dogs not allowed. **Facilities** Elevator, laundry service, safe at reception. **Parking** 50m. **How to get there** (Map 6): Bus: 22, 30, 32, 63 - Metro: Trocadéro, Victor-Hugo. **Open** All year.

This hotel was entirely renovated right down to the smallest detail and has now reopened its doors. Right in the middle of a business district and a few paces from the Trocadero and numerous museums, this is a place that will appeal to those appreciating comfort as much as simplicity, and who insist that a reasonable price should not preclude tasteful decor. The rooms are pleasantly arranged with navy blue carpeting against a background of yellow walls, white and blue bathrooms, and ox-blood red furniture specially designed for the hotel. A large number of the rooms face the avenue but those doubtful about the real efficiency of double-glazing can always ask for one at the back. The ground floor is where breakfast is served and it has received the same care and innovative decoration. Everywhere the inspiration has come from the south with some exotic features and a few references from the 1930's. As for the welcome, it is youthful and really friendly while this is also one of the best price-quality deals in the capital.

Hôtel Boileau

81, rue boileau
75016 Paris
Tel. (0)1 42 88 83 74 – Fax (0)1 45 27 62 98
M. Mahé Guirec

Category ★★ **Rooms** 30 (some with soundproofing) with telephone, bath or shower, WC, cable TV. **Price** Single 370F, double 430F, triple 550F. In August: –30%. **Meals** Breakfast 35F, served 7:00-10:00. **Credit cards** All major. **Pets** Dogs allowed. **Facilities** Bar, laundry service, safe at reception, room-service. **Parking** Avenue de Versailles. **How to get there** (Map 9): Bus: 22, 62, 72, PC - Metro: Exelmans. **Open** All year.

We appreciate the Hôtel Boileau for the convivial atmosphere found here thanks to Mahé Guirec, the young owner and all his team. We also like the warmth of the ground floor area where family furniture, pictures and other objects give a 'lived-in' feel. You enter first into the reception area and its corner lounge, then the bar and the very attractive and airy breakfast room lit from the patio. You cannot enter the latter but it forms an integral part of the decor. There are thirty rooms but for the moment we would only recommend those which have been fully or partially renovated, often with all-new bathrooms. They have matching wallpapers and fabrics, and some have cerused oak furniture. On our last visit these were rooms 101, 103, 121, 211, 212, 222, 224, 231, 232 and 234, but since then others have certainly been refurbished. The situation is quiet, the rates are reasonable and Oscar, the house parrot, will not fail to liven up the breakfast conversation.

Hôtel du Bois

11, rue du Dôme - 75116 Paris
Tel. (0)1 45 00 31 96 - Fax (0)1 45 00 90 05
e-mail: hoteldubois@wanadoo.fr
M. Byrne - M. Tarron

Category ★★★ **Rooms** 41 with soundproofing, bath or shower, WC, hairdryer, telephone, cable TV, minibar, safe (+10F). **Price** Single 495-525F, double 570-685F. Extra bed 150-160F. **Meals** Breakfast 49F, served 7:30-10:00. **Credit cards** Amex, Visa, Eurocard, MasterCard. **Pets** Dogs allowed. **Facilities** Laundry service, room-service. **Parking** At 34, rue Lauriston. **How to get there** (Map 6): Bus: 22, 30, 31, 52, 73, 92 - Metro: Kléber, Charles-de-Gaulle-Étoile - RER and bus for Roissy-Charles-de-Gaulle. **Open** All year.

A few meters from the Etoile you reach the little Rue du Dôme from the Avenue Victor-Hugo via a flight of steps, which gives a slight air of Montmartre to the area, even though it is in the most classical quarter of them all. The hotel is somewhat British in its style, not really surprising as the manager, Mr Byrne, comes from England. Spring-like fabrics and thick carpeting from across the Channel have been chosen for the room decor, to give them a very soft character, and even though they are not large you always feel at home in them. Some rooms can sleep up to four people, and all are comfortable and sound-proofed to better isolate the hotel from the noise of the major avenues around the Etoile. There is a ravishing lounge which doubles as the breakfast room, facing the reception area, and the welcome is both courteous and friendly. This offers a very good value deal for a hotel of charm in such a favored district.

Résidence Bouquet-de-Longchamp

6, rue du Bouquet-de-Longchamp
75016 Paris
Tel. (0)1 47 04 41 71 - Fax (0)1 47 27 29 09
Mme Tamzali

Category ★★★ Rooms 17 with telephone, bath or shower, WC, hairdryer on request, TV, minibar. **Price** Single 396-566F, double 432-622F. **Meals** Breakfast 50F, served at any time. **Credit cards** All major. **Facilities** Dogs allowed (+30F) - Elevator, laundry service, safe at reception, room-service, served 19:00-2:00. **Parking** At 65, avenue Kléber. **How to get there** (Map 6): Bus: 22, 30, 32, 63, 82 - Metro: Boissière, Iéna, Trocadéro. **Open** All year.

It is by its green shutters and flowering window-boxes that you will recognize this hotel, situated in a small street very close to the Trocadero. From the entry the tone is set, with the beige of the travertin floors matched by the leather of the armchairs, and the silk of the ample curtains marrying well with all the greenery flowing from the window-boxes. Through the wide windows partially veiled by voluminous silk curtains, you can see a pleasant corner lounge sharing the small welcoming hall with reception. There are a lot of bright colors in the rooms, nicely highlighted by the richer shades of the curtains and bedspreads. There's also beige lacquered furniture and beige wall fabrics (with a few exceptions in sky-blue) with small gilt wall-lamps. In the basement, but with a roof-light to encourage the green plants, the breakfast room is very elegant with its comfortable medaillon chairs and watered tones. You should avoid rooms 101 and 105 as they look only onto a blank wall. Prices are reasonable particularly in the low season and the welcome is friendly.

Hôtel Chambellan - Morgane

6, rue Keppler
75116 paris
Tel. (0)1 47 20 35 72 - Fax (0)1 47 20 95 69
Mme Christine de Lapasse

Category ★★★ Rooms 20 with bath or shower, WC, telephone, cable TV, minibar, 11 with hairdryer. **Price** Single and double 650-900F. Special rates in low season and weekends on request. **Meals** Breakfast (buffet) 50F, served 7:00-10:00. **Credit cards** All major. **Pets** Small dogs allowed. **Facilities** Elevator, laundry service, safe at reception, room-service, bar. **Parking** George-V. **How to get there** (Map 6): Bus: 22, 30, 32, 63, 73, 92 - Metro: George-V, Kléber - RER: Charles-de-Gaulle-Étoile - RER and bus for Roissy. **Open** All year.

Just behind Avenue Marceau and close to the Etoile, Rue Keppler is very quiet. You pass through a little hall before entering the Hôtel Chambellan-Morgane itself, where you discover a very pretty lounge with pink and pearl tones, covered with painted worked wood and furnished in the Louis XVI-style. Breakfast from a copious buffet is also served here. The bedrooms are harmonious and more modern with their cerused furniture, 'moiré' on the walls, quilted bedspreads and assorted curtains that are always floral and bright. Very comfortable and light, they are pleasantly sized and have impeccable bathrooms. In addition, whether on the back or even on the street, all are quiet and well sound-proofed. The welcome is very friendly and everything will be done to ease your stay.

Hôtel Étoile Maillot

10, rue du Bois-de-Boulogne
75116 Paris
Tel. (0)1 45 00 42 60 – Fax (0)1 45 00 55 89
M. Delfau

Category ★★★ **Rooms** 27 and 1 suite with soundproofing, telephone, bath or shower, WC, hairdryer, cable TV. **Price** Single 560-680F, double 600-720F, suite 820-860F. **Meals** Breakfast 45F (included some weekends in July and August), served 6:30-11:30. **Credit cards** All major. **Pets** Dogs allowed. **Facilities** Elevator, laundry service, safe at reception. **Parking** Foch, Palais-des-Congrès. **How to get there** (Map 3): Bus: 73 - Metro: Argentine, Porte-Maillot - RER: Charles-de-Gaulle-Étoile, Porte-Maillot. **Open** All year.

On a quiet street between the Arc de Triomphe and the Porte Maillot, this is a traditional hotel with a charming, old-fashioned, wooden elevator. Decent in size, the classic bedrooms have period furniture (mainly Louis XVI or Directoire) and small brass sconces, and each room has different fabrics. On the top floor, rooms have charming Mansard roofs, and corner are illuminated by two large windows. The immaculate bathrooms have modern comforts, and some are quite spacious. Breakfast is served in your room as the ground floor is used only for the reception area and the small lounge.

Hôtel Frémiet - Eiffel

6, avenue Frémiet
75016 Paris
Tel. (0)1 45 24 52 06 - Fax (0)1 42 88 77 46
Mme Fourmond

Category ★★★ **Rooms** 34 (18 with air-conditioning) and 2 suites with bath or shower, WC, telephone, TV, hairdryer, minibar - 1 for disabled persons. **Price** Single 550-750F, double 690-850F, suites 990F (1 pers), 1300F (2pers). Special rates in low season. Extra bed +170F (free for children under 13). **Meals** Breakfast 50F, served 6:30-12:00, snacks avalaible. **Credit cards** All major. **Pets** Dogs allowed. **Facilities** Elevator, laundry service, safe at reception. **Parking** 200m. **How to get there** (Map 6): Bus 32, 72 - Metro: Passy. **Open** All year.

In a neighborhood reminiscent of Montmartre, with its stairs climbing up a steep hill, the Hôtel Frémiet is located in one of the small, very quiet streets built at the turn of the century to connect the quays of the Seine with the Passy hill. Classic and cozy are the key words at the Frémiet, which has 18th-century-style furniture, wood paneling, high molded ceilings, and a beautiful stairway. The bedrooms are elegantly decorated and most have been redone with famous-name fabrics, beautiful carpets, gleaming bathrooms (especially in the newest rooms), and beautiful furniture, some of which has been produced by the owners' daughter, a decorator and designer. The bedrooms are quite cheerful, most are large, and all are immaculate. Guests in the two *Etamine* suites— one decorated in blue, the other in ecru—will enjoy outstanding quality for the price. Note that there are many museums nearby.

Hôtel Garden Élysées

12, rue Saint-Didier
75116 Paris
Tel. (0)1 47 55 01 11 - Fax (0)1 47 27 79 24
Mme Annie Martin

Category ★★★★ **Rooms** 48 with air-conditioning, bath, WC, telephone, TV satellite, hairdryer, minibar, safe - 2 for disabled persons. **Price** Single 850-1100F, double 1000-1600F. Special rates in August-December and weekends for the readers of this guide. Extra bed +150F. **Meals** Breakfast (buffet) 95F, served 7:00-10:30. **Credit cards** All major. **Pets** Small dogs allowed. **Facilities** Elevator, patio, laundry service, bar, room-service. **Parking** 4-car in the hotel (150F/day) and rue Lauriston. **How to get there** (Map 6): Bus: 22, 30, 82 - Metro: Boissière, Trocadéro. **Open** All year.

Modern, comfortable, and quite luxurious, the Garden Elysées is in a leafy courtyard near the Trocadéro. We loved the cerused furniture in the reception rooms and the bedrooms, which are elegant and have marble baths; the smaller rooms have a more conventional decor. The color scheme revolves around salmon, pink, and orange shades. The most recently redone rooms are decorated in a more fanciful spirit with elegant fabrics. All rooms are bright, with large windows overlooking either the courtyard or the garden. A special delight is the copious breakfast, which is served in the dining room/veranda overlooking the garden. In the winter, the lounge/bar is often brightened with a log fire in the fireplace.

Hôtel Gavarni

5, rue Gavarni - 75116 Paris
Tel. (0)1 45 24 52 82 - Fax (0)1 40 50 16 95
e-mail: gavarni@compuserve.com
Mlle Nelly Rolland

Category ★★ Rooms 30 with shower, WC, hairdryer, telephone, cable TV. **Price** Single 390-455F, double 480-500F. In low season and from Friday to Sunday excluding salon periods: Single 355-420F, double 420F. Extra bed +80F. **Meals** Breakfast 35F, served 6:30-12:00. **Credit cards** All major. **Pets** Dogs not allowed. **Facilities** Elevator, laundry service, safe at reception. **Parking** At 19, rue de Passy (50 m). **How to get there** (Map 6): Bus: 22, 32, 52 - Metro: Passy - RER: La Muette. **Open** All year.

Residential and quiet, the little Rue Gavarni joins onto Rue de Passy, reputed for its shopping. The Hôtel Gavarni was recently taken over by the young and very welcoming Nelly Rolland, and since then renovations have been pushing ahead. Sponged wallpapers have been put in the rooms, enhanced by a pretty frieze, the bedspreads and curtains are now bright and colorful, the floors covered with a thick moquette, and so on. One appreciates all the improvements made to the well-being of each room while forgetting the standardized small furniture and tight space of the shower rooms. All is well maintained and now comfortable and pleasant. You should not forget the quality breakfasts and above all, the general friendly and relaxed ambiance. This will certainly leave you with a good impression, while this "little address" with reasonable prices has not yet finished its improvements.

Le Hameau de Passy

48, rue de Passy
75016 Paris
Tel. (0)1 42 88 47 55 – Fax (0)1 42 30 83 72
Mme Cantuel

Category ★★ **Rooms** 32 with bath or shower, WC, telephone, cable TV - 1 for disabled persons. **Price** Single 450-550F, double 500-630F. January-March: −10%, July-August: −20%. Extra bed +80F. **Meals** Breakfast included, served 7:30-10:30. **Credit cards** All major. **Pets** Dogs allowed (+30F). **Facilities** Garden, elevator for some bedrooms, laundry service, safe at reception, room-service from 19:00. **Parking** At 19, rue de Passy. **How to get there** (Map 6): Bus 22, 32, 52 - Metro: La Muette, Passy - RER: La Muette. **Open** All year.

Between two boutiques on Rue de Passy, a discreet passage leads you into a cul-de-sac covered in greenery and occupied along its full length by the Hameau de Passy. Fully renovated, small modern rooms have been fitted out, and some of them can be joined together. Rooms are reached by the elevator or the spiral staircase, and they have green or blue cerused furniture with lush fabrics with geometrical motifs, a corner for writing and a print on the wall. The bathrooms are all well-equipped. All rooms enjoy the luxuriant greenery lovingly tended by M. Cantuel, father of the young owner, and from time to time you may find yourself with "your nose in the leaves". When installed in the small lounge-bar or breakfast room, or if you just choose to sit quietly outside, you will find it difficult to believe that you are only a few steps from the Trocadero, close to numerous museums; you won't notice any traffic noise at all.

Hôtel Libertel d'Argentine

1-3, rue d'Argentine
75016 Paris
Tel. (0)1 45 02 76 76 – Fax (0)1 45 02 76 00
M. Courtade

Category ★★★★ **Rooms** 40 with soundproofing, telephone, bath or shower, WC, hairdryer, cable TV, minibar - 1 for disabled persons. **Price** Single and double 870-930F. **Meals** Breakfast (buffet) 75F, served 7:00-10:30. **Credit cards** Amex, Visa, Eurocard, MasterCards. **Pets** Dogs allowed. **Facilities** Elevator, laundry service, room-service. **Parking** Avenue Foch. **How to get there** (Map 3): Bus: 22, 30, 31, 52, 73, 92 - Metro: Argentine, Charles-de-Gaulle-Étoile - RER: Charles-de-Gaulle-Étoile. **Open** All year.

The Hôtel d'Argentine is on a small, quiet street near the Etoile. It was named after the country whose fashionable set traditionally frequented this neighborhood in the 19th century. The hotel was completely renovated by the architect Frédéric Méchiche, who designed it in the manner of a private home. The lobby is neoclassical, with fluted columns, Greek staff, faux marble, and Empire mahogany furniture upholstered with Jouy fabric. In the adjacent bar, where the original rotunda ceiling and cornices have been retained, you will find 19th-century chairs, allegorical engravings, a thick carpet, and complimentary tea. The bedrooms are charming, with finely striped wall fabrics, coordinated check bedspreads, and calico curtains. The lovely, comfortable bathrooms are done in dark-gray and putty-colored marble. It's pleasant to enjoy a leisurely breakfast in a room (with areas for smokers and non-smokers) that is decorated in Consulate style: walls elegantly painted with large, Wedgewood-blue stripes with white pilasters, and marble medallions. This is a very fine address.

Hôtel Libertel Auteuil

8-10, rue Félicien-David
75016 Paris
Tel. (0)1 40 50 57 57 – Fax (0)1 40 50 57 50
Mme Lamotte

Category ★★★ **Rooms** 94 with air-conditioning, telephone, bath, WC, hairdryer, TV satellite, minibar, safe - 3 for disabled persons. **Price** Single and double 620-1200F, junior-suite 1490F. **Meals** Breakfast (buffet) 75F, served 7:00-10:30; snack availables. **Credit cards** All major. **Pets** Dogs allowed. **Facilities** Elevator, laundry service, room service until 4:00. **Parking** At the hotel (90 F). **How to get there** (Map 6): Bus: 22, 52, 70, 72 - Metro: Jasmin, Mirabeau - RER: Kennedy-Radio-France. **Open** All year.

This hotel was built in the 1930s style that is typical of the 16th *arrondissement,* a chic neighborhood where beautiful buildings line quiet, peaceful avenues. The decorator Frédéric Méchiche has focused on space and light: The reception area and the large lounge on the ground floor open onto the street and the patio. The white walls and the sleek, lacquered rattan furniture are highlighted by sun-yellow cushions and Matisse, Picasso, and Kline lithographs on the walls. The same elegant modernity can be found in the bedrooms with their pretty caramel-and-white striped bedspreads, coordinated drapes, and beautiful bathrooms. The hotel's clients are mainly business people, due to the proximity of the Maison de la Radio and the Beaugrenelle business center. Yet you are not far from the lovely banks of the Seine and the Pont Mirabeau, luxury boutiques along the Avenue Mozart, and colorful markets on the Rue de Passy. Note that on the other side of the Pont Mirabeau bridge, is the restaurant *La Plage,* with a view of the Statue of Liberty.

Hôtel Massenet

5 *bis*, rue Massenet
75016 Paris
Tel. (0)1 45 24 43 03 – Fax (0)1 45 24 41 39
M. Mathieu

Category ★★★ Rooms 41 (2 with terrace) with bath or shower, WC, telephone, cable TV, minibar, 35 with hairdryer. **Price** Single 450-715F, double 650-840F. Special rates in low season. Extra bed +180F. **Meals** Breakfast 40F, served 7:00-11:00. **Credit cards** All major. **Pets** Small dogs allowed. **Facilities** Elevator, laundry service, safe at reception, patio, bar. **Parking** At 19, rue de Passy. **How to get there** (Map 6): Bus 22, 32, 52 - Metro: Passy, La Muette - RER La Muette-Boulainvilliers. **Open** All year.

Monsieur Mathieu was born in this hotel, which was run by his grandparents and then his parents, and he loves to tell stories of the old hotel and the Passy neighborhood when he was a child. Some bedrooms have their original antique furniture, while others have been recently redecorated in a more modern spirit with a white-lacquer decor trimmed in blue. Most baths have also been redone. You will find pale fabrics—sometimes used as wall coverings—and beautiful engravings and paintings in the bedrooms, the corridors, and the reception rooms. There is a lovely, wood-paneled dining room that opens directly onto a small patio with tables. The bedrooms overlooking the back enjoy a view of the hotel's garden as well as those of neighboring buildings. But you'd do as well with Room 70 or 71: they are on the street side, but each has a small flower-filled terrace with a table and chairs, and the price is the same. There is a pleasant bar with sitting areas. This is a comfortable hotel that some guests might find somewhat expensive, but it offers good, traditional service, including a doorman to carry your luggage.

Hotel Le Parc

55-57, rue Raymond-Poincaré
75016 Paris
Tel. (0)1 44 05 66 66 – Fax (0)1 44 05 66 00
M. François Delahaye

Category ★★★★ Rooms 100, 17 suites and 3 duplex with air-conditioning, telephone, bath (1 with whirlpool), WC, hairdryer, TV satellite, safe - 4 for disabled persons. **Price** Standards 1990F, Superieures 2350F, Junior-suites 3200-3500F. **Meals** Breakfast 135F, served at any time. **Credit cards** All major. **Pets** Dogs allowed. **Facilities** Elevator, laundry service, fitness center, room-service (24h/24h). **Restaurant** "Le Relais du Parc": Service 12:30-14:30, 19:30-22:30. **Parking** Rue Raymond-Poincaré (125F). **How to get there** (Map 6): Bus: 22, 32, 52, 63, 80 - Metro: Victor-Hugo, Trocadéro. **Open** All year.

Composed of five Anglo-Norman-style buildings, Le Parc is truly a grand hôtel. It was designed in the style of an English manor house by the famous English decorator Nina Campbell. The beautiful Edwardian decor includes figured carpets, quilted chintzes, four-poster beds, antique engravings, and paintings. The only exception is a handsome modern sculpture by Arman at the reception desk, who also designed the tables and sconces at the bar. Suites, rooms and lounges are all superb and offer all the comforts. Alain Ducasse, the master himself, supervises the hotel's restaurant, Le Relais du Parc. Meals are served either on the Indo-English colonial-style veranda or on the terrace in a beautiful courtyard with trees. The hotel is run by a distinguished, efficient manager.

Hôtel Passy-Eiffel

10, rue de Passy
75016 Paris
Tel. (0)1 45 25 55 66 – Fax (0)1 42 88 89 88
M. and Mme Cantuel

Category ★★★ **Rooms** 48 and 2 suites with soundproofing (15 with air-conditioning), bath or shower, WC, telephone, TV satellite, hairdryer, minibar. **Price** Single 520-620F, double 580-680F, triple and suite 750-950F. –10% from December to February and weekends; –20% in August. **Meals** Breakfast 50F,served 7:30-10:30. **Credit cards** All major. **Pets** Dags allowed (+20F). **Facilities** Elevator, patios, laundry service, safe at reception. **Parking** At 19, rue de Passy. **How to get there** (Map 6): Bus: 22, 32 - Metro: Passy. **Open** All year.

The Rue de Passy is a neighborhood of fashionable boutiques and many gardens, including that of the Passy Eiffel. The bedrooms at the back of the hotel, which are always in demand, enjoy a good view of the hotel's garden. The hotel is tastefully decorated in a rather classic style, with some copper bedsteads, squat armchairs, and furniture in rattan and cherrywood. The raspberry carpeting is elegant and the quilted bedspreads with coordinated drapes are reminiscent of the colors at Monet's house at Giverny. The rooms are comfortable and have double-glazing, which is especially important on the street side. Room 2 enjoys the use of a small ground-floor patio, and Rooms 5 and 6 are spacious (but the stairway leading to them might pose problems for some). Several suites will soon be added, in the meantime, Room 60 is spacious enough for families with children. Engravings, a pleasant dining room/veranda, a small flower garden, a lovely 1930s lounge, and the homemade honey at breakfast (Monsieur Cantuel is an enthusiastic beekeeper) complete the pretty picture.

Hôtel Pergolèse

3, rue Pergolèse - 75116 Paris
Tel. (0)1 40 67 96 77 - Fax (0)1 45 00 12 11
web: http://www.webscapades.com/france/paris/pergoles.htm
Mme Vidalenc

Category ★★★★ **Rooms** 40 with air-conditioning, telephone, bath, WC, TV satellite, hairdryer, minibar. **Price** Single and double 950-1400F, "Pergolèse room" 1700F. Special rates weekends excluding salon periods. **Meals** Breakfast 70F, buffet 95F. **Credit cards** All major. **Pets** Small dogs allowed. **Facilities** Elevator, room-service. **How to get there** (Map 3): Bus: 73, 82, PC - Metro: Argentine - RER: Porte-Maillot. **Open** All year.

Close to the Palais des Congrès, the Pergolèse is only ten minutes walk from the Place de l'Etoile; this is a fine hotel in a quiet location. Its success owes a lot to the devotion and professionalism of Mme Vidalenc, who has called on leading contemporary designers and interior decorators, including Rena Dumas, who designed the layout and furniture. The entry area opens onto two lounges with superb leather armchairs, and the bar is set around a very fine carpet designed by Mac Connico. It declines the full range of dark blues and sets off the comfortable armchairs and the brown woods of the furniture. In the breakfast room the underwater scenes painted once again by Mac Connico set the tone. The rooms have also been freshened up with both pastel and sharper colors matching those of the armchairs, the lightshades and even the little rings decorating your porcelain teacups. The bathrooms in white marble are all very refined, while the service and litttle attentions are those of a 'four-star' hotel, but still pleasantly non-fussy.

Hôtel Raphaël-Paris

17, avenue Kléber
75116 Paris
Tel. (0)1 44 28 00 28 - Fax (0)1 45 01 21 50
M. Alain Astier

Category ★★★★ **Rooms** 64 and 23 suites with soundproofing, air-conditioning, bath or shower, WC, telephone, hairdryer, TV satellite, minibar. **Price** Double "Charme" 1950F, "Boudoir" 2350F, "Alcove" 3150F, "Salon" 4200F, apart. and suite from 6300F. **Meals** Breakfast 135F and 175F. **Restaurant** "La Salle à Manger": gastronomic cooking. **Credit cards** All major. **Pets** Dogs allowed (+120F). **Facilities** Laundry service, room service, bar. **Parking** At 8, avenue Foch. **How to get there** (Map 6): Bus: 22, 30 - Metro: Kléber - RER: Charles-de-Gaulle-Étoile - RER and bus for Roissy-Charles-de-Gaulle. **Open** All year.

The Raphaël has its devotees and we are among them; it remains one of the 'Grands Hôtels' of France. In the main gallery you will find a classical decor of worked wood pieces, mantels, and armchairs in the Louis XV-style, all against a background of Persian carpets. While waiting for the elevator, do not fail to admire the Turner painting! The rooms are spacious and of great opulence and comfort. The suites can convert into apartments with private terraces; the 'Chanel Suite' has a view of the Arc de Triomphe. The latest renovations include the opening of two duplexes, their walls covered with painted wood, while the hand-finished faience tiles in the bathrooms all repeat the same 18th-century motifs. Once again you have private terraces over the roofs of Paris. You should also note the new open-air restaurant on the top floor open in fine weather. More traditionally, the bar continues to be a very chic meeting place, and taking a glass there allows you to discover one of the most elegant addresses of the capital.

Hôtel Saint-James Paris

43, avenue Bugeaud
75116 Paris
Tel. (0)1 44 05 81 81 – Fax (0)1 44 05 81 82
M. Tim Goddard

Category ★★★★ **Rooms** 24 and 24 suites, with air-conditioning, soundproofing, telephone, bath, WC, hairdryer, safe, minibar, cable TV. **Price** Single 1650F, double 1900 and 2150F, suite 2650 and 3000F. **Meals** Breakfast 110F, buffet 135F, served 7:00-10:00 (in room at any time). **Credit cards** All major. **Pets** Dogs allowed. **Facilities** Elevator, laundry service, bar, health center, room-service (24h/24). **Restaurant** Gastronomic - Menu 250F, also à la carte. **Parking** At the hotel. **How to get there** (Map 6): Bus: 52 - Metro: Porte-Dauphine - RER C: Avenue-Foch. **Open** All year.

It was on the initiative of the widow of President Thiers that this 19th-century private house was built in the style of a chateau. It is close to the Bois de Boulogne but that does not prevent the Saint-James from adding its own touch of greenery, offering its guests the privilege of a large garden just a few minutes away from the Champs-Elysées. The interior has preserved the ambiance of a very select club (notably the sumptuous bar-library), and this was its role before becoming a hotel in 1992. The size of the public spaces are impressive, with high windows onto the garden, and an oval dining room extending out doors. Some of the rooms are in a cleverly contemporary style due to the very sure taste of designer Andrée Putman. Those under the glass roofing of the top floor are astonishing with their terrace-gardens. Others are very British and very warm, and all have superb 'retro' bathrooms. The cuisine is noteworthy (served under the trees in summer) while the welcome is just as pleasant.

Hôtel Square

3, rue de Boulainvilliers
75016 Paris
Tel. (0)1 44 14 91 90 – Fax (0)1 44 14 91 99
M. Patrick Derdérian

Category **** **Rooms** 18 and 4 suites with air-conditioning, soundproofing, telephone, fax, bath, WC, hairdryer, minibar, safe, cable and satellite TV - 2 for disabled persons. **Price** Double 1350-1950F, suite 2250-2500F. **Meals** Breakfast (buffet) 60F (90F in room), served 7:00-11:00. **Credit cards** All major. **Pets** Small dogs allowed. **Facilities** Elevator, bar, laundry service, room-service. **Restaurant** Menu 250F, also à la carte. **Parking** At the hotel. **How to get there** (Map 6): Bus: 70, 72 - RER C: Kennedy-Radio-France. **Open** All year.

Just a few meters away from the Seine and the Maison de la Radio, you'll find this small building with its rounded forms, entirely covered with grey marble and named the Square Hôtel. It is a perfect example of the best contemporary trends in interior decor with curved lines, soft furniture matched with ethnic items (pottery, lights, fabrics, etc.), and a touch of lively color here and there. The vast rooms have three tone schemes : grey and ivory, gold and bronze, or brick and saffran. The overall effect is one of total comfort, including the bathrooms in white marble veined with anthracite. You should also note they have a gallery of contemporary art and a very fashionable restaurant, also used for breakfasts, on the ground floor. A very fine address that fully justifies its rates.

Hôtel Résidence Trocadéro

3, avenue Raymond-Poincaré
75116 Paris
Tel. (0)1 47 27 33 30 – Fax (0)1 47 27 80 85
Mme Taillère

Category ★★★ **Rooms** 27 with air-conditioning, bath or shower, WC, telephone, TV satellite, hairdryer, minibar, safe - 2 for disabled persons. **Price** Single 520-670F, double 630-780F. Special rates in July-August and some weekends. Extra bed +170F. **Meals** Breakfast (buffet) 54F, served 7:00-10:30. **Credit cards** All major. **Pets** Small dogs allowed. **Facilities** Patio, elevator, laundry service, bar, fax, minitel. **Parking** At 65, avenue Kléber (price for the night 18:00-9:00 39F). **How to get there** (Map 6): Bus: 22, 30, 32, 63, 82 - Metro: Trocadéro. **Open** All year.

This hotel is on the corner of the bustling Place du Trocadéro. The rooms at the back are quiet, while those on the busy Avenue are less so but enjoy a panoramic view from the Trocadéro to the Eiffel Tower and the Champs-de-Mars. The newly redone bedrooms are decorated with taste and simplicity, with beautiful carpets and coordinated fabrics in tones of blue, green, sienna, or golden yellow. The hotel throughout is fresh and well kept. The bathrooms, with large cream and navy tiles, are simply elegant. A corner bar and a breakfast room opening onto a patio with tables add to the pleasure of the Résidence-Trocadéro, a friendly place to stay near many points of interest.

La Villa Maillot

143, avenue de Malakoff
75116 Paris
Tel. (0)1 53 64 52 52 - Fax (0)1 45 00 60 61
M. Éric Greselin

Category ★★★★ **Rooms** 39 and 3 suites with air-conditioning, soundproofing, telephone
with answering machine, bath or shower, WC, hairdryer, TV satellite, minibar, trouser-
press - 2 for disabled persons. **Price** Single 1580F, double 1800F (900F Friday to Sunday
and 1200F Monday to Thursday for the readers of this guide, breakfast included), suite (2-
4 pers.) 2400-2 600F. Extra bed 300F. **Meals** Breakfast (buffet) 110F, served 7:00-10:00.
Credit cards All major. **Pets** Small dogs allowed. **Facilities** Elevator, laundry service, bar,
safes at reception, room-service. **Parking** In hotel (6 places, 110F/day), avenue Foch. **How
to get there** (Map 3): Bus: 73, 82, PC - Metro and RER: Porte-Maillot - Navette Air France.
Open All year.

The building dates from 1987 and was specifically designed as a hotel
with large airy spaces. The ground-floor reception area with its
light-oak worked wood leads into the lounge-bar and breakfast room
extending onto a veranda. The decor is modern and inspired by the Art
Deco-style. Whether in the lounge or rooms, the colors are ivories while
the furniture is in clear or black cerused wood. The marble bathrooms
are ultra-modern with numerous attractive details adding to the comfort
of each. As for the rooms, they are impeccably sound-proofed and
spacious, but those with a number ending in a '2' are smallest. All are
very comfortable with huge windows in those rooms on floors 1 to 5
opening onto the local garden of trees. A large framed picture on silk
personalizes the decor. This is a rather luxurious and expensive hotel
but offers very interesting price deals. The welcome is very friendly and
the breakfast hearty.

Hôtel Ampère

102, avenue de Villiers
75017 Paris
Tel. (0)1 44 29 17 17 - Fax (0)1 44 29 16 50
M. Chavalier

Category ★★★ **Rooms** 102 with air-conditioning, soundproofing, telephone, bath or shower, WC, cable TV, minibar, safe, hairdryer - 3 for disabled persons. **Price** Single 770F, double 860F, triple 1060F. **Meals** Breakfast (buffet) 45F, served 7:15-10:00. **Credit cards** All major. **Pets** Dogs allowed (+15F). **Facilities** Elevator, bar (piano-bar), laundry service, patio, room-service. **Restaurant** Menus from 110F. **Parking** Private (80F per day). **How to get there** (Map 3): Bus: 84, 92, 93 - Metro and RER C: Pereire. **Open** All year.

On the corner of Place Pereire, the Résidence Ampère-Villiers has just celebrated its first birthday. This is a big-capacity hotel with a modern decor a little short on charm. The large and light reception area leads into the lounge (which doubles as a piano-bar at cocktail time), the dining room and an attractive garden where you can enjoy your drink. The rooms are not very large, even those catering for three people, but are well laid-out with attractive furniture designed for the hotel. All are similar but in alternating colors of blue or green depending on the floor level. The Avenue de Villiers is lively and so it is better to sleep on the courtyard side. The young women at reception are attentive and very efficient, handling a mainly family clientele visiting Paris.

Hôtel Astrid

27, avenue Carnot – 75017 Paris
Tel. (0)1 44 09 26 00 – Fax (0)1 44 09 26 01
web: http://www.webscapades.com/france/paris/astrid.htm
Mme Guillet

Category ★★★ **Rooms** 40 with soundproofing, telephone, bath or shower, WC, hairdryer, cable TV, safe. **Price** Single 520-585F, double 625-750F, triple 800F, 4 pers. 885F. Special rates in winter and July 15. – August 31. **Meals** Breakfast included, served 7:00-10:00. **Credit cards** All major. **Pets** Dogs allowed (+35F). **Facilities** Elevator. **Parking** 50m. **How to get there** (Map 3): Metro: Charles-de-Gaulle-Étoile - Bus: Air France to Roissy at 50m. **Open** All year.

Avenue Carnot is certainly the quietest in the Etoile district, but only some 100 hundred meters from the Arc de Triomphe at its lowest point, it gives onto the very busy Rue des Acacias. The Hotel Astrid is on this very corner. Each room has its own particular style and it was clearly with much pleasure that the owners chose all the fabrics, furniture, lamps, etc. In one room, curtains with blue leafy patterns have been matched with a fine yellow wallpaper and Directory-style furniture pieces, on which you find a small repeat in blue patina. In another room, a Provencal theme is chosen, and in a third, gilded bedsteads are used to create a romantic ambiance much closer to the guest room at home than the usual hotel standard. The last area to benefit from the renovation program, the rooms with showers have now been finished. Despite their small size they are pleasant, possibly a bit less personal than the others but also fully recommendable. To this well maintained overall effect, you can add the charming view of the chestnut trees, and on the ground floor an attractive breakfast room with its large bright bay windows.

Hôtel de Banville

166, boulevard Berthier – 75017 Paris
Tel. (0)1 42 67 70 16 – Fax (0)1 44 40 42 77
web: http://www.webscapades.com/france/paris/banville.htm
Mme Lambert

Category ★★★ **Rooms** 39 with air-conditioning, soundproofing, bath or shower, WC, telephone, TV satellite, hairdryer, safe. **Price** Single and double 635-860F. Special rates the weekend and in low season on request. **Meals** Breakfast 60-80F, served from 6:30; snacks available. **Credit cards** All major. **Pets** Dogs allowed. **Facilities** Room service (24h/24), bar (piano-bar the Wednesday evening). **Parking** At 210, rue de Courcelles. **How to get there** (Map 3): Bus: 84, 92, 93, PC - Metro: Pereire and Porte-de-Champerret - Bus for Roissy-Charles-de-Gaulle at Porte Maillot. **Open** All year.

The Hôtel de Banville is a superb accommodation in the Porte Maillot district animated by the Palais des Congrès. Lined with its plane trees, the Boulevard Berthier is however quiet, and the hotel is in a small 1930's building. You are immediately won over by the elegant lounge fitted out as in a private house with fine antique furniture, pictures and beautiful fabrics from Chez Rubelli. The original elevator gives access to the spacious rooms, which are light and open onto the trees. All deliberately different, they do have one common feature in their perfectly chosen fabrics and wallpapers (very far from the usual hotel standards), pretty furniture and of course fine bathrooms. Breakfast is taken in the romantic setting of a fascinating trompe-l'oeil that transforms the dining room into a winter garden. You should note the very reasonable prices and a particularly friendly welcome that make this one of our favorite hotels in Paris.

Centre-Ville Étoile

6, rue des Acacias – 75017 Paris
Tel. (0)1 43 80 56 18 – Fax (0)1 47 54 93 43
e-mail: http://www.hcv@giga–planet.fr
M. Michaud

Category ★★★ **Rooms** 20 with air-conditioning, bath, WC, telephone, cable TV, minibar, safe. **Price** Single 590-790F, doubles 690-890F. **Meals** Breakfast 55F. **Credit cards** All major. **Pets** Dogs allowed. **Facilities** Elevator, laundry service, patio, room-service, restaurant. **Parking** At 24, rue des Acacias. **How to get there** (Map 3): Bus: 73 - Metro: Argentine, Charles-de-Gaulle-Étoile - RER: Charles-de-Gaulle-Étoile - RER and bus for Roissy airport. **Open** All year.

Originally, this hotel consisted of two buildings facing each other and connected on each floor by an exterior passageway. The owners have now enclosed this space with a high, glass wall and skylight. Serving as the reception area, the new space is bathed with natural light and beautified with lush green plants. The rest of the decor is black and white, contemporary, airy, and sleek, with black leather club chairs in the lounge and the small dining room, and bedrooms with wide beds, black lacquered furniture, white or brown walls, and handsome carpets. The monochrome effect elegantly off sets the brightly colored contemporary posters and luminous wall sconces. Some guests might find the rooms rather small, but they are very comfortable. Equally lovely are the small, all–white bathrooms with their unusual RATP (Paris Public Transportation System) tiles outlined with a black border; others are gray and bordered with mirrors. Special mention should be made of the staff, who turn down your bed covers, fill the ice bucket and, as a small finishing touch, place chocolates on your pillow.

Hôtel Champerrey-Héliopolis

13, rue d'Héliopolis
75017 Paris
Tel. (0)1 47 64 92 56 - Fax (0)1 47 64 50 44
Mme Rennie

Category ★★ **Rooms** 22 with telephone, bath or shower, WC, hairdryer, TV - 2 for disabled persons. **Price** Single 350-385F, double 450-495F, triple 495-580F. Special rates the weekend and in low season on request. **Meals** Breakfast 38F, from 7:00. **Credit cards** All major. **Pets** Dogs allowed. **Facilities** Patio, bar, safe. **Parking** Private (2 places), Porte de Champerret. **How to get there** (Map 3): Bus: 83, 84, 92, 93, PC - Metro: Porte de Champerret - RER: Pereire. **Open** All year.

A white facade with small windows on two floors gives this hotel a homey air. Having once lived in Madagascar, the owner loves sunshine and bright colors: The luxuriant decor of green plants, flowers in bright pots, and a small, colorful birdcage make the Champerrey Héliopolis seem very far from the big city. The warm, inviting lounge-bar, comfortably furnished and decorated with personal objects, is brightened by exotic green and blue cacti in the entrance, and the corridors are cheerfully decorated with blue carpets. The bedrooms are simple, modern, and comfortable. In some, a small square balcony overlooks the patio, and you can enjoy your breakfast here. Breakfast is also served in the bar and at a single, much coveted table on the patio, also popular at cocktail time.

Hôtel Cheverny

7, villa Berthier - 75017 Paris
Tel. (0)1 43 80 46 42 - Fax (0)1 47 63 26 62
web: http://www.webscapades.com/france/paris/cheverny.htm
M. Gillot and M. Brillant

Category ★★★ **Rooms** 48 with air-conditioning, telephone, bath or shower, WC, TV satellite, minibar. **Price** Single and double 390-580F, 430-660F; triple 660-750F. **Meals** Breakfast (buffet) 55F. **Credit cards** All major. **Pets** Small dogs allowed. **Facilities** Elevator, patio. **Parking** Porte-de-Champerret (200m). **How to get there** (Map 3): Bus: 83, 84, 92, PC - Metro: Porte-de-Champerret - RER: Pereire. **Open** All year.

In an impasse set back from the Avenue de Villiers, the Cheverny's facade is brightened by the geraniums tumbling from the window boxes. The small patio is a gardener's delight, too, with ivy cascading down the wall in the back, a small fountain, and tables and chairs to enjoy the leafy scene, which can also be seen from a glassed-in loggia with rattan armchairs upstairs. The rooms have recently been enhanced with white-leaded oak furniture and brightened with lively colored fabrics. The rooms for three people are especially attractive but more expensive. In the basement you will find the bar and the breakfast room beneath a stone cradle-vault. Breakfast is also served in a pale-pink lounge with beige cerused furniture. The hotel is in the immediate proximity of the Espace Champerret.

Hôtel Eber-Monceau

18, rue Léon-Jost
75017 Paris
Tel. (0)1 46 22 60 70 - Fax (0)1 47 63 01 01
M. Jean-Marc Eber

Category ★★★ Rooms 13, 3 suites and 2 duplexs with bath, WC, telephone, cable TV, minibar. **Price** Double 640-690F, suite 1050F, duplex 1150-1360F. **Meals** Breakfast 55F. **Credit cards** All major. **Pets** Dogs not allowed. **Facilities** Elevator, small patio, laundry service, room-service. **Parking** At 100, rue de Courcelles. **How to get there** (Map 3): Bus: 30, 31, 84, 94 - Metro: Courcelles - RER and bus for Roissy. **Open** All year.

The *habitués* who come back time and again to the Eber-Monceau are surely attracted by the homey atmosphere. This is largely due to the small, intimate size of the hotel and to the lovely reception area and lounge, which is especially charming with its beautiful, polychrome beam ceiling and neo-Gothic oak fireplace. Cane chairs, decorative objects, and interesting paintings add further to the welcoming ambiance, as do the tiny bar and patio (that could do with a few chairs in summer). But we have some reservations about the bedrooms. They are tastefully furnished, it's true, but they're somewhat too small and cheerless. On the other hand, the lovely white bathrooms, which have warm terra cotta floors and modern conveniences, make up for this drawback. The suites, and especially the duplexes, are larger and very pleasant but, of course, you'll pay the price.

Hôtel Étoile-Pereire

146, boulevard Pereire
75017 Paris
Tel. (0)1 42 67 60 00 – Fax (0)1 42 67 02 90
M. Pardi

Category ★★★ **Rooms** 20, 1 suite and 4 duplexs (with air-conditioning) with telephone, bath or shower, WC, cable TV, safe, minibar. **Price** Single and double 590-690F, 790F, suite 1090F. Special rates in low season (Easter, Christmas, July-Aug. and weekend 2 nights) single 500F, double 600F, duplex 850F (breakfast included). **Meals** Breakfast 54F. **Credit cards** Diners, Visa, Eurocard, MasterCard. **Pets** Dogs not allowed. **Facilities** Elevator, laundry service, bar, room-service. **Parking** At 30, rue Rennequin. **How to get there** (Map 3): Bus: 43, 83, 84, 92 - Metro and RER: Pereire - Bus for Roissy. **Open** All year.

With one exception, all the bedrooms at the Etoile Pereire overlook a quiet, interior courtyard. As in a private home, the bedrooms vary in size. The blue suite with two windows overlooks the courtyard. The magnificent duplexes have sitting areas on the ground floor and beds upstairs. The decor is tasteful: walls covered in beige, blue, or rose fabrics with matching curtains, white piqué bedspreads, and beautiful lithographs of exotic birds. There is a very comfortable lobby and bar, and a charming dining room where outstanding breakfasts–with a choice of 40 different preserves–are served.

Hôtel Excelsior

16, rue Caroline
75017 Paris
Tel. (0)1 45 22 50 95 – Fax (0)1 45 22 59 88
M. Le Ralle

Category ★★★ **Rooms** 22 with soundproofing, telephone, bath or shower, WC, hairdryer, TV satellite. **Price** Single 380-420F, double 420-450F. **Meals** Breakfast 32F. **Credit cards** All major. **Pets** Dogs allowed. **Facilities** Elevator, safe at reception, drink machine. **Parking** At 18, rue Caroline. **How to get there** (Map 4): Bus: 30, 66 - Metro: Place-de-Clichy, Rome. **Open** All year.

Once through the door of the Excelsior you must not be put off by the first impression that the reception area-lounge may give you. Certainly, its Louis XIII-style furniture and the old rustic cupboard are not without charm, but the overall effect remains rather cold and stuffy, while the brown tiled floor does not help. In contrast, the rooms are very much warmer and cosseted, often with navy-blue or raspberry draped fabrics, all with small furniture pieces, and impeccable speckled carpeting that is matched by the bedheads, pretty curtains and the printed or white piqué bedspreads. You often find a marble fireplace or moulded ceilings, but avoid room 502 which is the smallest. Some look onto the street while those on the courtyard enjoy the quiet greenery of a rather 'bohemian' garden which is large for Paris. The bathrooms are well maintained and some have windows. As almost always, the breakfast room is in the basement. The welcome is friendly and relaxed.

Hôtel Flaubert

19, rue Rennequin
75017 Paris
Tel. (0)1 46 22 44 35 – Fax (0)1 43 80 32 34
M. and Mme Niceron

Category ** **Rooms** 37 with bath or shower, WC, telephone, TV, minibar - 1 for disabled persons. **Price** Single 425-480F, double 500-650F, triple 750F. **Meals** Breakfast 40F, served 6:30-10:00. **Credit cards** All major. **Pets** Dogs allowed. **Facilities** Elevator, patio. **Parking** in front of hotel. **How to get there** (Map 3): Bus: 30, 31, 43, 84, 92 - Metro: Ternes. **Open** All year.

The Flaubert is a small local hotel whose best features are found inside and beyond the reception area, in the luxuriant small patio. Here, cascades of Virginia creeper and ivy geraniums tumble down from the balconies, mingling with flower beds of aucuba, impatiens and annuals. We recommend the ten bedrooms looking out over this refreshing scene: Numbers 1 to 3, on the garden level with windows overlookig the garden; and those on the 'gangway'. They are brighter and you reach them via an outside passageway on the patio. All are identically fitted out with good bathroom facilities. Tiled in beautiful terra cotta, the breakfast room has the ambiance of a conservatory/bistro, with small bamboo chairs and green plants, offering an exotic spot from which to observe the activity on the street.

Hôtel Libertel Monceau

7, rue Rennequin
75017 Paris
Tel. (0)1 47 63 07 52 – Fax (0)1 47 66 84 44
Mme Frédérique Péchenart

Category ** **Rooms** 25 with bath or shower, WC, hairdryer, telephone, minibar, cable TV.
Price Single 600-825F, double 600-890F. Extra bed 220F. **Meals** Continental breakfast
45F, buffet 75F, served 7:00-10:30. Snacks available from 80F. **Credit cards** All major.
Pets Small dogs allowed. **Facilities** Elevator, bar, laundry service, safe at reception, room-
service, patio. **Parking** Fiat ou Wagram. **How to get there** (Map 3): Bus: 30 - Metro: Ternes,
Wagram. **Open** All year.

Close to the Place des Ternes, Rue Rennequin leads into Avenue
Wagram. All freshly renovated with some rooms still being worked
on during our visit, the Libertel-Monceau offers 25 small sound-proofed
rooms with most looking onto the street, or over a flowery patio. Blues
for some, yellows for others, but all have shimmering fabrics and acajou-
style furniture, or else simple white cane pieces. The ravishing bathrooms
in white faience are also all new, delicately enhanced by a frieze in
'azulejos' tile, while their beautiful basins are inspired by turn-of-the-
century designs. A warm bar in the British style allows you to relax in
armchairs and on sofas while reading the French and foreign press. In
summary, one can say that this hotel is comfortable and cosseted, while
the attention of the welcome even goes as far as giving you a weather
forecast with your breakfast.

Hôtel Magellan

17, rue Jean-Batpiste Dumas
75017 Paris
Tel. (0)1 45 72 44 51 – Fax (0)1 40 68 90 36
Mme Anne-Marie Borgen

Category ★★★ **Rooms** 75 with telephone, bath or shower, WC, TV satellite. **Price** Single 595F, double 630F, +145F extra bed. **Meals** Breakfast 40F, buffet 55F. **Credit cards** All major. **Pets** Dogs not allowed. **Facilities** Elevator, garden. **Parking** Privated by reservation (85F/day). **How to get there** (Map 3): Bus: 84, 92, 93, PC - Metro: Porte-Maillot, Porte-de-Champerret - RER C: Pereire. **Open** All year.

The many contemporary wood panels, elegant lithographs, and small 1930s-style lounges augur well as you enter the beautiful lobby of the Magellan. Just behind it, you can glimpse the lovely garden, with trees, rows of iris, rose bushes, and tables with umbrellas where you can enjoy a drink. The rooms are all decorated in the same way, and the standard hotel furniture in oak or burred walnut is rather dated, but the rooms are vast, bright and well maintained. The other main attraction of the Magellan is the small pavilion in the garden, and almost all the bedrooms overlook this lovely scene. The rooms are quiet, and with the first good weather, you can enjoy the garden. The welcome by the personnel is friendly and attentive.

Marmotel Étoile

34, avenue de la Grande Armée
75017 Paris
Tel. (0)1 47 63 57 26 - Fax (0)1 45 74 25 27
M. Rogert

Category ★★ Rooms 22 with telephone, bath or shower, WC, TV, minibar, safe. **Price** Single 395F, double 450-470F. In weekend and August (except for Salon periods) 350F, 400F and breakfast offered for readers of the guide. **Meals** Breakfast 29F, served 7:00-11:30. **Credit cards** Amex, Visa, Eurocard, MasterCard. **Pets** Dogs allowed. **Facilities** Garden. **Parking** Charles-de-Gaulle (at 500m.). **How to get there** (Map 3): Bus: 22, 30, 52, 73, 92 - Metro: Argentine - RER: Charles-de-Gaulle - Bus Air France. **Open** All year.

Almost hidden between a café and an automobile parts store, the Marmotel could easily be missed by passers-by. This very simple hotel has its *habitués,* including a good number of business people who enjoy the quiet atmosphere and the garden, where breakfast is served. You won't find many "two stars" who offer this kind of service and have this location–just a few yards from the Arc de Triomphe. The bedrooms are spacious and have the conventional modern comforts, but their decor is only functional. For a quiet room, ask for one overlooking the garden; Rooms 112, 114, 122, 124, 132 and 134 are noisy, with their windows directly over the busy Avenue de la Grande Armée.

Hôtel Méderic

4, rue Médéric
75017 Paris
Tel. (0)1 47 63 69 13 – Fax (0)1 44 40 05 33
M. Rolin

Category ★★ **Rooms** 27 with bath or shower, WC, telephone, TV satellite. **Price** Single and double 425-495F, 4 pers. 750F. **Meals** Breakfast 45F, served 7:00-11:00. **Credit cards** All major. **Pets** Dogs not allowed. **Facilities** Elevator. **Parking** At 50 meters. **How to get there** (Map 3): Bus: 84, 30 - Metro: Courcelles. **Open** All year.

Many passers-by on the Rue Médéric stop to look in the window of this hotel's lovely breakfast room, with its Provençal décor; yellow walls and tablecloths, blue-gray patinated chairs, 19th-century landscape paintings, and a comfortable small lounge beckon you inside to investigate further. The bedrooms are quite pleasant; aside from the two family suites on the top floor (tall people can enjoy the view from the roof windows), the other rooms are very small. The walls are beige or tapestried in Japanese straw and are adorned with lovely mirrors and wall sconces in gilt, antiqued wrought-iron. The furniture is only functional, with small beige chairs, but there are period armchairs in some rooms. The Méderic is a simple, family-style hotel, and the prices are reasonable.

Hôtel Mercédès

128, avenue de Wagram
75017 Paris
Tel. (0)1 42 27 77 82 - Fax (0)1 40 53 09 89
Mme Gisela Prigent

Category *** **Rooms** 37 with air-conditioning, bath or shower, WC, telephone, cable TV, minibar, hairdryer. **Price** Double 690-750F, triple 840F, suite-bureau (2 pers.) 850F, duplex (2-4 pers.) 1200F. **Meals** Breakfast (buffet) 55F, served 7:00-10:30. **Credit cards** All major. **Pets** Dogs allowed. **Facilities** Elevator, laundry service **Parking** Wagram. **How to get there** (Map 3): Bus: 31, 92 - Metro: Wagram. **Open** All year.

The Mercédès is a superb example of 1930s architecture. Steps at the corner of the building lead to a huge lounge and lobby with small contemporary chairs in multicolored leather and a decor of yellow and green plasterwork. The bedrooms are in softer colors, with lime-green wall fabrics and green carpets and headboards and dressing tables in varnished burl. In the larger rooms, several pieces of 1930s furniture have been added, and the smaller rooms have a very charming outside loggia. Special mention should be made of the extraordinary duplex suite, whose bedroom is on a platform overlooking the lounge and a huge, glassed-in, semi-circular area with a panoramic view of Paris. Another stunning architectural feature is the basement rotunda with four magnificent stained-glass windows by the turn-of-the-century glassmaker Gruber. The delicious breakfast buffet is served here, and next to this room is an inviting bar.

Hôtel de Neuville

3, rue Verniquet – 75017 Paris
Tel. (0)1 43 80 26 30 – Fax (0)1 43 80 38 55
web: http://www.webscapades.com/france/paris/neuville.htm
Mme Beherec

Category ★★★ **Rooms** 28 with telephone, bath, WC, cable TV – 1 for disabled persons. **Price**
Single 586-706F, double 592-712F. Weekends and August 480F. **Meals** Breakfast (buffet)
55F, served 7:00-11:00. **Credit cards** All major. **Pets** Dogs allowed (+60F) **Facilities**
Elevator. **Parking** Private at 20m. **How to get there** (Map 3): Bus: PC, 53, 83, 84, 92, 94 –
Metro and RER: Pereire. **Open** All year.

Just in front of the Hôtel de Neuville the very green Boulevard Pereire
opens up slightly to allow a small triangular space for Place Verniquet.
Up a flight of steps to reach the reception lobby, you find an elegant
room where light oak worked wood pieces mingle with basket seating
in the 1930's spirit, and the beige marble of the bar, all create a peaceful
ambiance. Two steps and a pair of columns mark the bar off from the
lounge, with contemporary canvasses regularly exhibited on the walls,
but the finest picture of all remains the luxurious patio which you cannot
tire of looking at through the large rectangular window in the center of
the lateral wall. On the floors above the bedrooms are attractive, simple
and functional. Three of them have amusing beds with copper canopies,
while those with a number ending in a '5' or '6' overlook the rows of
trees on the Boulevard. The ground-floor breakfast room is charming
in its winter garden style, while the welcome is particularly pleasant.

Hôtel Pierre

25, rue Théodore-de-Banville
75017 Paris
Tel. (0)1 47 63 76 69 - Fax (0)1 43 80 63 96
M. Alain Lagarrigue

Category ★★★ **Rooms** 50 with soundproofing (4 with air-conditioning) with bath, WC, telephone, hairdryer, cable TV, minibar, safe - 4 for disabled persons. **Price** Single 810-830F, 870-890F (special rates for weekend). Extra bed 100F. **Meals** Breakfast (buffet) 68F, served 7:00-10:30, snacks available: room-service meal trays 70-200F. **Credit cards** All major. **Pets** Dogs allowed. **Facilities** Elevator, patio, laundry service. **Parking** At 20 m. **How to get there** (Map 3): Bus: 31, 92 - Metro and RER: Pereire. **Open** All year.

With its entrance flanked by the American, British, Japanese and European Community flags, the Hôtel Pierre is a luxurious establishment on a human size. In the attractive lobby, there are deep, comfortable chintz sofas, a large selection of newspapers, and a coffee machine at guests' disposal. Equally tasteful, the bedrooms have thick red carpets with small green motifs, chintz curtains and bedspreads, elegant brass sconces, and Impressionist reproductions. The overall decor is somewhat conventional, but there are attractive small details in the bedrooms and bathrooms; the rooms overlooking the courtyard (especially those on the lower floors) enjoy a view of a charming patio with its magnolia tree and flowers. Double-glazed windows ensure a quiet night's sleep, and when you awake, you'll enjoy breakfast in a delightful room with large bay windows and floral drapes, which look out onto the garden.

Hôtel Princesse Caroline

1 *bis*, rue Troyon
75017 Paris
Tel. (0)1 43 80 62 20 - Fax (0)1 42 27 49 53
M. Lascaux

Category ★★★ **Rooms** 63 with air-conditioning, soundproofing, telephone, bath or shower, WC, hairdryer, TV satellite, minibar, safe - 13 for disabled persons. **Price** Single 660-730F, double 730-930F. **Meals** Breakfast (Buffet) 60F, served 7:00-11:00. **Credit cards** Visa, Eurocard, MasterCard, Amex. **Pets** Dogs not allowed **Facilities** Elevator, laundry service. **Parking** Wagram. **How to get there** (Map 3): Metro: Charles-de-Gaulle-Étoile - Bus: Air France Roissy. **Open** All year.

The Princesse Caroline is on one of the few small streets (just off the Place de l'Etoile) whose tranquillity contrasts with the bustling avenues that converge on the Arc de Triomphe. It thus enjoys an exceptional location without the usual disadvantages. Recently renovated, it is luxurious, with corner lounges with elegant 1930s armchairs, beige marble floors, and light-oak wall paneling. On each floor, the huge landings are also paneled in oak, and have thick green carpets. The bedrooms, regardless of size, are appointed with comfort and taste: beautiful Louis XVI- or Directoire-style cherrywood furniture and immaculate baths for example. The best rooms overlook the courtyard where the view is pleasant and the rooms are totally quiet. Breakfast is served in a small, bright room in the basement, with tasteful Louis XVI medallion-back chairs and charming fruit-motif tablecloths.

Hôtel Regent's Garden

6, rue Pierre Demours
75017 Paris
Tel. (0)1 45 74 07 30 – Fax (0)1 40 55 01 42
M. Condy

Category ✶✶✶ **Rooms** 39 (some with air-conditioning) with telephone, bath, WC, hairdryer, TV, minibar. **Price** Single 680-980F, double 740-980F. **Meals** Breakfast 50F. **Credit cards** All major. **Pets** Dogs not allowed. **Facilities** Elevator, laundry service, garden, safe at reception. **Parking** Private (8 places) or public (30m). **How to get there** (Map 3): Bus: 30, 31, 43, 83, PC - Metro: Charles-de-Gaulle-Étoile, Ternes. **Open** All year.

Behind the Avenue des Ternes, this is the beautiful mansion that Napoléon III built for his doctor. Flanked by chestnut trees, the several entrance steps lead into an elegant lobby occupied by the reception area and the lounge, which open onto a large garden. To your right, the blue lounge is used for breakfast. Half of the bedrooms overlook the garden, while the others are sound-proofed with double glazing and overlook a courtyard with trees. The rooms have high, molded ceilings, and vary in size, but all are pleasant, (some rooms have just been fully renovated) and have new bathrooms. In good weather, breakfasts are served in the large garden whose luxuriant flowers and 19th-century ambiance quickly make you forget that you are in the center of Paris, two minutes from the Etoile.

Hôtel Tilsitt Étoile

23, rue Brey - 75017 Paris
Tel. (0)1 43 80 39 71 - Fax (0)1 47 66 37 63
web: http://www.webscapades.com/france/paris/tilsitt.htm
Christine Lafosse

Category ★★★ **Rooms** 39 with air-conditioning, bath or shower, WC, telephone, TV satellite, minibar. **Price** Single 610-735F, double 850F, suite 990F. −10% in low season and weekends except in Salon periods. **Meals** Breakfast 60F. **Credit cards** All major. **Pets** Small dogs allowed. **Facilities** Elevator, laundry service, room-service. **Parking** Wagram. **How to get there** (Map 3): Bus: 22, 30, 31, 43, 52, 73, 83, 92 - Metro: Ternes, Charles-de-Gaulle-Étoile - RER: Charles-de-Gaulle-Étoile - RER and bus for Roissy airport. **Open** All year.

The Rue Brey is small and discreet but only a few paces from the Arc de Triomphe and the Champs-Elysées, and just the kind of place to look for a quiet central hotel. This is surely what Mme. Lafosse and Mme. Cot said to each other when they opened the Tilsitt Etoile, and by adding in all their taste and practical skills they have managed to create a calm and modern establishment where one quickly feels at ease. Right from the entrance you will appreciate the large reception lounge with its bar and grey-pearl worked wood integrating mirrors and wide windows that exploit the limits of the room to the full. It has armchairs in 1930's style arranged around small octagonal tables to form various small corners for taking a drink. The decor is predominantly in greys and beiges, and you find it again in the small rooms but with an added colored or flowered note from the cotton fabrics and lightshades. The rooms on the courtyard are rather sad and remain a bit standardized, but the hotel as a whole is irreproachably maintained and the welcome particularly attentive.

Ermitage Hôtel

24, rue Lamarck
75018 Paris
Tel. (0)1 42 64 79 22 - Fax (0)1 42 64 10 33
Family Canipel

Category ★★ Rooms 12 with bath or shower, WC, telephone, hairdryer. **Price** Single 415F, double 480F, triple 600F, 4 pers. 700F; small bedroom with shower and WC outside the room: 380F (2 pers.). **Meals** Breakfast included, served 7:00-9:00. **Credit cards** Not accepted. **Pets** Small dogs allowed. **Facilities** Terrace, safe at reception. **Parking** At 20, rue Lamarck (60F/day). **How to get there** (Map 4): Bus: 80, 85, Montmartrobus - Metro: Lamarck-Caulaincourt. **Open** All year.

This mansion was built in the reign of Napoléon III for "a beloved lady." From the entranceway, the frescos by Roland du Buc evoke Montmartre scenes from right outside the door: steep streets and famous stairways that take you up to the vineyards, the Montmartre Museum and, of course, Sacré Cœur, which is less than 200 yards away. For 25 years, the Ermitage has been a family-style hotel, with only twelve bedrooms, decorated with English fabrics and figured or solid-blue wallpaper. There are alcove beds in two of the large rooms, 1900s-style or more contemporary furniture, carpets, and small pieces of furniture on the stair landings. Seven rooms overlook the garden; those on the ground floor are directly on the garden and are always very much in demand in good weather when breakfast can be served there. The rooms upstairs have a magnificent panorama over Paris. The small lounge with its old kneading trough and Provençal buffet is also at your disposal. The overall effect is somewhat old-fashioned, but the hotel is very well-kept, the staff is courteous, and we felt at home here.

Hôtel Prima Lepic

29, rue Lepic
75018 Paris
Tel. (0)1 46 06 44 64 – Fax (0)1 46 06 66 11
Mme Renouf

Category ★★ **Rooms** 35 and 3 suites familiales with soundproofung, bath or shower, WC, telephone, TV, hairdryer. **Price** Single 350-380F, double 400-420F, triple 500F,4 pers. 500-700F, 5 pers. 700F. **Meals** Breakfast (buffet) 40F, served 8:00-10:30. **Credit cards** Visa, Eurocard, MasterCard. **Pets** Dogs allowed. **Facilities** Elevator, safe, drink machine. **Parking** Impasse Marie-Blanche. **How to get there** (Map 4): Bus: 30, 54, 68, 74, 80, 95, Montmartrobus - Metro: Blanche, Abbesses. **Open** All year.

The Rue Lepic bustles with an animated outdoor food market, but the entrance to this Montmartre hotel is very discrete. The ground floor, which is illuminated by a skylight, is occupied by the reception area, a small corner lounge, and a large breakfast room with garden furniture in white lacquered rococo wrought iron, green plants, and frescos depicting the famous sites of the neighborhood. The bedrooms on both the courtyard and the street side are bright, and have lovely wallpaper–including Laura Ashley designs in the most recent rooms–and white piqué bedspreads; all are tasteful and most are a good size. In addition to the rattan furniture, you will find period furniture that Madame Renouf enjoys bringing home from antiques markets: small Louis Philippe and Louis XVI wardrobes, antique tables. Some rooms have a lovely headboard, others a bed canopy that harmonizes with the curtains. The bathrooms are adequate, and the corridors have been newly carpeted in blue and dark red.

Hôtel Regyn's Montmartre

18, place des Abbesses
75018 Paris
Tel. (0)1 42 54 45 21 - Fax (0)1 42 23 76 69
M. Michel Cadin

Category ★★ Rooms 22 with bath or shower, WC, telephone, cable TV, hairdryer, safe. **Price** Single 375-395F, double 440-460F. Extra pers. +30%, free for children under 13, «Carte club» of the hotel: 11th night free and many personalized services. **Meals** Breakfast 45F, served at any time. **Credit cards** Visa, Eurocard, MasterCard, Amex. **Pets** Dogs allowed. **Facilities** Elevator, laundry service. **Parking** Impasse Marie-Blanche. **How to get there** (Map 4): Bus: 30, 54, 67, Montmartrobus - Metro: Abbesses. **Open** All year.

On the Place des Abbesses, facing the Saint-Jean-l'Evangeliste Church, a masterpiece of Art Nouveau–Regyn's is the ideal base for visiting Montmartre. The bedrooms are bright and well-kept, with many small details that add to your comfort and pleasure: double-glazed windows on the street side, good beds, a corner for writing, stylized bronze light fixtures, and immaculate bathrooms. The rooms are decorated in soft colors–beige, pink, or salmon–with velvet fabric on the walls and pale curtains and bedspreads. (The *Lie de Vin* floor may not be to everyone's taste.) Most rooms overlook the tree-covered square and the church, those on the *quatrième* and *cinquième étages* enjoy a panoramic view of Paris. Eight rooms overlook the courtyard–garden, and Room 50 has a view of Sacré Cœur. Very fond of his neighborhood, Michel Cadin founded the association "A Village In Paris, Montmartre," which publishes a small guide, organizes events, and promotes the preservation of Montmartre. You would be well advised to visit Montmartre, which, you'll learn, is much more than Sacré Cœur and the Place du Tertre: The *Butte* is full of passageways and tiny, hidden streets that are the heart and soul of this picturesque *arrondissement*.

Terrass Hôtel

12, rue Joseph de Maistre
75018 Paris
Tel. (0)1 46 06 72 85 - Fax (0)1 42 52 29 11
M. Binet

Category ★★★★ **Open** All year. **Rooms** 88 and 13 suites (50 with air-conditioning) with bath or shower, WC, telephone, TV satellite, hairdryer, minibar. **Price** Single 1070F, double 1280F, suite 1600F. Extra bed +450F. **Meals** Breakfast (buffet) included, served 6:15-10:30 (continental breakfast in room at any time). **Credit cards** All major. **Pets** Dogs allowed. **Facilities** Panoramic terrace, elevator, laundry service, individual safes at reception, bar. **Restaurant** Menu 130F and 160F, also à la carte, terrace restaurant in good weather (à la carte). **Parking** 10 spots at the hotel (100F per day), and impasse Marie-Blanche. **How to get there** (Map 4): Bus: 80, 95 - Metro: Place-de-Clichy.

Lying at the foot of the Butte Montmartre, this hotel offers guests an extraordinary garden and terrace restaurant with a splendid view over the rooftops of the capital. On good days, you can enjoy gourmet meals there. The ground-floor restaurant, however, is less expensive, and is pleasantly decorated in a Provençal style. The reception area is adjusted with numerous corner lounges and a snug bar. Many bedrooms have somewhat classic furniture and floral fabrics. The more recent rooms are embellished with Souléiado fabrics on the walls and built-in oak furniture. All rooms have beautiful carpets and magnificent bathrooms in Italian tiles. The rooms vary in size but not in price (except for the huge suites); the largest and most beautiful are those whose numbers end in 10. You will enjoy a magnificent view over all of Paris if you stay on the street side on the *quatrième étage*. The breakfast is delicious.

Hotel George Sand

18, avenue Marceau
92400 Courbevoie - La Défense
Tel. (0)1 43 33 57 04 - Fax (0)1 47 88 59 38
Mme Teil

Category ★★★ **Rooms** 31 with telephone, bath or shower, WC, TV satellite, minibar. **Price** Single 410-450F, double 460-500F. Friday, Saturday and in low season 360-380F (1-2 pers.). **Meals** Breakfast (buffet) 40F, served 7:00-11:00. **Credit cards** All major. **Pets** Dogs allowed. **Facilities** Elevator, laundry service, room-service, patio. **Parking** In hotel 30 m (7 places, 25F/night). **How to get there** (Map 3): Bus: 176 - Metro and RER: La Défense - Rail station: Gare Saint-Lazare/Courbevoie. **Open** All year.

The George Sand is located in a suburb very near Paris and a fifteen-minute walk from the Grande Arche of La Défense; with its offices and business complex, this modern quarter today is an important part of the capital. Named after the writer George Sand, the hotel is a veritable small museum in homage to her. In a romantic 19th-century decor, the lounge is beautified with antiques and decorative objects of her time: sculptures by David d'Angers and Jean-Baptiste Clesinger, a pastel portrait of George Sand, several books and a letter that belonged to her, a portrait of Liszt, a bust of Chopin. The bedrooms are decorated with floral wallpaper and antique furniture in the style of the writer's country house at Nohan. There are comfortable amenities and useful services for business people staying at the hotel, including fax and photocopy machines, and the breakfast buffet is delicious.

Le Jardin de Neuilly

5, rue Paul-Déroulède
92200 Neuilly-sur-Seine
Tel. (0)1 46 24 51 62 - Fax (0)1 46 37 14 60
Mme Rouah

Category ★★★ **Rooms** 29 with soundproofing (20 with air-conditioning), bath or shower, WC, telephone, cable TV, hairdryer, safe, minibar. **Price** Single and double 600, 900, 1200F. **Meals** Breakfast 90F, served 7:30-10:30; snacks available. **Credit cards** Amex, Visa, Eurocard, MasterCard. **Pets** Dogs allowed. **Facilities** Garden, room-service, bar. **Parking** At 210, rue de Courcelles. **How to get there** (Map 3): Metro: Sablons, Porte-Maillot - Bus for Roissy-Charles-de-Gaulle and Orly at Porte-Maillot. **Open** All year.

This former private residence, separated from the street by a pretty garden, now offers an ideal base for those going to the Congress Center but wanting a charming, quiet hotel for the evenings. Spacious even though a little impersonal, the reception area does not lack charm and leads into a lounge soberly fitted out in an 18'th Century-style . The rooms are warmer with some of them elegant, others more provincial, and all are different but all very comfortable and personalized with antique furniture pieces. The 'standard' rooms are a little small for their price but conversely the 'luxes' are often large. The marble bathrooms are modern and functional. A very attractive connecting veranda runs beside the garden and can be enjoyed in all seasons, notably when breakfast is served outside on elegant groupings of tables and chairs in cane and wrought-iron. You should note that the hotel is particularly quiet at weekends when Neuilly is deserted by its inhabitants.

Hôtel Princesse Isabelle

72, rue Jean-Jaurès
92800 Puteaux
Tel. (0)1 47 78 80 06 – Fax (0)1 47 75 25 20
M. Philippe Vaurs

Category *** **Rooms** 35 and 1 suite with soundproofing (7 with air-conditioning), telephone, bath or shower, WC, hairdryer, safe, minibar, cable TV. **Price** Single and double 685F, suite (max. 5 pers.) 950F. Extra bed 100F. **Meals** Breakfast (buffet) 50F, served 7:00-10:00. **Credit cards** All major. **Pets** Dogs allowed. **Facilities** Elevator, laundry service, bar, patio, room-service, fitness center. **Parking** 20 places (5 mn). **How to get there** (Map 3): Bus: 73 - Metro: Esplanade de La Défense - RER: Grande Arche.

Despite a rather grey facade this hotel hides a much more attractive interior where you find a 'bourgeois'–decorated lounge bar and a selection of rooms very different in size and styling. Our favorites are on the ground floor in the two small facing buildings reached via a flowery alleyway behind the hotel. We also liked those in the annex apart (from No. 703), sited across the road and around the courtyard of the Hôtel Le Dauphin under same ownership. The small rooms of the main building are more classical and pleasant, especially on the courtyard side. Their decor is cosseted with light oak worked wood, wall fabrics and small pictures, but the furniture, often white-lacquered, is now rather dated. We should also refer to a huge family suite with lounge and kitchenette, along with a vast communal terrace on the courtyard side, ideal for taking a drink or reading in the sunshine. Breakfasts are served inside or in a charming garden on the Hôtel Le Dauphin side.

Syjac Hôtel

20, quai de Dion-Bouton
92800 Puteaux
Tel. (0)1 42 04 03 04 – Fax (0)1 45 06 78 69
M. Olivier Lesaffre

Category ★★★ **Rooms** 29, 1 suite and 3 duplex with soundproofing, telephone, bath or shower, WC, hairdryer, safe, minibar, TV satellite - 2 for disabled persons. **Price** Single 570-670F, double 670-1500F, triple 850F, suite (5 pers.) 1500F. **Meals** Breakfast (buffet) 60F, served 7:00-10:00. **Credit cards** All major. **Pets** Dogs allowed. **Facilities** Elevator, laundry service, bar, patio, room-service, sauna. **Parking** Godefroy. **How to get there** (Map 3): Bus: 73 - Metro: Esplanade de La Défense. **Open** All year.

Beside the Seine, the Quai de Dion-Bouton is a very busy fast road but the Hôtel Syjac has protected itself effectively from such a noisy background, and you reach it via a small counter-alley just before the Pont de Puteaux. The entry hall leads into a very attractive lounge with an open fireplace. Furnished and abundantly decorated as in a private house, it is completed by a small bar opening onto a patio. Comfortable and cosseted, the rooms are generally more standard but with attractive small bathrooms, and we recommend those giving onto the courtyard. Very successful, the apartments have a more personalized decor seen perfectly in the corner lounges and open fireplaces for winter use. You will also appreciate the elegant breakfast room with an abundant buffet, on the ground floor and decorated with a vast Italian xxx as a 'trompe-l'oeil'. Lastly, for relaxing and keeping fit, there is a sauna and a fully equipped work-out room for your use.

INDEX

I N D E X

C

D

E

F

NEIGHBORHOOD INDEX

RIVE GAUCHE

NOTRE DAME - ILE DE LA CITÉ

QUARTIER LATIN

JARDIN DES PLANTES - LES GOBELINS

L U X E M B O U R G

S A I N T - G E R M A I N - D E S - P R É S

F A U B O U R G   S A I N T   -   G E R M A I N

PORTE D'ORLÉANS - PLAISANCE

GRENELLE

PASTEUR - VAUGIRARD

RIVE DROITE

CHÂTELET - LES HALLES

LOUVRE - TUILERIES

ILE . SAINT - LOUIS

M A R A I S

M A D E L E I N E   –   O P É R A

G A R E   S A I N T   –   L A Z A R E

P L A C E   V I C T O R   H U G O

P A S S Y   –   T R O C A D É R O

G O O D V A L U E
I N D E X

HOTELS WITH RESTAURANT

Notes

Notes